BIG, HOT, CHEAP, and RIGHT

BIG, HOT, CHEAP, and RIGHT

WHAT AMERICA CAN LEARN from the STRANGE GENIUS OF TEXAS

ERICA GRIEDER

PublicAffairs
New York

Published in the United States by PublicAffairs™,
a Member of the Perseus Books Group.

Printed in the United States of America.

PublicAffairs books are available at special discounts for bulk purchases in
the U.S. by corporations, institutions, and other organizations. For more
information, please contact the Special Markets Department at the Perseus
Books Group, 2300 Chestnut Street, Suite 200, Philadelphia, PA 19103, call
(800) 810-4145, ext. 5000, or e-mail special.markets@perseusbooks.com.

Book Design by Cynthia Young

Library of Congress Cataloging-in-Publication Data
Grieder, Erica.
Big, hot, cheap, and right : what America can learn from the strange genius of
Texas / Erica Grieder.—First edition.
        pages cm
Includes bibliographical references and index.
ISBN 978-1-61039-192-4 (hardcover)—ISBN 978-1-61039-193-1
(e-book) 1. Texas—History.   2. Texas—Politics and government.   3. Texas—
Social conditions.   I. Title.
F391.G847 2013
976.4—dc23

                                                          2012044312

First Edition

10 9 8 7 6 5 4 3 2

For my brothers:
Daniel, John, Mark, and David

CONTENTS

INTRODUCTION

AT NOON ON MARCH 16, 1861, Sam Houston, the governor of Texas, sat down to write his professional obituary. He was nearly seventy years old. Within three years he would be dead, and that afternoon his life's work was being undone just outside his office, on the grounds of the Texas capitol.

On February 1, delegates to a state convention had voted to secede from the Union, by a crushing margin. A referendum held three weeks later found that nearly three-quarters of voters agreed. Texas formally left the United States on March 2, 1861, the twenty-fifth anniversary of the day Texas declared its independence from Mexico. The day in question, March 16, was to be the day the governor of Texas swore his oath of allegiance to the Confederate States of America.[1]

That governor, however, would not be Houston. For more than a year, since the 1859 election, he had been trying to stamp out the secessionist fervor that had taken hold of the state, first by argument, and finally by stalling; in the end, it was the legislature that called for a state convention to vote on the question. And now the secessionists were calling for him to come forward and be sworn in as the governor of Texas in the Confederate States of America. But the governor could acknowledge how Texas had voted more readily than he could accept it.

"Fellow citizens, in the name of your rights and liberties, which I believe to have been trampled upon, I refuse to take this oath," Houston wrote. "I love Texas too well to bring strife and bloodshed upon her."

Houston was concluding one of the oddest and most unlikely political careers in American history. He grew up as a fatherless boy from Tennessee, then as a teenage runaway lived with the Cherokees for several years before joining the infantry to fight in the War of 1812. From these semiferal beginnings he went on to power, fame, and, briefly, respectability. He was a congressman from Tennessee, then the governor of that state, until he had his heart broken and took off for the frontier, where he lived in a wigwam and drank himself half to death. Several years later, he roused himself and went to Texas, where he took up arms again and led the revolutionaries to their decisive victory at the Battle of San Jacinto. He became the first official president of Texas, then the governor of Texas, then the state's first senator, then the governor again. By the time he finished writing his letter of resignation, that was all over: when he didn't turn up outside, the convention delegates vacated his office, and Houston's lieutenant governor was sworn in instead.

"It is, perhaps, meet that my career should close thus," Houston continued. "I stand the last almost of my race . . . stricken down because I will not yield those principles which I have fought for."

The principle at hand was union. Despite having been the president of Texas, Houston was the state's most devoted American. He had gone to Texas to see if it could be won for the United States, and he had fought for Texas assuming that it would be. He had called for annexation in his inaugural presidential address.

And for the past several years, although he supported slavery, Houston had been fighting to preserve the Union. He was the only Southern governor who opposed secession. At first, he had said that the state had no right to secede, that Texas had joined the United States, not the North or the South. Several years later, he modified his pitch: maybe the states had that right, he conceded, but the war would be bloody, expensive, and ruinous.

Few were swayed. Texans didn't like to listen.

Neither, for that matter, did Houston. For his whole life he had maintained an idiosyncratic, stubborn, and occasionally self-defeating sense of principle. On his wedding night his wife had confessed to him that she was in love with someone else. He was too humiliated to stay in Nashville, but he took an ad in the papers, warning that anyone who questioned her virtue "would pay for the libel with his heart's blood." As he prepared to lead the Texans into the Battle of San Jacinto in April 1836, he knew they would be badly outnumbered, again. Twice in the preceding six weeks, the Mexican army had massacred the revolutionaries—first at the Alamo, where the Texans hadn't surrendered, and then at Goliad, where they had. In light of that, Houston took only one precaution: he ordered his troops to burn the bridges behind them.

And when the Mexican army surrendered, when the monstrously erratic president and general Antonio López de Santa Anna was finally captured, it was Houston whom he asked for mercy. "That man may consider himself born to no common destiny who has conquered the Napoleon of the West," said Santa Anna, "and now it remains for him to be generous to the vanquished."

"You should have remembered that at the Alamo," Houston said. He had been wounded in the battle and was lying on a blanket under an oak tree. A biographer would later write that "a ring of savage Texans had pressed around, with ominous looks on their faces and ominous stains on their knives."[2] But Houston spared Santa Anna's life and laid out the terms of the armistice that ended the revolution.

And now Houston was wounded again. "The severest pang," he wrote, "is that the blow comes in the name of the State of Texas."

IT'S COMMON FOR STORIES about Texas to start at the siege of the Alamo, and for good reason. That half-accidental battle is at the emotional core of the state's story about itself, and in Texas, as in the United States, origin stories have been reified by belief and devotion.

But this isn't just a story about the state. One of the fundamental truths about Texas is that, although the state is genuinely sui generis, and self-consciously different from the other states, it is, in many ways, the most American of all. Texas is part of the United States. This is a story about both of them. That's why it makes sense to start with Houston. He was among the first people to see that Texas was part of the United States, even before the United States was committed to it, and even if Texans wavered along the way.

In retrospect, he was right. Today, Texas sometimes looks like the United States taken to its logical conclusion, with Texans themselves being an exaggerated version of Americans—the revolutionaries among the revolutionaries, the fighters who never left the ring, the inmates taking over the asylum. These are "the Super-Americans," as *New Yorker* writer John Bainbridge put it in his 1961 book of the same title. "America on steroids," agreed *The Economist* in 2002.

If people are resistant to this conclusion, you can hardly blame them. Texas is, despite Florida and New Jersey, America's most controversial state, and when skeptical outsiders look at it, they have plenty to pick on. It has creationists on the State Board of Education. It has evangelicals in the governor's mansion, except during those episodes when the governor has to move to a taxpayer-funded McMansion because someone threw a Molotov cocktail over the gates (2008–2012). It has America's biggest prison population and its busiest death row. It grew rich on oil and worked that wealth on behalf of cronies, dirtying itself and the nation in the process.

Meanwhile, if you want to talk about schools, about health care, about poverty, Texas is at the bottom of the pack, keeping company with its bedraggled southern neighbors. The politicians all wish they were cowboys, and on the rare but unfortunate occasions when they get to national office, they go hog wild. They start wars. They take the rule of law out for target practice.

When confronted with any of these charges, Texas's leaders are blithely unconcerned. They might even take them as a compliment and think about running for president. "It's like a whole other country," as one of the official slogans puts it. When compelled to self-reflection—if, for example, you specify one of the many metrics where Texas is among the worst in the nation—they just joke about it. "Thank God for Mississippi," as Rick Perry might put it. That casual belligerence, that reflexive stupidity: further grounds for offense.

Texas's boosters, meanwhile, can't stop bragging. They would brag no matter what, probably, but over the past ten years they've had a lot to hang their hats on. In 2002, Texas accounted for 7.4 percent of the country's economy; by 2012, that figure had jumped to 8.7 percent.[3] Between June 2009 and June 2011, the lone state of Texas created 40 percent of America's net new jobs. Since 2000, several million people have moved here, drawn by the factor that has always drawn people to Texas—the chance to find work and wrestle a new life out of this inhospitable soil. This is where America goes for jobs, for energy, for land, for soldiers, for industry, for growth.

And Texas manages all that, the boosters note, without any special favors. The state is a net contributor to federal tax receipts. When scrapping with Washington, the state is often trying to turn down federal funds: Texas would rather not have the money if doing so means taking the rules that go with it. And the state does its share in the face of special challenges. The land border between the United States and Mexico, for example, runs for some 2,000 miles, about 1,200 of them in Texas. Yet it's Arizona and California that are the squeaky wheels when it comes to unauthorized immigration and border security.

It's hard to say which side is right, because there are a lot of mixed signals.

This is the state that gave America George W. Bush. Republicans control every statewide office, and the religious right has a chokehold on the state GOP. Yet it's also the state that produced Lyndon Johnson, who signed a lot of the laws that today's Republicans are so angry about.

Texas's oil industry is as powerful as ever. In 2011, in the wake of the Deepwater Horizon oil spill, one of the state's congressmen apologized to BP, the British oil giant that was leasing the rig in question, for all the hassle. Texas is also America's top state for wind power, and it was Texans who kicked off the shale gas revolution that is currently killing Big Coal.

Texans are sticklers for law and order, yet the state has maintained one of the nation's most moderate policies toward unauthorized immigration. Texas has the fourth-highest incarceration rate in the nation, but in the past ten years some two dozen states have pursued sensible criminal justice reforms—more treatment, fewer mandatory sentences—based on an initiative that started in Texas.

The cheerleaders dismiss Texas's inequities, its glibness, its hubris. The state's critics minimize Texas's entrepreneurial ethos, its openness, its confidence. There is one thing everyone can agree on: Texas punches above its considerable weight. Over the past fifty years, three Texans have held the White House. More have held fearsome power in the halls of Congress. The state's powerful oil interests have had their grimy fingers all over America's foreign policy, and the religious right comes here to field-test its messages. If Texans figure out a way to sell something, be it shale gas or science textbooks or criminal justice reforms, you can bet they'll try to foist it on your state. Even worse, the state just keeps getting bigger and stronger and, apparently, angrier, like Bowser in Super Mario 3.

At the same time, Texas is clearly getting some things right. Over the past century, it came from nowhere to become one of America's biggest, most dynamic, and most important states. Over the past ten years, it's posted an economic performance that most states would love to see. Jobs are available. Household incomes are rising. The schools are improving. The cities are thriving. Between 2000 and 2010, Texas added 4 million people, between the migrants and the babies. Because of this staggering growth, it picked up 4 new seats in the House of Representatives during the most recent round of congressional redistricting. It's become a cliché to say that people are voting with their feet, but nonetheless, if a couple million people move to a state, this starts to look like a pattern.

The possibility that Texas is doing some things well is not, in itself, a menacing one, and the bluster about how the nation has nothing to learn from Texas is just willfully obtuse, almost prima facie absurd.

Much of the nation, though, still wants to ignore or discount Texas's success. That's understandable—it's a lot more fun to talk about sex ed and the death penalty than the structural economy, and it would be myopic to admire a state's economic growth if it comes at the expense of the working and middle classes, the environment, the rule of law, and so on. That hasn't been the case in Texas, though. The state is getting better for everyone. It's strange that other Americans can't seem to see that. Maybe something about this state just clouds people's judgment.

Even so, even if the nation is tired of Texas, the state shouldn't be ignored. Despite its idiosyncrasies, today's Texas looks more like the future United States than any other state except, perhaps, California. America's two biggest states have already been trying to figure out how to deal with a young, urbanizing, and increasingly heterogeneous population in the face of globalization, recession, realignment, and structural economic change. If neither of them can manage the transition, the United States is going to have a big problem. If either of them can, the United States should pay attention.

And I hate to be gloomy, but California . . . well, given its economic problems, maybe we should look elsewhere for ideas. Texas is the logical choice. Even if some of its politicians don't believe in evolution, it's already managed to evolve. A hundred years ago, for many Texans, infrastructure meant having a pail for water. Fifty years ago, it was the last state in the country with a poll tax. During the second half of the twentieth century, though, it clawed its way out of poverty and backwardness—thanks to luck and federal support, but also to a lot of old-fashioned bootstrapping and individual initiative.

Today Texas is one of America's genuine powerhouses, and it has all the tools it needs to keep that up as long as it plans accordingly. Texas is, despite its rhetorical flare-ups, a pragmatic and largely reasonable state. It has a deep-seated suspicion of government and, not coincidentally, unusually high confidence in the private sector and in individuals, but as far as that goes, it's an exaggeration of American tradition rather than a break from it.

Texas, in other words, is not a menace. There's no reason to be scared. There's no reason to be jealous. There are, however, plenty of reasons to pay attention. Texas might not be a role model for every state, but most places could use a little more of this state's spirit, drive, and determination. The United States isn't doing itself any favors by keeping its scrappiest state at arm's length. That's not preaching, by the way. Texans are Americans, so we can't say it's their loss. It's ours.

1

MAN-MADE MIRACLE

"I'M PRETTY SURE that to Washington, DC, Texas is an outlaw state," said Rick Perry, the governor of the rogue place in question. It was June 2012, and he was giving a keynote address at the state Republican convention, in Fort Worth. The audience, some 6,000 strong, laughed and cheered.

It had been only a few months since he had face-planted in the race for the Republican presidential nomination, but Perry, with his smug grin and expensive suit, was looking like the cat that ate the canary. For the previous ten years—a period that neatly overlapped with his tenure as governor—the state of Texas had been having such a good run that pundits, and not just local ones, had taken to calling it the "Texas Miracle." The state had added millions of people, and hundreds of thousands of jobs; the year before, its GDP, according to the Bureau of Economic Analysis, had hit $1.3 trillion. For the sake of comparison, Texas's economy was bigger than that of Mexico or South Korea, and almost as big as, say, Australia's.

The state's unemployment rate had been lower than the national average every month since February 2007.[1] The number of jobs in

Texas had been growing more or less steadily for about a decade. In January 2002, there were 10.04 million workers in the state; in August 2011, the figure was 11.45 million.[2]

Texas had never been short on self-love, perhaps its greatest natural resource, but it had also been basking in praise from America's business community. "In *Chief Executive*'s eighth annual survey of CEO opinion of Best and Worst States in which to do business, Texas easily clinched the No. 1 rank, the eighth successive time it has done so," wrote the magazine's editor.[3] In November 2011, it claimed the number one spot in *Site Selection* magazine's annual ranking of "top business climates."[4] A few months later, *Business Facilities* magazine agreed: Texas was the "best business climate," according to its 2012 ranking.[5] CNBC gave Texas top honors in its survey of "top states for business" in 2008, 2010, and 2012.[6]

Texas's cities had also been singled out. In 2011, demographer Joel Kotkin, writing at *Forbes*, announced that Austin was America's number one "next big boom town." San Antonio, Houston, and Dallas were number four, number five, and number seven, respectively. That same year, the Milken Institute, an economics think tank based in California, took a different view: San Antonio was America's best-performing big city, followed by El Paso (number two); Austin was only fourth.[7] A 2012 list of the twenty-five best cities for business and careers, also from *Forbes*, included five in Texas.[8]

At the state convention, Perry didn't bother to run through the entire list of tributes to the state, but he did highlight one that he seemed to particularly savor: "Even the *New York Times* let it slip on its pages." He was referring to a blog post, "Texas Is the Future," published a few days earlier, that had noted the state economy had grown by 3.3 percent in 2011 ("not just oil, not just manufacturing").[9] There was more laughter, more cheering.

The governor smirked. The Texas economic engine was still humming along, and so it didn't matter whether he was a laughingstock for the nation. The nation was still a laughingstock for Texas.

THE STATE'S FLOURISHING ECONOMY was only one of the reasons that many Republicans had been delighted when Perry announced in August 2011 that he would run for the Republican presidential nomination. Since the 1970s and 1980s, America's Republican Party had come to rely on a coalition of fiscal and social conservatives as the two pillars of its political base. Under normal circumstances, it was an equable marriage of convenience. The fiscal conservatives brought the money and the social conservatives brought the passion. Even if the two groups weren't perfectly aligned—why would they be?—at least they managed, for the most part, to stay out of each other's way. When they didn't, though, the Republican coalition could seem like a Faustian bargain.

That was the party's position when Perry entered the race. The gentlemen's agreement between the fiscal conservatives and the social conservatives had been challenged by the sudden appearance, in 2009, of the Tea Party movement, which applied the social conservatives' traditional zeal to the fiscal conservatives' traditional issues—taxes, spending, regulation. For months the Republican power brokers had been hoping for a new candidate. It was looking like the Republican presidential nominee would be an ideologically suspect Mormon from Massachusetts unless somebody else came along. As Mitt Romney slogged along in the polls, the far right—the social conservatives and Tea Partiers—were increasingly out of temper. For Republican moderates, this presented a dilemma. If the far right voters got their way, the party would end up with an unelectable nominee, such as Rick Santorum. If the base was ignored, though, those voters might sulk or even sit out the election altogether. Now here was a socially conservative evangelical southerner, a red-meat politician who had just hosted a massive prayer rally. He was the longest-serving governor of America's biggest red state—a state that just happened to be leading the nation, by a whopping margin, in job creation.

As it happened, the power brokers and pundits had slightly exaggerated his social credentials. Perry had never cared as much about the culture wars as people expected him to, given his biography and job title. The fact was that, although the governor had always described himself as a social conservative, he had rarely been asked to prove it, and he had never much exerted himself over those issues. Even in announcing his candidacy, he didn't pander to the religious right; he was there to talk business. "Since June of 2009," he said, "Texas is responsible for more than 40 percent of all of the new jobs created in America."[10]

It was a pretty good line. At the time Perry joined the race, the nation, and almost every state in it, had been struggling for several years with high and intractable unemployment. The national unemployment rate had jumped from 5.4 percent in May 2008 to 9.4 percent one year later and wouldn't drop below the 9 percent threshold until October 2011.[11] The figures were even higher for certain subsets—young people, minorities, and people without much education. The underemployment rate, meanwhile, was hovering around 16 percent.[12] Millions of Americans, after months of unemployment, had just given up.

The unemployment rate, of course, is a key indicator of social welfare, arguably the most important one. Anyone who can afford not to worry about it is someone who hasn't had to worry about his or her own employment status. And the question of whether a job is "good" enough for someone probably should be answered by the person in question. So given that jobs were the absolutely critical issue for so many Americans in the years after the 2008 financial crisis, wouldn't Democrats have been genuinely curious about how Texas had managed it, on the off chance that any aspects of the situation could be replicated elsewhere?

But it turns out that Democrats don't believe in miracles. And so the national left's reaction to Rick Perry's narrative of jobs and growth in Texas looked like Elisabeth Kübler-Ross's five stages of grief.

First there was denial. "What you need to know is that the Texas miracle is a myth," wrote Paul Krugman in the *New York Times*, "and more broadly that Texan experience offers no useful lessons on how to restore national full employment."[13] Other left-leaning critics concurred: the statistics had to be misleading. After all, Texas had all that oil, and all those people, plus the governor spent all of his time poaching jobs from other states.

Besides, why get excited about an economy that wasn't even that great? As of June 2011, Texas's unemployment rate was 8.2 percent, not much below the national average. "While Texas has created more jobs than any other state in the past two years, the increase is far less than advertised," wrote Merrill Goozner at the *Fiscal Times*. "The rate of increase is not much higher than a number of other states, including former rustbelt centers like Pennsylvania or liberal sanctuaries like Vermont."[14] Another version of this line of argument was that oil-rich Texas would naturally be buffered against a recession. While high energy prices hurt most states, the few that produce most of America's fuel tend to be countercyclical; they do well precisely when other states struggle, and vice versa. North Dakota, for example, was thriving too; it had even less unemployment than Texas, but no one was strutting around talking about a North Dakota Miracle.

Then anger arose. Those weren't good jobs; they were insulting, minimum-wage "McJobs." Kevin Drum, at *Mother Jones*, explained that the whole thing "looks a lot less miraculous once you put it under a microscope—and pretty soon it won't just be churlish lefties pointing this out."[15] Harold Meyerson, in the *Washington Post*, argued that Texas was no role model for a developed country. If the state was creating jobs, he said, it was only because Perry was wielding "a range of enticements we more commonly associate with Third World nations—low wages, no benefits, high rates of poverty, scant taxes, few regulations and generous corporate subsidies."[16] Anyway, Democrats weren't powerless to create jobs. Barack Obama had presented a jobs plan to Congress (about a month after Perry got in the race, surely unrelatedly). He could pass it if only Republicans in Congress would quit stonewalling.

Then came bargaining. The Center for Immigration Studies (CIS), which is nominally nonpartisan but calls for less immigration, released a report saying that of the jobs created in Texas since 2007, 81 percent had gone to immigrants. In other words, "immigrants (legal and illegal) have been the primary beneficiaries of this growth since 2007, not native-born workers."[17] On hearing this, the right joined the left in having a problem with Texas, and both sides indulged in a little spasm of self-righteous xenophobia, even though, by CIS's own account, half of those immigrants who were taking up American jobs were legally authorized to do so. Over the next few weeks, another, even more desperate theory surfaced. These were drug-war jobs. Of the 4 million people who had moved to Texas in the preceding decade, some very significant share were traffickers or kingpins.

Before the Democrats could reach the depression stage, though, they got a real miracle. Perry's presidential campaign totally collapsed. Future pundits will recall that it was a woeful debate performance that did him in. Asked to specify the three federal agencies that he wanted to cut—a bit of bluster that had been part of his standard stump speech forever—he confidently named two. Pressed for the third, he flailed for about a minute before giving up. "Oops," he added, by way of an explanation. (See? That's what limited government looks like.)

In truth, Perry's tumble had started before he stepped on stage.[18] For weeks, for example, he had been hammered by other Republicans for a couple of moderate positions from his past. In 2001, he had signed a law allowing certain undocumented students to pay in-state tuition rates at Texas public colleges and universities. Ten years later, defending that decision during one of the primary debates, he seemed taken aback when everyone else on stage denounced him for it. It was a nice bit of situational irony; the left had feared Perry because it thought he was from the far right, but the far right had landed the first few swings at the piñata.

After the "oops" debate, however, Perry's remaining support fell off a cliff. Herman Cain, an executive from Georgia who had made his fortune in the pizza industry, took over as the next Republican not-Romney. Democrats lost interest in the supposed Texas miracle. As long as Perry wasn't going to be the nominee, there was no longer any reason to worry about it.

THAT WAS TOO BAD. The Texas Miracle wasn't a masterpiece of central planning. It was to some degree due to a series of happy coincidences, and given that every state is different, it couldn't have been precisely replicated elsewhere. At the same time, it wasn't exactly dumb luck. While Texas was fortunate to have natural resources, it had also been cagey enough to create an economy that was about more than just oil. Two of the frequent observations—that Texas was creating lots of minimum-wage jobs and that it was doing well because it had managed to avoid the housing crisis—were effects of the phenomenon rather than causes.

The job creation numbers themselves, to start, were real. The data, which came from the Federal Reserve Bank of Dallas, have withstood every critique. "For obvious reasons, this has become a subject of intense interest to the national media," said Richard Fisher, the president of the Dallas Fed, in an August 2011 speech in Midland. "My staff and I are being hounded by the national press corps for data and commentary."[19] Nevertheless, if you looked at the period from June 2009 to June 2011, he continued, Texas actually accounted for 49.9 percent of the nation's net new jobs.

Of course, a number of states continued to lose jobs after the recession technically ended. In other words, their losses were dragging down the national net jobs figures. That would make the states that were gaining jobs seem stronger than they actually were. So Fisher went on: if you looked only at the states that had net job growth over the period in question, the figure was still impressive: 29.2 percent of the new jobs in states that had net new jobs were in Texas.

It was a soup of figures, but Fisher's point was clear: any way you wanted to cut the numbers, Texas was creating a lot of jobs—more than anyone else, at least. The Texas Miracle's skeptics, in other words, would be better off asking what kind of jobs they were and how they were acquired.

The other question—whether Texas's jobs were good jobs—was more relevant. Texas does have more minimum-wage jobs than any other state, and it ties with Mississippi as the state with the most minimum-wage workers per capita. That's a problem because a person who earns the federal minimum wage ($7.25 an hour) ends up making about $15,000 a year, assuming a standard forty-hour workweek for fifty-two weeks a year. For a single mother with one child, for example, that's not even enough to hit the federal poverty line.

Around the country, as of 2011, 5.2 percent of workers aged sixteen or older who were paid on an hourly basis earned $7.25 or less per hour.[20] In Texas, the figure was 8 percent.[21] In California, it was just 1.6 percent—although by state law the minimum wage was $8.00 an hour, so that's how California pulled off the lower figure. A better comparison would be to New York. There, as in Texas, the minimum wage was the same as the federal standard, but just 5.1 percent of hourly workers fell into the minimum-wage-or-less category, which was almost exactly the same as the country as a whole. The usual explanation for this is that everything is more expensive in New York, including labor, and that Texas's workforce is different from New York's (younger, less educated, and so on). The usual defense is that it's a lot cheaper to live in Texas than in New York—which is true, but the cost of living isn't that low. If you were living in Texas and making $15,000 a year, you would still be poor.

Most of the jobs created in Texas during the previous decade, however, were not minimum wage jobs. Lots of them were government jobs, as Democrats pointed out. Lots of them were emphatically white collar. All told, according to a Dallas Fed analysis based on BLS statistics,

28 percent of jobs created in Texas between 2001 and 2011 were in the lowest wage quartile. Another 28 percent were in the lower-middle group. The rest were in the upper-middle and highest wage quartiles (24 percent and 21 percent respectively). It's true, then, that Texas created a lot of minimum- and low-wage jobs during the span in question. Of course, the state's population had been growing, and the bigger the population, the greater the demand for food, sundries, movies, and so on. And the population growth was driven by the state's broad-based economic growth; it wasn't the other way around. In terms of median household income, by the way, Texas ranks in the middle of the pack.

Krugman, in his *Times* column debunking the "miracle," had put the population growth down to "a high birth rate, immigration from Mexico, and inward migration of Americans from other states, who are attracted to Texas by its warm weather and low cost of living, low housing costs in particular."[23] Texas does get some of the sun-loving retirees known as "snowbirds," most visibly in the Rio Grande Valley, but if Krugman thinks Texas's *weather* is a key driver of domestic in-migration to Texas, he should come visit some time, really any time, in the long summer. Sure, businesses are drawn to the low cost of living and the low cost of housing; they make for a cheaper workforce. But if these were big draws by themselves, more people would be moving to South Dakota. Instead, people are moving to Texas en masse for the same reason people have always moved to Texas en masse: to work.

The state's population growth was also one of the two big reasons that Texas avoided the worst of the housing crisis. Millions of people were moving to the state; that braced demand and kept housing prices stable. As a mildly ironic point of interest, note that Texas's bad reputation had helped keep housing prices from overheating before the crisis—the state always grew, but outsiders could never have predicted that so many people would want to move to Texas, so real estate investors and developers tended to focus their efforts on California, Florida, and Arizona.

The other thing that helped Texas on the housing front was its lending laws. As many people have observed, these were surprisingly strict, at least relative to the laws that other states had, which stipulated that people had the inalienable right to buy as much of a McMansion as they wanted even if the application was scribbled in crayon. Texas didn't allow balloon mortgages, it didn't allow prepayment penalties, and, perhaps most importantly, it severely restricted cash-out refinancing. During the housing collapse, Texas had a greater share of subprime mortgages than the national average, but its subprime mortgages were faring better than most. In 2005, about 8 percent of Texas's subprime loans were past due or in foreclosure, right in line with the national figure. By 2008, the Texas figure had jumped to 14 percent, but the national figure was 20 percent.[24]

Some analysts noted that these laws were a break from Texas's professed ideas. "I find it very ironic that places like the AEI are using Texas as the role model for The Way States Should Conduct Themselves in the future, which is by association bootstrap-tugging laissez-faire financial capitalism," wrote Mike Konczal, a fellow at the Roosevelt Institution, a progressive outfit inspired by FDR and Eleanor. He continued: "The research produced at the Dallas' Federal Reserve, by economists on the ground, points out the exact opposite— consumer protection is a major reason why Texas isn't Arizona or California or Florida."[25]

Of all the reasons that Texas isn't California, its consumer protection regime isn't the biggest culprit, but Konczal was right to say that Texas sometimes breaks with strict laissez-faire capitalism. That's always been the case; the state has never really pretended otherwise. A minimalist design is still a design. Texas calls for limited government, which is distinctly not the same thing as calling for *no* government, and Texas has often done things that are the opposite of laissez-faire.

Historically, that is, Texas wasn't a straightforward probusiness state. It was (and is) pro–Texas business, whether the business was farming or oil or microchips. And if the government had to get involved to help the private sector along, well, for many Texans, that's what government was *for*. At the end of the nineteenth century, for example, an antitrust movement emerged in the United States. The young country was no longer the agrarian republic of Thomas Jefferson's vision. Big business interests had coalesced in the industrial Northeast and old Northwest, and they had the size to muscle the little guys aside. In Texas at that time, everyone was a little guy. Many of the people were small farmers who saw themselves as the victims of outside monopolies. In 1889, Texas became the second state in the country to get an antitrust law. Two years later it established a regulatory agency, the Texas Railroad Commission (TRC), that was intended to give small farmers an advocate in their dealings with the northern railroads and soon took on oversight of the state's oil industry, thereby becoming the most important state regulatory agency in the country, as well as a textbook example of the value of government oversight.

We'll return to that later, though. For now, let's just observe that today, of course, Texas's oil industry is a behemoth—the state's most lucrative natural resource and a key reason that outsiders are skeptical when Texans pretend that the Texas Miracle is about anything other than oil.

BECAUSE OF TEXAS'S filthy oil riches, outsiders assumed that a lot of the jobs created in Texas must have been oil and gas jobs. Energy is a major driver of the state economy, as we all know, and buoyant oil prices helped keep Texas thrumming along while most states were struggling.

As an aside, this is an odd line of critique. Just because Texas has a lot of oil and gas, while most states don't, doesn't mean that the Texas economy writ large is somehow an illusion. No one would agree with that logic if extrapolated to the United States, a resource-rich country, as a whole. Maybe the idea is that because Texans didn't make the oil, it somehow shouldn't count. Let's be fair, though. Maryland didn't create the federal government. New York didn't invent finance. California didn't create its spectacular beauty. Every state has assets, and challenges. It would be nice if the governor of New Mexico could travel back in time four hundred years and lay the foundations for some world-class universities—instead, like Texas, like every state, it has to play the hand it was dealt, dance with the one that brung it, and so on.

But even if we set that aside, oil isn't sufficient to explain the Texas Miracle. The oil industry, like most of the energy industry, is capital intensive rather than labor intensive. Oil rigs create jobs (relatively high-paying ones, because the work is dangerous, dirty, and difficult). But the expensive part of a drilling operation is the drilling, not the driller. The Texas Miracle might have sputtered if oil and gas hadn't been doing well, but the energy industry isn't sufficient to explain all the jobs growth. In June 2011, according to an analysis from economist Karr Ingham, the Texas oil and gas industry was at a high point, with some 224,000 workers; since June 2010, the energy industry had added more than 28,600 jobs or about 13 percent of the state's net jobs in that span.[26]

That's probably fewer than people would expect, even in Texas. The state is less dependent on energy than it once was. That's partly because other industries have emerged naturally. When Texans discovered their first oil gusher, in 1901, there was barely anything else in the state, but that was bound to change.

But it's also because Texas has made a deliberate effort to diversify, particularly after oil prices collapsed in 1986. When that first gusher was hit, Texans weren't thinking of the long term. The nineteenth century had been a grueling one for Texas. It had staged a successful revolution and logged nine years as an independent republic. No sooner had Texas been annexed than it went to war with Mexico on behalf of its new country. Then there was the Civil War, after which Texas, thoroughly defeated, was reconstructed by hostile carpetbaggers. And for all those decades, the average Texan was eking out a living by growing cotton, farming corn, or catching feral cattle. The state's priority in 1901 was to catch up, and putting itself in charge of its newfound wealth was one way to do that. By 1901, there was a feeling that if Texas were to be colonized again, it should, at least, be colonized by Texans. The antitrust law from 1889 provided a way for the state to keep the nation's extant oil companies, which had started sniffing around, firmly out.

The state's leaders succeeded well enough that by the 1970s the state's economy was still dangerously lopsided. The oil industry carried Texas through the national recession of the 1970s (a national recession that was triggered and exacerbated by high energy prices, which meant that Texas was well hedged against it). When the price of oil collapsed, however, Texas was caught flat-footed. The state spent years in the doldrums, even as the national economy roared back to life in the 1980s.

It was a real learning experience. "Fool me once, shame on . . . shame on me. Fool me twice . . . won't get fooled again," as George W. Bush would say years later. Between 1970 and 1987, according to a 2011 analysis by two economists at the Dallas Fed, a 10 percent uptick in the price of oil boosted state GDP by 1.9 percent and employment by 1 percent. Between 1997 and 2010, however, a 10 percent increase in the price of oil boosted Texas GDP by 0.5 percent and employment by 0.39 percent.[27] As those figures show, the state's economy has diversified. The diversification began naturally, but it was helped along by state policy. Helping business is, in a sense, the overarching goal of what Texans describe as "the Texas model"—the secret to the state's success, according to many Republicans, and a model so simple that even Perry knows it by heart.

2

THE TEXAS MODEL

TEXAS'S REPUBLICAN LEADERS can describe their governing philosophy in three words ("the Texas model") or four if they need to explain what the Texas model is ("low taxes, low services"). In Perry's telling, the Texas miracle was proof of how well the Texas model works. During his brief presidential campaign, he offered a four-part "recipe" for economic stewardship as part of his stump speech: low taxes, low regulation, tort reform, and "don't spend all the money." That had worked in Texas, he said, and it could work for the whole country.

The idea is almost as simple as he described. The state's Republicans don't like taxes. Texas is one of the seven states that don't collect an individual income tax (the others are Alaska, Florida, Nevada, South Dakota, Wyoming, and Washington). It's also one of four that don't collect a corporate income tax; it has a gross receipts tax instead, meaning that most businesses pay a small tax on all of their sales, rather than only on their profits. About two-thirds of the state's general revenue funds come from the sales tax.

Texas's taxes are indeed low, albeit regressive. For FY 2009, the Tax Foundation put the Texas tax burden at $3,197 per capita (the thirty-ninth highest in the nation), compared to $4,160 in the United States as a whole and $4,910 in California (the sixth highest).[1] Texas's aversion to taxes is partly principled, partly structural (the state constitution severely limits state taxing authority), and partly pragmatic. The idea is to create a business-friendly climate. That's also why Texas isn't big on regulation or lawsuits.

This model mostly predates Perry. Texas never had high taxes. Technically speaking, he's even raised a few little taxes over the years.[2] His biggest move came in 2006 when he engineered a "swap" that lowered property tax rates—Texas has some of the highest property tax burdens in the country—with the intention of offsetting those declines via an increase on the cigarette tax and a new margins tax on most businesses. Those new revenue streams haven't made up for the decline in property-tax receipts, though; Republicans describe the swap as a net tax decrease, and Democrats call it a structural deficit.

Similarly, the governor inherited the state's minimal regulatory framework. His administration has resisted new federal regulations, in some cases by offering new state regulations as an alternative. Perry also signed a major tort reform bill in 2003 and a follow-up "loser pays" reform in 2011.[3] The connection between tort reform and job creation is empirically dubious, but these reforms may have served as what economists call a "signaling device"—a sign that the state was serious about its commitment to conservative principles. The reforms certainly sent some signals to the Texans for Lawsuit Reform, one of the state's most powerful lobbies.

As far as being business friendly, Texas has succeeded. The Tax Foundation rates it as the nation's ninth best climate for business. Notably, the state gets top-ten billing even as the Tax Foundation also dings Texas for high corporate taxes; though the state's gross receipts tax has plenty of exemptions and loopholes, it still yields the thirty-seventh highest business tax burden in the country. The reason the state's business climate is regarded so highly might have more to do with the lack of a personal income tax, which millionaires like just as much as anyone else does, and the lackadaisical regulatory climate.

As far as taxes and spending go, Texas practice what it preaches, for the most part. Outsiders sometimes assume the state must be hypocritical, that its leaders rail on about taxes and spending while begging for federal money—which is true of many red states, including most of the American South. "Among states that voted Republican in the last three elections, all but one gets more money back from the federal government than it pays in taxes," noted Jonathan Cohn, a progressive journalist, on the eve of the 2012 elections. "For most Democratic states, it's the opposite."[4] So when Perry accepted stimulus funds after railing against the stimulus for months, the schadenfreudists did some smirking.

But as Cohn mentioned, there is one red state that gives more to the federal government than it takes. From 1990 to 2009, according to a 2011 analysis from *The Economist*, Texas was among the twenty states that paid more in federal taxes than they received in federal funds.[5] Many of the state's recent battles with the federal government have been in defense of its right to run a tight-fisted ship. The stimulus package, for example, involved supplemental money for the states' unemployment insurance funds. Texas took some of that money, but only the funds that came without federal strings attached. Taking all of the money on offer would have required the state to change its eligibility standards for unemployment funds. When the federal money dried up, after a few years at most, Texas would be on the hook for more spending—indefinitely. For Texas's Republican leadership, that wasn't an acceptable trade, especially given that Texas still had some money in its unemployment fund. (In South Carolina, by contrast, Governor Mark Sanford had joined Perry in threatening to turn down some of unemployment funds but soon backed down because the state fund was running dry.)

People can agree or disagree with the Texas Republicans on that position, but it wasn't an incoherent argument. Perry later argued—logically enough—that it was fair for Texas to accept some of the other stimulus funds. Texas didn't want the stimulus, he explained, but if it was happening anyway, Texas taxpayers might as well get their share of it.

If we're trying to figure out whether Texas is sincere in its commitment to limited spending, we can look at earmarks as another proxy. Of course, federal pork reflects a lot of things other than state policy—the specific composition of a state's congressional delegation, perhaps, or unusual infrastructure needs. There are blue states that don't get many earmarks (New York and Illinois) and red states that do (Alaska, North Dakota, Utah). With that said, an analysis by the *Congressional Quarterly* found that Texas had the ninth-lowest rate of earmarks per capita in the country in FY 2010: $17.03, compared to, say, $64.37 in New Hampshire, where it seems they live free or die on other people's dime.[6]

Texas has been assiduous in seeking federal contracts, but that's not quite the same thing as seeking federal support. The state has, for example, been the beneficiary of significant increases in military spending. Since 2005, when the military had its most recent round of Base Realignment and Closure, the federal presence at Fort Hood (just outside the town of Killeen), Fort Bliss (El Paso), and Fort Sam Houston (San Antonio) has ballooned. But the army isn't the Works Progress Administration. The Center for the Intrepid—a new rehab facility for veterans returning from combat, at Fort Sam—isn't just there for show. And the Department of Defense isn't expanding its presence in Texas in some kind of misguided effort at redistribution; it's picking the sites that make sense. One of the reasons for the expansion at Fort Bliss, for example, is that the post offers access to miles and miles of training and testing space at the White Sands Missile Range, just across the border in New Mexico.

Texas is also serious about transparency, at least when it comes to government spending. The ongoing State Integrity Investigation gives it an "A" for internal auditing, although its overall grade on the "corruption risk report card" is a D+, and in 2012, the United States Public Interest Group ranked Texas first among all the states for government spending transparency.[7] Overall, on fiscal matters, it's fair to say that the state's actions correspond to its rhetoric. And again, keep in mind that Texas is paying more into the federal government than the federal government is returning. Stupid, maybe. Hypocritical, no.

State Republicans have fought efforts to tweak their model, even during lean times. The state budgets on a two-year cycle, starting with the year after the budget in question. At the beginning of the 2011 legislative session, Texas was expecting the biggest budget shortfall in its history, as much as $27 billion, for the 2012–2013 biennium, not to mention the gap in the budget already in progress.

At the time, these numbers were only estimates based on projections of spending obligations and expected revenue. Still, regardless of how big or small the shortfall turned out to be, the Republicans were determined to make it up by cuts, and for the most part they did. Democrats thought the effects would be devastating, given that the state's per capita spending was already among the lowest in the nation. They didn't dare call for tax increases; in Texas, that's a tough spell. But, they pointed out, there was some $10 billion sitting in the state's "rainy day" fund, and it wouldn't be difficult to argue that a global economic downturn counted as a rainy day.

The legislature eventually, grudgingly, took about $4 billion out of the state's well-padded rainy day fund but left more than $6 billion untouched. The legislators also deployed a few transparent accounting tricks for good measure. But the budget that eventually got through cut $15.2 billion in spending for the 2012–2013 biennium, and state spending was so stingy to begin with that almost every agency was whittled down.

Further proof of the Republican commitment to austerity came almost immediately. Within weeks of the session's end, the Comptroller's Office reported that sales tax receipts were higher than expected. The public sector fleetingly thought it might get a reprieve; if the governor would just call a special session, the legislators could restore the education spending, at least. In real terms, the schools budget looked the same, but Texas's school-age population was growing, so per-pupil spending had declined. That turned out to be a nonstarter, though, and in 2012 the Republican leadership confirmed that everyone should proceed as though the cuts would take place.[8]

As mentioned, however, the state occasionally breaks with its own model. The secret ingredient in Perry's recipe for making Texas business friendly is industrial policy. In 2003 and 2005, the legislature established two funds that allocated money the governor could use to woo (or poach, if you'd prefer) businesses from elsewhere via subsidies and incentives. The Texas Emerging Technology Fund (TETF) was designed to steer money to half a dozen industry clusters—aerospace and defense, biotech and life sciences, and so on.[9] The Texas Enterprise Fund (TEF) was a general-purpose pool, which Republicans called the "deal-closing fund" and everyone else called the "slush fund."

Both funds were slightly unsound, doctrinally speaking, but the lapse would have been surprising only to someone who hadn't noticed all the other ways Texas abandoned its professed ideology when doing so became inconvenient.

Both also seemed ripe for crony capitalism, especially the TEF, with its freewheeling mandate. Texans for Public Justice (TPJ), a watchdog group based in Austin, reports that in 2010, forty-three companies, which had received $333 million in rewards from the governor's office, had donated a combined $7 million to Perry's reelection campaign and the Republican Governors Association.[10] Good Jobs First, a national organization focused on government accountability for economic development policies, cited the TEF and the TETF as two of the nation's most wasteful subsidy programs.[11]

Adding insult to injury, the return on taxpayer investment hasn't been what the governor's office predicted. In a subsequent report, Texans for Public Justice noted that Perry claimed to have created 54,600 jobs by distributing a mere $440 million in grants to support sixty-five projects in 2010. In reality, according to TPJ's analysis, the TEF had doled out $350 million over the course of that year, with only 22,349 jobs created by the end of it.[12]

The state also picks winners and losers through more conventional economic development tools. In 2001, a new law authorized property-tax credits for companies that created facilities for manufacturing, R&D, clean coal, renewables, and so on, as long as they were willing to locate in certain parts of the state and expected to create a certain number of jobs.[13] In 2010, the Comptroller's Office reported that the state had awarded $733 million to sixty-four renewable projects since that time, most of them related to wind power, yielding a grand total of 487 jobs—a cool $1.5 million per job.[14]

At the same time, the goal of the law wasn't strictly to create jobs; it was to goose certain industries. In that respect the credits were more successful. Texas now leads the nation in wind power production. Even the governor's funds have got some things right. In 2009, Texas A&M University received a $50 million award from the TETF to build the National Center for Therapeutics Manufacturing. The award looked like an instance of overt cronyism. "Unfortunately, the infusion of taxpayer money is showing some disturbing symptoms that have been found in other state economic development deals," wrote Loren Steffy, the business columnist for the *Houston Chronicle*, describing a tangle of connections between A&M and the governor's office. The university's new associate chancellor for economic development had just come over from the governor's office, where he had served as the TETF's director; in 2008, A&M had announced a partnership with Introgen Therapeutics, whose founder was on the finance committee for Perry's reelection campaign.[15] Even apart from that—Texans can be oddly sanguine about cronyism—the grant seemed overly optimistic. A&M was well positioned to expand its research in life sciences. The university's expertise is in subjects such as agriculture and engineering. But it had already stumbled several times in its attempts to become a vaccine hub. Three months after A&M announced the partnership with Introgen, for example, the company filed for bankruptcy.

In 2012, though, the federal Department of Health and Human Services announced that A&M was one of three sites around the country to become a new national biodefense center (the other two sites would be led by companies: Emergent Manufacturing Operations in Maryland and Novartis in North Carolina).[16] The federal grants to Texas would add up to $285 million, $176 million over the first five years; the state's expected contribution was estimated at $40 million. The first part of the Texas center opened in July 2012. The university's chancellor, John Sharp, explained that part of the reason A&M won the contract was because it had already built some of the relevant facilities—sterile pods and so on—using the money from the 2009 grant.[17]

Such direct supports can be controversial, even among the beneficiaries. "We're not really big believers in huge subsidies," said one executive at a solar company in Austin; it had received a property-tax abatement from the city of Austin and a grant from the governor's slush fund, but neither sweetener, she argued, was big enough to keep the company going if its products weren't selling.[18] The subsidies and incentives might not be strictly necessary either. Texas's greatest competitive advantage, in the end, might be that it's come closer than most states to mitigating policy uncertainty. You don't have to wonder what's going to happen in Texas next year or ten years from now or, probably, a hundred years from now: what's good for business is what's going to happen. In the end, that's the gift Texas gives business executives once the direct handouts run dry.

ONCE THE TEXAS MIRACLE started, it proved to be somewhat self-fueling. People looking for jobs moved to Texas in droves. Over the years, the rate of population growth actually exceeded the rate of job growth, causing Texas's unemployment rate to rise and further muddle Rick Perry's figures. Even so, by being here, these newly minted Texans saved the state a lot of trouble. Once there, their presence helped to create even more jobs—in restaurants, in retail, in the schools, and so on.

On balance, some of the critiques of the Texas Miracle were salient, but none were sufficient to explain it away entirely. Some factors in the miracle were put in place when Perry was still a Democrat. Others demonstrably had nothing to do with him. Oil and gas are still major drivers of the state economy, but Texas has diversified from its oil, land, and cattle traditions. These days, its riches also come from technology, renewable energy, and defense and from manufacturing, trade, and transportation, with the latter having been transformed since the North American Free Trade Agreement (NAFTA) was passed in 1994. In 2011, Texas's exports totaled $251 billion—17 percent of America's total and up 21.3 percent from the year before.[19] So when one industry takes a hit—as manufacturing did during the recession or as agriculture is during the current drought—Texas is well hedged.

As for whether the Texas model is safe for export, Krugman was correct when he observed that some of the factors that helped Texas through the recession can't be simply extrapolated to other states or scaled to the nation as a whole. Even if the Texas model could be exported, other states might not want it. Texans have gotten used to having a limited government; the state constitution, which was written in 1876, effectively guarantees that. The people of this state are accustomed to the virtues and the flaws of this approach (which are, of course, two sides of the same coin): the model means that Texas is open to aspirational upstarts, in business and in politics, but sometimes the people who seize the opportunities in either sphere are cranks, crooks, or cronies. People in other states might prefer a more predictable system, even if the result is more static.

The most effective critique of the Texas model is just that jobs aren't everything. It may be that keeping taxes low and regulations scarce and services minimal is a good way to attract business. It nonetheless has consequences, because it means the state inevitably has less money for health care and education and infrastructure than some of its peers. All told, Texas spends less per capita than all but two other states (Nevada and Florida)—$3,703 per fiscal year in 2010. The national average then was $5,251, which was just about where California came in.[20]

And Texas does lag behind the nation as a whole in many respects. It famously ranks poorly on a lot of indicators of social welfare: one of the worst poverty rates, one of the worst high school dropout rates, dead last for the percentage of people with health insurance.

For Democrats, this is no coincidence—it's proof that low taxes can have a high cost. Republicans, however, maintain that the abstemious approach is the best one. A bigger safety net would require more spending, which would require more taxing, which they're against. When it comes to helping people in the most dire straits— feeding the poor or housing the homeless—their suggestion is that other actors, such as churches, charities, or community groups, should pick up the slack. While Texas Republicans do agree with Democrats that the state needs better schools, they're often skeptical about whether money is the answer, especially because Texas's public schools aren't actually that bad. If you control for demographics, they sometimes look quite good.

One thing's for certain, though: the Texas model isn't going to change in the short term. Indeed, there are some serious structural barriers to change. The state constitution calls for an extremely limited government, one of the most limited in the country. Texas Democrats would like to see some changes, but they are so far out of power that sometimes they seem like the state's third party, after the Republicans and the Tea Party.

Perhaps more to the point, even Texas Democrats don't want to change the model altogether. Compared to their national counterparts, they're in favor of business and skeptical of taxes. If transplanted to California, a typical Texas Democrat would be reclassified as a moderate Republican.

The Texas model isn't an accident, in other words, even if the state constitution does call for a very stark version of it. Texas has a long tradition of looking outside the government for support—and often finding it. That predates the Texas revolution and was reinforced by the rise of the cattle kingdom and the oil booms. In the twentieth century, Texas's sense of self-sufficiency persisted, even as federal money helped Texas dredge its ports, build its highways, power its farms, and steer America to the moon. To understand Texas in the twenty-first century, then, we have to understand how it became the state that it is today.

3

THE TROUBLESOME TERRITORY

"IT'S SMALLER THAN I THOUGHT."

That's the universal reaction from first-time visitors to the Alamo. Once a Spanish mission, then the cradle of Texas liberty, it is now the state's most popular tourist attraction, wedged in downtown San Antonio across the street from a Ripley's Believe it or Not! Though the building may be less imposing than its history, the grounds were big enough to doom the small force of men who tried to defend it in 1836.

They were Anglos and *Tejanos*, English-speaking Americans and Mexicans living in Texas, who wanted to break free of the volatile young Republic of Mexico. There weren't that many of them, only about 200. When they lined up around the walls of the fort, wielding their cannons and rifles, there were yawing gaps between each station. Yet even facing off against more than 2,000 soldiers from the Mexican army under the command of General Antonio López de Santa Anna, the Texans were defiant. When the Mexican army warned that there would be no quarter—no mercy would be shown, no surrender allowed—they responded by firing a cannon. No one, inside or outside the walls, thought it was going to be much of a contest. The defenders of the Alamo didn't have a chance. They had, at first, hoped for reinforcements, that more Texans would come or that the Americans would send supplies, and thirty-two soldiers had arrived from a garrison at Gonzales, but as the days passed, it became apparent that no more were coming. The Mexican soldiers could afford to take their time. In the thirteen days leading up to the final attack, they milled around outside the stone walls of the mission, building ladders, in plain sight of the Alamo's increasingly distressed commander, William Barret Travis.

Today the Alamo itself is still about the size of the small church that it once was. Visitors are often disappointed by that, after all the movies and the books and the myths and the sloganeering. At first glance, the Alamo might even seem overhyped. Texans do, after all, make a virtue of bragging. And the casual whoppers most commonly told in Texas schoolrooms have nothing do to with evolution or abstinence, but with the details of the Texas revolution, the bits of apocrypha that have been blithely repurposed as fact.

Texan teachers might say, for example, that Commander Travis was uncomplicated, noble, and brave. (Actually, he had abandoned his wife and child back in Louisiana after running up a series of debts as a lawyer, although he did, apparently, occasionally think about sending for them.) Jim Bowie, the Tennessee frontiersman, stricken by illness, was supposed to have fought from his deathbed, slashing the invaders with his famous knife. (In fact, when the Mexican soldiers stormed the walls, he was lying under blankets, possibly in a coma, possibly already dead.)

And as the day drew near, or so the legend goes, the defenders of the Alamo knew what was coming. They were lethally outnumbered. Travis had written to American newspapers, begging for help, vowing that the Texans would defend the Alamo at any cost. "Victory or Death!" he had promised, and now he gathered everyone around and used his sword to draw a line in the sand. If anyone wanted to leave, he said, this was his chance. Only one man took him up on it, the cowardly Moses Rose. (The truth is that history can't confirm whether the line in the sand was literal or figurative. The detail came from Rose's own account, and he was, after all, a coward.)

The rest of it, though, is true. It adds up to a pretty good story, and one that Texans cherish. "This is the West, sir," says a newspaperman in an old John Ford movie. "When the legend becomes fact, print the legend."

Even the historians who don't romanticize the Texas revolution tend to describe the Alamo solemnly. William C. Davis, for example, sometimes seems exasperated by the Texans (or Texians, as they were then known). They were, in his view, disorderly, self-interested, and illogical. Yet when he takes on the Alamo, he softens:

> It was to be the stuff of legend, a virtual replay of the ancient tale of a desperate few selling their lives to buy precious time for the many, a story enacted as far back as Thermopylae if not beyond. Yet nowhere in the American Saga would so many important elements be in play at the same time to ensure the creation of such a truly epic legend, the cornerstone of Texian mythology and reality at one and the same time. Men who were already living semimythical heroes were here in the persons of Bowie and Crockett. Around them stood a small cadre of men seemingly willing to risk all in defense of ideals of liberty and democracy. Arrayed against them were the myrmidons of absolutism led by a cynical incarnation of brutality. It was good and evil, the future and the past, freedom and slavery, all locked in mortal combat, an epic in the making that was ripe for begetting the cornerstones of Texian identity, and pride. It may have been a small event in the course of history, but it would loom paramount in defining Texas and its people now and forever.[1]

Though the loss of the Alamo was a foregone conclusion, defending it turned out to be critical from a strategic perspective. The battle itself was indeed as short as everyone expected. Once the Mexican army breached its walls, the defenders were slaughtered within about half an hour. But during the two weeks General Santa Anna's army spent building fortifications, the Texian revolutionaries elsewhere had time to gather and plan. The siege also gave Travis time to make a case for Texas, via the press, directly to the people of the United States. The United States didn't offer any help, but the letters Travis had written from inside the walls drew attention to the territory and were dramatic enough—"Victory or Death!"—to be reprinted in papers around the country. Americans were watching when the Texas revolutionaries sacrificed themselves in exactly the way that Travis had promised they would.

And over time, the story of the Alamo has come to seem as important as the battle itself. A hopeless fight proves the sincerity of the fighters, if not the prudence of their judgment. That's what the revolutionaries had been missing up to that point. In October 1835, the Mexican government asked the increasingly unruly Texian colonists to return a cannon that had been provided, in 1831, for their protection. In response, the Texians raised a flag emblazoned with words of defiance—"Come and take it"—that Leonidas, a king of Sparta, had used more than two thousand years before. That triggered the Battle of Gonzales, which is counted as the first official fight of the Texas revolution. But it is the Alamo that is remembered as the Texan version of Thermopylae.[2]

Before that it had been possible, indeed reasonable, for Americans to dismiss the Texans as a bunch of roustabouts, malcontents, and speculators. The quixotic attempt to defend the mission, and the startling brutality of the slaughter there, upended the narrative. Five weeks later, when Sam Houston led his troops to their decisive battle at San Jacinto, the Alamo was their rallying cry; the battle of the Alamo had put Texans in the right, which is where they still see themselves today.

They were also opportunists, of course, but in that respect they were no different from anyone who had come before.

IN 1519, HERNÁN CORTÉS had planted the Spanish flag on Mexico's Yucatan Peninsula. In the decades following, Spanish conquistadores made several forays into the interior, skirmishing with Indians and suffering from exposure. "Five Christians, of a mess on the coast, came to such extremity that they ate their dead," reported Álvar Núñez Cabeza de Vaca, reflecting on his own travels in Texas; he had been among the first conquistadores to explore the territory after shipwrecking on Galveston Island, which he dubbed the "Isle of Misfortune," in 1528. He continued: "This produced great commotion among the Indians, giving rise to so much censure that had they known it in season to have done so, doubtless they would have destroyed any survivor, and we should have found ourselves in the utmost perplexity."[3] To its earliest visitors from abroad, Texas was a disappointment.

Indian tribes—the Caddos, the Comanches, and the Lipan Apaches, among many others—had been living in Texas for hundreds of years. But the land was better suited to their purposes, hunting and gathering, than to the Spaniards' hobbies of acquiring treasure or building empires. Later European explorers complained there were too many mosquitoes, not enough wood, no maize, muddy water, and nothing to be found but cows and empty plains and people eating prickly pears.

When conquistadores approached Texas from the west, from what is now New Mexico, they were similarly unimpressed. "What I am sure of is that there is not any gold nor any other metal in all that country," reported Francisco Vásquez de Coronado in 1541, "nothing but little villages, and in many of these they do not plant anything and do not have any houses except of skins and sticks, and they wander around with the cows."[4]

That being the case, Spain took little interest in Texas until 1689, when it learned that the French had claimed part of the territory as its own. The French had actually been poking around Texas for longer than that, but the threat of formal encroachment into the

Texas territory, along with the ongoing possibility of Indian campaigns against the more heavily populated areas of what is now northern Mexico, spurred Spain to act. It built a series of missions, including the Mission San Antonio de Valero, the first incarnation of the Alamo.

The priests sent to man the stations were soon as frustrated as their predecessors. In 1781, Fray José Franco López wrote an irritable report to the bishop in the Mexican province of Leon, explaining that, while their missionary work was proceeding well enough ("The evil habits that remain are only those that seem to have been inherent"), the prosperity of the settlements was less than it could be. The Indians were willing to plant corn, beans, cantaloupe, and watermelon, but they were lazy, Lopez continued, and they wouldn't plant wheat because it interfered with the corn. The Spanish had brought cows, but the Comanches and Apaches kept killing them. The sheep were hard to raise because they kept running off into the forests, where "even the gentlest sheep" would get tangled up in the brush.[5]

Even if conditions were more hospitable, it would have been hard for Spain to continue holding on to Texas. The age of European colonization in the Americas was coming to an end. The American Revolution, in 1776, had shown other colonies that independence could be won. Some in Mexico were catching on already.

The young republic of the United States was also beginning to push its boundaries, out of perceived necessity. America's population was small, its infrastructure minimal, its wealth inconsequential, but in those days land was money, and power.

Jefferson was the first American president to take an interest in the Texas territory, although his 1803 Louisiana Purchase ultimately left Texas on the table; Napoleon had expressed claims to parts of it, but the risk of triggering a confrontation with Spain wasn't worth it. The same spirit of caution led the United States to pass over Texas again in 1819, when John Quincy Adams, as secretary of state under James Monroe, negotiated the purchase of Florida under the

Transcontinental Treaty. The United States was keen to rid the continent of European powers, but not quite ready to risk a war to do so. The treaty instead arranged for America to take control of the Oregon territory. It formally left Texas to the Spanish, establishing the Sabine River as the eastern border of the territory and the Red River as its northern limit.

Meanwhile, the Spanish and mestizo residents of Texas were becoming steadily more frustrated by what they saw as arbitrary and unhelpful Spanish authority. They had started to think of themselves as Mexicans, and like the rest of Latin America, they were getting ready for revolution. In 1813, Texas declared independence for the first time. The document, which only called for Texas to be a distinct state in what was not yet an independent Mexico, gave a vehement critique of Spanish rule:

> Unable to defend itself on the Peninsula, much less to protect its distant colonies; those colonies are abandoned to the caprice of wicked men, whilst there exists no power to which they may be made responsible for the abuse of their authority, or for the consequence of their rapacity. Self preservation, the highest law of nature, if no other motive, would have justified this step. But, independent of this necessity, a candid world will acknowledge that we have had cause amply sufficient, in the sufferings and oppression which we have so long endured.[6]

Yet no sooner had Mexico become independent, in 1821, than it became clear that the new country, a poor, fragile, but stubborn state, had even less capacity to control Texas than the Europeans.

MUCH LIKE THE NEW United States in 1776, the young nation of Mexico in the early 1820s needed to shore up its borders and bottle up its restive neighbors. To keep the Indians at bay, it would need "civilized" settlement to hold its northern frontier. People had been trickling into the territory anyway, as hunters and traders from the Louisiana territory cast an acquisitive eye over the coastal plain. Accordingly, Mexico opened its borders to Anglo settlers.

Among these was Moses Austin, an entrepreneur from Missouri. He had been observing the tensions in the Texas territory before Mexico's independence and reasoned that, although Spain was skittish about American negotiators, it might be open to a businessman. He negotiated a land grant with Spain and a permit to bring three hundred Catholic families to the territory. Then, in 1821, Moses abruptly died. For his dying wish, he insisted that his son, Stephen F. Austin, take over his dream of becoming an *empresario* (the Spanish word for "entrepreneur"), meaning a businessman who received land grants from the crown and hoped to make his fortune by convincing other settlers to join him.

There is no indication that Stephen F. Austin, who would become known as the father of Texas, had set out for Texas with any revolutionary impulses or even political aspirations. Of all the heroes of the era, he was the least audacious. A lawyer by trade, he had settled in New Orleans in a bid to build up a practice there. If not for his father's high-pressure negotiation tactic of imminent death, he probably wouldn't have had any interest in Texas at all. For years before the revolution, and even after the revolution was afoot, he tried to soothe tensions with Mexico. Even when he was imprisoned in Mexico City—authorities suspected him of revolutionary activities, and he was held for almost a year—he was sure it was all just a misunderstanding.

Back in 1821, though, Austin was anticipating nothing of the sort. The Mexican authorities had agreed to accept him as an *empresario* in his father's stead. It was, perhaps, precisely because his motive was so transparent that Mexican authorities were willing to work with him, making Austin an early example of what would later emerge as a cornerstone of Texas political reasoning: with businessmen, at least, you know what to expect.

Signing up other settlers was no problem. Thousands of Americans, with their debts mounting or their soil depleted or their luck running out, were looking at Texas as a place where they could make a fresh start. Most were farmers, and some were frontiersmen—most of these were from Appalachia, giving Texas an infusion of Scots-Irish irascibility. Some chalked "GTT" (Gone to Texas) on their abandoned homes by way of explanation.

American politicians, too, were once again eyeing the territory. They had never made any treaties with Mexico. In 1828, President Adams had sent a negotiator to see about buying Texas. The negotiator, however, bumbled the job. One of his arguments was that if Mexico got rid of Texas, it would have less to worry about; by lopping off a big chunk of land, the federal district in Mexico City would be closer to its own borders and thereby easier to manage. Worse, under instruction to talk up the virtues of the American system as part of an effort to purchase the Texas territory, he ended up vigorously trashing Mexico in the comparison. He was asked to leave the country immediately.

John Quincy Adams's successor uncharacteristically let the issue languish, though not out of any lack of interest. Andrew Jackson had become a hero during the War of 1812, and he was the key figure in America's new Democratic Party, a decentralized, antielitist party that bears little resemblance to the one we know today. As a nationalist and an expansionist, he had long been interested in Texas, but when he became president in 1829, he waited. Not starting a war with Mexico would be one of his greatest acts of diplomacy. Still, he kept a close eye on the situation—and his old protégé Sam Houston. The men had been close for years: Houston had served under Jackson during the War of 1812, and Jackson, who had no children, saw the fatherless Houston as something close to a son.

WHEN HE WAS INAUGURATED president of the newly independent Republic of Texas, on October 22, 1836, Sam Houston assured his fellow Texans that Americans would welcome their call to be annexed.

"They have already bestowed upon us their warmest sympathies. Their manly and generous feelings have been enlisted in our behalf. We are cheered by the hope that they will [receive] us to a participancy of their civil, political, and religious rights, and hail us welcome into the great family of freemen. Our misfortunes have been their misfortunes—our sorrows, too, have been theirs, and their joy at our success has been irrepressible."

This was overstating the case. Americans had some appreciation for the glory of the Texas revolution, but not so much that they were going to start hailing the Texans, much less receiving them to participancy. There was a concern that annexing Texas would trigger a war between the United States and Mexico (the annexation of Texas would eventually be a major cause of the Mexican-American War, although not the only one.) The overarching issue was just that Americans were ambivalent about Texas. They may have been sympathetic, but the majority didn't think that this hot, scrubby, and sprawling territory was worth the trouble.

Even Jackson, for so long a leading advocate of expansion in general and Texas in particular, continued to err on the side of caution. He did not extend official recognition to the Republic of Texas until March 1837, shortly before he left office. His successor, the Democrat Martin van Buren, was opposed to annexation and rejected Texas's first bid for annexation later that year.

It was an unexpected blow for the Texans, and they were stung. In 1838, Texas elected a new president, Mirabeau Lamar, who officially withdrew the offer Houston had made. But interest in Texas would grow in the years to come. The United States was restless to expand.

SINCE THE EARLY DAYS of the republic, politicians had occasionally held that Providence had entrusted the continent to the American settlers. According to this vision, they were a uniquely virtuous people who were qualified, and indeed obligated, to spread the fruits of liberty and democracy from shore to shore. The term "manifest destiny" was coined in an 1845 article by journalist John L. O'Sullivan, who used it in an essay specifically calling for the annexation of Texas.

Manifest destiny, however, never enjoyed universal support. America's expansionist tendencies have always been complicated, and in some cases curtailed, by prudence and self-interest. At this point Americans were worried the United States, still a young country and certainly not yet populous or rich, was getting too unwieldy as it was. And the Texas case brought extra concerns; American politicians were worried about the diplomatic consequences of acknowledging an independent Texas, much less annexing it.

The far bigger problem was slavery. Slavery was legal in Texas, and the population of the republic included about 5,000 slaves. Texas was less dependent on the institution than the southern states, not because it was enlightened, but because its underdeveloped economy had not given rise to the plantations that were thriving in the South's cotton belt. Still, Texas was clearly committed to slavery. If it were to be admitted to the United States, it would have to be on those terms. "Should Texas be annexed to our country," wrote William Ellery Channing, a Unitarian pastor, in an open 1837 letter to Henry Clay, "I feel that I could not forgive myself, if, with my deep, solemn impressions, I should do nothing to avert the evil."

On this front, Texas's timing was terrible. Anglo settlers had started moving to Texas when the abolitionist movement was in its infancy. Twenty years later, the country wasn't quite on the edge of civil war, but the debate over slavery's expansion was increasingly fraught. American politics had started to organize along the Missouri Compromise line. Historian Joel H. Sibley has gone so far as to make the case that the controversy over Texas was precisely what made it impossible to ignore this tension—that the annexation of Texas was, in fact, the proximate cause of the Civil War. At the least, the Texas issue exacerbated the questions.

Similarly, Texas would also be the proximate cause of a further political realignment. In 1836, the United States had two major parties, the Whigs and the Democrats. The Democrats were stronger in the South and West; the Whigs, who had formed in opposition to the Jacksonian Democrats, were more heavily represented in the North. But both parties were national rather than regional—until Texas came along.

The annexation of Texas split the nation down the middle. The South supported the idea because southerners supported slavery. The Democrats meanwhile shared Jackson's general interest in territorial expansion and his confidence that a country with a limited, decentralized government could absorb such additions. Whigs generally disagreed. So when Texas became a major issue, it reinforced the connection between the South and the Democrats, and further polarized American politics along starkly regional lines.

From the Texans's point of view, none of this mattered. They didn't see themselves as a far-flung territory, or at least not far-flung enough to elicit a backlash; the United States already owned the Oregon territory, and that was farther west than Texas. The question of whether slavery should be extended to additional states after Texas was not much of a priority.

The majority of Texans considered themselves Americans and had expected to be welcomed accordingly. Once it became clear that welcome was not forthcoming, many resigned themselves to life as an independent nation. In 1838, when Mirabeau Lamar was inaugurated as the second president of Texas, he asserted his belief in an independent Texas: "I have never been able myself to perceive the policy of the desired connexion, or discover in it any advantage either c[i]vil, political or commercial, which could possibly result to Texas," he said. As president, he sought alliances with settlers in other western territories, fixed the capital, and signed treaties with other governments. Both France and Britain recognized the Republic of Texas during Lamar's tenure.

When William Henry Harrison, an annexation-wary Whig, succeeded Martin van Buren in 1840, Texas's continued independence seemed inevitable. Then fate took a turn.

The importance of the American vice presidency has historically been underrated. That fact can partly be blamed on Texas; it was a Texan vice president, John Nance Garner, who served under Franklin Roosevelt for two terms and later derided the office as "not worth a bucket of warm piss," which is the quote political journalists can always turn to when they need to explain how unimportant the vice president is. The next vice president from Texas, Lyndon Johnson, proved Garner wrong. He coolly calculated, before becoming JFK's running mate, that nothing boosts a person's chances of being elected president so effectively as being next in line, not to mention the chance that vice presidents might have to assume the higher office in the event of an unexpected death. In 1841, John Tyler was the first person to become preseident that way.

Harrison served for barely a month before dying, abruptly, of pneumonia. Tyler, his vice president, was a troublemaker. He was a southerner and a former Democrat who had fallen out with his party. He had been put on the 1840 ticket only because the Whigs thought he would balance out Harrison and help broaden their electoral coalition. As no president had died in office at that point, no one had considered what Tyler might do if he were in charge. It was an oversight the Whigs would regret.

With Harrison dead, the party faced a point of order: Did the Constitution mean that the dead president's vice got the job, or was he a placeholder? While the Whigs were arguing, Tyler took action. He darted back to Washington, took the oath of office in his hotel room, and assumed the presidency.

That was the last thing the Whigs wanted. Unwilling to support his reelection, they threw him out of the party the same year he became president. This left Tyler free to pursue his own interests. Chief among them was the annexation of Texas.

Given that Texas was a country, the correct protocol would have been for the United States and Texas to sign a treaty on the subject. This would have been difficult, though. The Constitution says that any international treaty has to be approved by the Senate with a two-thirds supermajority—difficult at the best of times, but particularly so on such a polarizing issue.

Tyler and his supporters lobbied the senators for the next two years. They played up the economic benefits of national expansion, particularly with European powers skulking around the continent. They downplayed the slavery issue. Some supporters even argued that annexation of Texas would actually mitigate the political power of southern slaveholders. As they migrated to Texas, their influence would be diluted. But this was a risky argument, and ultimately the treaty that Tyler drafted made no mention of slavery at all.

By early 1844, Tyler thought he had the votes in the Senate for annexation. Texans, despite their pride, were amenable enough. "The Treaty I do not like," wrote Anson Jones, then president of the Republic of Texas, in a letter to Houston, "but suppose we must 'thank God and not look the gift horse in the mouth.'"

And then there was another twist. An explosion aboard the USS *Princeton* killed Tyler's secretary of state. To replace him, Tyler swiftly and carelessly picked John Calhoun, the South Carolina politician who was already among the preeminent southern voices in support of slavery. As tensions mounted and the prospect of secession was openly discussed, he would become one of the South's leading voices in favor of that too.

Unsurprisingly, Calhoun was not much of a diplomat, and within two months of joining the Tyler administration, he would prove it. Britain had established a presence in Texas—an alarming development for the United States, which still had uneasy relations with the empire. France was also taking a solicitous interest in the young republic. In April 1844, Calhoun sent a stern letter to Richard Pakenham, the British envoy in Washington, scolding him for the Crown's attempt to interfere with a land that was American in every sense but the legal one.

"So long as Great Britain confined her policy to the abolition of slavery in her own possessions and colonies, no other country had a right to complain," Calhoun wrote. But the United States, he continued, had the right to set its own policies. Technically speaking, Calhoun admitted, the policy was that every state in the Union could decide about slavery for itself. As the letter went on, however, he explained that freed slaves "have invariably sunk into vice and pauperism, accompanied by the bodily and mental inflictions incident thereto."

Calhoun's support of slavery and his hopes that Texas would be admitted to the Union as a slaveholding state were therefore made clear. Historians are divided on his motive for writing the letter, given that if it became public, it was bound to incite a backlash among those who were already suspicious of the argument that the annexation of Texas had nothing to do with slavery. In any case, the letter did become public, just days after it was written, and the Senate summarily rejected Tyler's treaty.

Tyler, however, had one more idea. It was an election year, and he had no chance of reelection. But in those days presidents were inaugurated in March rather than January. Congress could pass a resolution in favor of annexation—that would require only a simple majority. The president would simply need to sign it. Texas could agree to the offer later.

The resolution squeaked through just days before Tyler's time was up. The next president, James K. Polk, was a Democrat and an ardent expansionist. He was in favor of annexing Texas, and had campaigned on a promise to do so, and given that Congress had already passed a resolution in favor of the idea, all Polk had to do was keep the plan on track. In the end, that was easy.

Between 1844 and 1845, that is, the ground had changed. Some of the northern Whigs were worn down; despite their best efforts, the annexation issue hadn't gone away. Others had realized that Texas itself wasn't going away, and as an independent republic left to its own devices, it was bound to ally with someone, which wouldn't necessarily be in America's interests either. The British were sympathetic, and in May 1845, Mexico had offered Texas a deal: Mexico would recognize Texas's independence, finally and fully, as long as Texas didn't join the United States.[7]

Texas, however, still preferred annexation to independence, especially since all of the twists and turns of 1845 meant that the United States was suddenly prepared to extend its welcome on fairly favorable terms. Under the terms of the February resolution, the United States had offered to take on Texas's debt from the revolution, for example, and had agreed that Texas would be allowed to keep its public lands under state, rather than federal, control. In October 1845, Texans officially voted in favor of accepting America's offer, by an overwhelming margin, and on December 29, 1845, after Polk's sign-off, Texas was officially admitted to the Union as America's twenty-eighth state.

The legal union, however, didn't resolve all of the tensions between Texas and the United States. By the time Texas was annexed, after nine years as an independent republic, its nature was written in the bloody ground of the revolution and hardened by humiliation and rejection. Most of the weird things about Texas—the skepticism about the federal government, the hostility to elites, the ambitious entrepreneurs, the pushy religionists, the mean streak, the informality, the arrogance—had been inherited from the United States, but they were reinforced in the Republic of Texas, and they hold true today.

Not only that, but the uneasy relationship between an independent Texas and an adolescent United States of America had enormous ramifications. As we've seen, the debate about whether to accept Texas exposed and heightened the divides that would eventually bring the country to civil war.

And in addition to bringing those historic grievances into sharp relief, the annexation debate itself had created some new and lasting suspicians between America and what was then its newest, biggest state. These, too, would persist for years to come, with dramatic consequences.

4

STATE OF HATE

AS THE MOTORCADE CREPT along Houston Street in downtown Dallas, Nellie Connally, the wife of the Texas governor, turned to John Kennedy.

"Mr. President," she said, "You can't say Dallas doesn't love you!"

There was something wistful about the comment, or even apologetic. The fact was that Kennedy was in Texas because Dallas didn't love him. He had carried the state by a whisker in 1960, despite being joined on the ticket by Lyndon Johnson. The intervening years had done little for his standing in the state. With another election year looming, Kennedy decided to go back to Texas for a five-city tour.

Plenty of people in Dallas, like so many around the country, were wild for the young president and his beautiful wife. Thousands of them had packed the downtown streets that morning, November 22, 1963, to catch a glimpse of the motorcade. As the police escorts crept alongside the open cars, they were bumped by hundreds of hands, reaching and waving. And the business community, as business communities are wont to do, had set aside its more skeptical feelings for lunch. Across town, about a hundred people were awaiting the president's arrival for a bipartisan luncheon at the Trade Mart. Jackie Kennedy would later recall that her husband had warned her she would have to look as "marvelous" as all the rich, Republican wives who would be there: "Be simple—show these Texans what good taste really is."[1]

But there was an angry undercurrent in Dallas that day. It was the most conservative city on Kennedy's Texas tour, and a slightly venomous one. A month earlier, Adlai Stevenson, then the US ambassador to the United Nations, had been booed and heckled by an angry mob. One man spat on him, and a woman hit him with a sign. City leaders had apologized, profusely; one city councilman said the fracas was "the conduct of an ill advised and ridiculous group which has given the city of Dallas a national black eye."[2] The Secret Service had swept through Texas before the trip, working with local law enforcement to try to figure out if the city's right-wing rabble-rousers were going to cause any trouble. That day's paper had carried a full-page ad from some local businessmen accusing Kennedy of communism. Another ad accused him of treason. It was, one observer later noted, like inviting someone for dinner and greeting him with a cream pie in the face.

Still, no one could have expected what happened just seconds after Nellie Connally turned away from the president.

In the wake of the Kennedy assassination, people have taken a darker view. "A kind of fever lay over Dallas country. Mad things happened," wrote William Manchester in his 1967 account, *Death of a President*. "Radical Right polemics were distributed in public schools; Kennedy's name was booed in classrooms; corporate junior executives were required to attend radical seminars."

People had warned Kennedy he shouldn't even go to Dallas; it was just too sinister, too homicidal. Judge Sarah Hughes, summoned that morning to swear in Lyndon Johnson before *Air Force One* went back to Washington, was among the locals who agreed. Dallas was "a city of hate," she said, "the only American city in which the president could have been shot."

Even now, the idea persists that it was something about Dallas, and the city's right-wing reactionary politics, that led to the assassination. The theme was revived during the rise of the Tea Party movement. "To me, the similarity between Dallas in 1963 and today's unhinged Obama hate is downright chilling," wrote Eric Boehlert, a senior fellow at Media Matters for America, a progressive outfit that aims to counter conservative media, in 2009.[3] His headline spelled it out: "A President Was Killed the Last Time Right-Wing Hatred Ran Wild Like This." Essayist Frank Rich returned to the subject in 2011, tracing a connection between "Oswald's Dallas" and what he saw as the toxic climate being stoked by the Tea Party.[4]

Besides being unfair—in spite of its sometimes-invidious rhetoric, the Tea Party hasn't killed anybody—this claim is misleading. Lee Harvey Oswald, the man who killed Kennedy, simply wasn't a product of the right wing. He was a leftist who had married a Soviet woman and advocated on behalf of Cuba. After the assassination, moreover, it emerged that Oswald had once tried to shoot Edwin Walker, a far-right, segregationist, anticommunist retired army general. Although Oswald was apparently aware that Kennedy was unpopular among conservatives in Dallas, he had no affiliation with them.

Oswald didn't have much affinity with anybody in Dallas, for that matter. He had moved to the area because his mother lived nearby, in Vernon, but he had few friends and struggled to keep a job. People seemed to find him personally unpleasant. And his political leanings were distinctly leftward. "Oswald's writings and his reading habits clearly indicate that he had an extreme dislike of the rightwing," concluded the Warren Commission Report, "an attitude most clearly reflected by his attempt to shoot General Walker."[5]

The Warren Commission nonetheless agreed that at that time Dallas had a "general atmosphere of hate." Texans weren't even getting along with each other. One of the purposes of Kennedy's trip had been to force Governor John Connally and Ralph Yarborough, the state's junior senator, to at least pretend to get along in public. Both were Democrats, as most Texans were at the time, but Connally was from what would later emerge as the Republican wing of the Texas Democratic Party.

If there was a causal connection between the atmosphere in Dallas and the assassination, it was that police were so worried about the right-wing lunatics that they didn't bother to keep an eye on the lone weirdos. Regional law enforcement agents had a file on Oswald for various bits of communist agitation, but when it came time to scan the region for threats to Kennedy, they dismissed him. James P. Hosty, the investigator assigned to keep tabs on Oswald, later testified that even if he had realized the motorcade was going to pass by the Texas Book Depository, where Oswald worked, he wouldn't have notified the Secret Service.[6] Oswald was just a low-level commie, and there were plenty of those around. He had never made any threats against the president or the vice president, or the governor for that matter. (The Warren Commission ultimately disagreed with Hosty on this point. He was among the dozen FBI agents disciplined.)

The assassination is still a painful subject for Dallas. The sixth floor of the Texas Book Depository, where Oswald was perched that morning, has been turned into a museum, and it attracts hundreds of thousands of visitors each year. But the city doesn't support the Sixth Floor Museum financially, nor has it paid much attention to Dealey Plaza, across the street, which is still a slightly junky-looking area at the edge of the freeway. Given the blitz of development that's happened in Dallas in the intervening decades, the omission is notable, a monument to the city's ambivalence about how great its sense of guilt should be.

In a 1983 essay for *Texas Monthly*, Lawrence Wright, a writer for the *New Yorker* who is originally from Dallas, recalled going to church the day after. The pastor gave a sermon accepting blame, on behalf of the city, for being complicit in the city's murderous climate. Wright's father, sitting next to him in the pew, seemed resistant to this explanation, and just before the end of the sermon the pastor relayed a message he had just received: Jack Ruby, a local restaurateur, had shot Oswald. If Dallas killed anyone, Wright wrote twenty years later, it was Oswald. That one was fairly clear-cut. Ruby was apparently motivated by a desire to avenge the nation and defend the city's honor. The police could have stopped him if they had been more careful in moving Oswald around.

Rough justice for Oswald didn't save Dallas's reputation, however. Wright was among those who had some sympathy for the city. "The hatred directed at our city was retaliation for many previous grievances," he wrote, and then explained further:

> The East hated us because we were part of the usurping West, liberals hated us because we were conservative, labor because we were nonlabor, intellectuals because we were raw, minorities because we were predominantly and conspicuously white, atheists and agnostics because we were strident believers, the poor because we were rich, the old because we were new. Indeed there were few of the world's constituencies that we had failed to offend before the president came to our city, and hadn't we compounded the offense again and again by boasting of those very qualities? In that case we were well silenced now.[7]

The silencing wouldn't last. America's misgivings about Texas, however, have proven persistent.

Nearly fifty years on, the trauma of the Kennedy assassination is starting to fade, yet Texas is still seen as more or less a rogue state. There's a widespread impression that Texas is corrupt, callous, racist, theocratic, stupid, belligerent, and, most of all, dangerous. All of the horrible stuff it does ends up creeping into the nation as a whole through the underhanded strategies of textbook distribution and national elections. While there's a germ of truth to these charges, most of them are scare stories. But why would people be scared of a state?

Well, as we've seen, Americans had reason to be uneasy about Texas before it even joined the country. The fact that Texas seceded from the union almost immediately thereafter didn't really improve matters. But something else happened at the beginning of the twentieth century. Texas started to get rich. The first oil gusher in Texas was discovered in 1901, at Spindletop. Thirty years later, the state's oil industry became even bigger, with the discovery of gargantuan reservoirs in the East Texas oil field. Before oil, Texas didn't have enough wealth or power to influence the country one way or another. After oil, it did. The state could no longer be dismissed as merely eccentric.

We'll come back to the oil industry later, so the important point for now is just that the discovery of oil in east Texas left the state with a clutch of superempowered businessmen—superempowered not just economically, but also politically. Rich Texans weren't shy about using their newfound wealth to push for favors, and they were successful enough at doing so that the nation started to pay attention.[8] As early as 1933, when Franklin Roosevelt became president, national politicians were trying to end the various loopholes that were helping this new crop of wildcatters become wealthier than seemed reasonable. They didn't succeed. Over the decades, as the special treatment for the oil industry continued, the nation's resentment of it, and Texas, only strengthened.

Making matters worse was that after the oil industry brought wealth and influence to Texas, Texans started getting ambitious about other things. An episode that has special resonance in the wake of the 2008 housing crisis is the savings and loan (S&L) debacle. In 1982, Ronald Reagan signed a law that briefly made life easier for America's savings and loan institutions by adopting new regulations that were modeled after Texas's freewheeling rules on the subject. Some years before, the state had loosened up its rule by reducing the amount of deposits S&Ls were required to keep on hand and allowing the thrifts to lend money for commercial real estate projects.

This financial deregulation had seemed to be working in Texas. Greater access to capital had given more Texans a chance to hunt for oil. Others focused on real estate development: all those people who were getting into oil would surely want to buy fancy condos and office towers to suit their new station.

What happened after the nation followed suit could probably, in retrospect, have been predicted. Interest rates were relatively high in 1982, so investors were saving more money than usual. The S&Ls, being flush with cash and having more discretion as a result of Reagan's new rules, lent more money than usual. When interest rates came back down, however, investors wanted to move their money elsewhere. More than 1,100 of America's savings and loans institutions, having lent out most of their deposits, abruptly failed.

In 1989, George H. W. Bush—Reagan's Texan vice president, who had been elected president himself the previous year—signed what was at that point the largest federal bailout in US history. According to ProPublica, an investigative journalism group, the final tab worked out to about $220 billion. Texas was home to nearly a quarter of the failed institutions and came in for nearly half of the bailout funds. That really rankled the rest of America, because the wealthy Texans who had had the bright idea to deregulate in the first place had spent much of the 1970s lolling around on piles of oil money, building skyscrapers, and drinking rivers of wine with names they couldn't even pronounce as their fellow citizens in other states shivered through the winters because oil prices were so high that no one wanted to turn the heat up. Adding insult to injury was the fact that Texas got to keep all its tacky new buildings.

The result was a very low point for US-Texan relations. In 1990, Seth Kantor, a reporter for the *Austin American-Statesman*, summarized the mood in Congress as one of "mouth-foaming distemper over Texas." He quoted Frank Lautenberg, a Democratic senator from New Jersey: "This massive theft of New Jerseyans' pocketbooks was not some random bolt of lightning from God. It was largely the result of conscious, calculated decisions made by Texas itself."[9]

In a withering 1990 complaint, Kantor added, the *Chicago Tribune*'s editorial board wrote, "The Midwest will get no direct benefit in return for exporting its wealth to the Southwest. In fact, we'll have to work that much harder to keep our own economies growing. Meantime, our dollars will help keep Texas oilmen in rattleskin boots and fancy cars."

Yet time has shown that even a groundswell of popular enmity can't chasten Texas plutocrats. In fact, to judge from their public statements, they actually think people ought to show them more respect. "What I find interesting about the U.S. relative to other countries is in most every other country where we operate, people really like us," said Rex Tillerson, the CEO of Exxon Mobil, in a 2012 interview with *Fortune*'s Brian O'Keefe.[10] "And they're really glad we're there. And governments really like us. And it's not just Exxon Mobil. They admire our industry because of what we can do. They almost are in awe of what we're able to do. And in this country, you can flip it around 180 degrees. I don't understand why that is, but it just is." If he's really perplexed, of course it shouldn't be that hard to find someone who'd be happy to offer an explanation.

LET'S SET THOSE ISSUES aside for the moment, however, because to focus on the excesses of Texas businessmen is to ignore all the other things Americans dislike about Texas. When they're not castigating Texans for plutocracy, moral hazard, and corruption, the critics often protest that the state leads the nation in theocracy.

The state's highways are studded with billboards featuring babies who say, via thought bubbles, that they could dream before they were born, and there are occasional roadside clutches of white crosses, graveyards for the victims of abortion. In October, traditional haunted houses jostle alongside Christian "hell houses"—passion plays about the terrible things that will happen to people who drink or have sex.

The actors are, typically, local high school students. Most coveted is the role of the girl who, having lost her virginity, screams her way through an abortion as Satan exults from a corner of the tableau. A friend and I once straggled into an all-night donut shop on the outskirts of San Antonio at the tail end of a long road trip during college. The clerk asked where we had come from. New York, we said. "Well," he said, thinking it over. "You're in God's country now. And once you're in God's country, y'ain't ever wanna leave."

More to the point, Texas is the only large state where the religious right has enough power to push the policy agenda. It's a relatively recent development, and Christian conservatives generally don't take priority over business interests, but they do have more influence in Texas than in most states. "Where did this idea come from that everybody deserves free education, free medical care, free whatever?" wondered Debbie Riddle, a Republican state representative, in 2003. "It comes from Moscow, from Russia. It comes straight out of the pit of hell."[11]

Another frequent charge is that Texas is a morally degrading influence on the rest of the United States, given its fondness for executions, its expansive prison system, and its proclivity for firearms. No aspect of criminal justice in Texas excites more national and international criticism than the death penalty. In 1972's *Furman v. Georgia*, the US Supreme Court had held that the death penalty was being applied in an arbitrary way, making it cruel and unusual punishment and therefore unconstitutional—a ruling that effectively suspended all executions until a subsequent Supreme Court decision, 1976's *Gregg v. Georgia*, which held that it was possible to apply the death penalty fairly. Since the courts thereby reinstituted capital punishment, Texas has executed more people than any other state—491, as of November 16, 2012. That's more than four times as many executions as Virginia, the state with the second-largest number of executions, which has put 109 people to death in that time.[12] If Texas were a separate country, it would almost lead the world.

All of Texas's executions take place in Huntsville, a small city in east Texas—the final resting place of Sam Houston and home to a small university that bears his name. Up the road, the Texas death penalty museum holds a handful of exhibits that celebrate the city's history—photos of the old prison rodeos and the electric chair itself, Ol' Sparky.

Up to five journalists are allowed at each execution, although there's usually fewer—the Associated Press, a reporter from the Huntsville paper, and maybe one or two from the city where the crime was committed. Sometimes a handful of protesters turn up outside the facility. One such group included a pair of black-clad Europeans who had somehow brought the piano John Lennon used while composing "Imagine"; it was sitting next to them there on the sidewalk. Their employer, musician George Michael, had purchased the piano at auction. On his directions, they explained, they were taking it to sites of violence around the United States for a film project.

Around dusk everyone heads to the killing building. The front offices feel like a portal to 1960. There's a picture of John Wayne on the wood-paneled wall. At the appointed hour everyone—the officials, the relatives of the victim and of the offender, and the journalists—files in to the viewing area, where the offender, dressed for a trip to the hospital and draped in a white sheet, is already laid out on a bed. The victim's relatives watch from a window on the left side of the execution chamber (that is, the offender's left); the offender's relatives are on the other side.

The first person I saw executed, in March 2007, was Joseph Nichols, who had been convicted of a 1980 Houston murder.[13] Asked for his last words, he named one of the guards and snarled at her, "Fuck you, dyke-ass bitch."[14] The injections began. His breathing became raspy for a few moments; then he gave a gurgling death rattle and died.

The second person was James Clark. Asked for his last words, he seemed confused, if not mentally handicapped. "I didn't know anybody was there," he said. "Howdy."[15] He had only one witness, an elderly man with spatters of dried paint on his fingernails and a comb's tooth marks in his hair. The old man was crying, but trying not to so that he could smile and wave at Clark as he died.

The death penalty is an area where Texas truly stands apart from public opinion in the rest of the country. According to a November 2011 poll from the Pew Research Center for People and the Press, 62 percent of Americans support the death penalty for people convicted of murder and 31 percent are opposed.[16] A May 2012 University of Texas/*Texas Tribune* poll, by contrast, found that 73 percent of Texans were either "strongly" or "somewhat" in favor of the death penalty; just 21 percent were opposed.[17]

And Texas's use of the death penalty is in keeping with its generally punitive approach to crime. The state's prison population is dropping slightly—in August 2012, there were about 154,000 people behind bars, down from 156,500 a year before—but Texas nonetheless has the largest prison population of any state and the fourth-highest incarceration rate in the country.[18] Prison conditions are for the most part overcrowded, unpleasant, and, occasionally, abusive. Most of the state's prisons have no air-conditioning, for example, making them brutal places to stay in the scorching summers. Several inmate deaths have been attributed to heat, leading to ongoing lawsuits against the state.[19]

The state's disproportionate prison population is partly due to disproportionate crime. In every major category, Texas's crime rates exceed the national average.[20] It's also due to the state's historically draconian approach. Texas drug laws, for example, have been notorious not only for their severity but also for their use in neutralizing people who were suspected of socially disruptive behavior but who had only been pipped for drugs.[21] That is to say, political types. The most famous case is that of Lee Otis Johnson, a black activist and organizer from Houston who in 1968 received a thirty-year prison sentence after passing a joint to an undercover cop.[22] (He served four years before being freed on appeal.) "Felony malicious mischief" has been another catchall charge used to crack down on perceived troublemakers, usually black or Hispanic ones. That supposed crime, which generally refers to property damage or vandalism, carries a sentence of up to twenty years.

Despite the fact that Texas's rate of gun deaths per capita is higher than the national average, Texans support the right to bear arms. They always have: one of the grievances that triggered the revolution was that Mexico didn't want the settlers to be armed. According to one study, about 35.9 percent of Texas households are armed.

One of the few modern governors to be skeptical of Texas's gun culture was Ann Richards, a Democrat. She was tough on crime—she built new prisons and made it much harder to get parole—but she also vetoed a concealed-carry law in 1994, even after advocates tried to convince her that the law would be a particular help for women who were looking to ensure their personal safety. "Well, I'm not a sexist," she responded, "but there is not a woman in this state who could find a gun in her handbag, much less a lipstick."[23] That was during her campaign against George W. Bush, who promised that he would sign the law. He won and did. In 2010, as a security measure, the state added metal detectors at the entrances to the capitol building in Austin. People who have a concealed handgun license, however, are allowed to enter at the side.[24]

The state has expanded gun rights further since then. In 2007, it passed a new "stand your ground" law, the kind that became notorious in 2012 after a Florida man shot and killed Trayvon Martin, an unarmed black teenager who apparently hadn't been doing anything more suspicious than being a black teenager in public at night. The Texas version of the law, to be clear, is vastly less permissive than Florida's. It only allows you to stand your ground in your house, rather than wherever you happen to be at the time.

Most Texans aren't bothered by this. In fact, in a state that never saw a budget cut it didn't like, law and order is one thing they've been willing to pay for. "When it's a question of malnutrition, hookworm, or illiteracy against new equipment for the Texas Rangers, the Rangers always get what they need," explained journalist Molly Ivins in 1975.[25] That's still true; in FY 2010 Texas devoted 9.3 percent of its general revenue spending to corrections, two ticks higher than the national average.

WITH CRONYISM, Christianism, and a unique state outlook on how to deal with crime, Texas seems to have just about enough strikes against it in the popular imagination. Americans might be able to overlook some of this if not for the fact that Texans themselves seem to go out of their way to offend everyone as much as possible. The easiest way to do so seems to be by casually bringing up secession. And few figures are more infamous for mentioning the issue than Rick Perry.

April 15, 2009, was a bright, sunny day in Austin. Governor Perry was at city hall addressing a rally for people who were against the stimulus package, one of the nation's proto–Tea Party events. As the governor was leaving, Kelley Shannon, a reporter with the Associated Press, asked him what he thought about the idea that Texas could secede. Somebody in the crowd had shouted something to that effect, and Perry was known to be a big proponent of states' rights.

"Oh, I think there's a lot of different scenarios," Perry replied. "Texas is a unique place. When we came in the union in 1845, one of the issues was that we would be able to leave if we decided to do that."

"You know, my hope is that America and Washington in particular pays attention," he continued. "We've got a great union. There is absolutely no reason to dissolve it. But if Washington continues to thumb their nose at the American people, you know, who knows what may come out of that? So. But Texas is a very unique place and we're a pretty independent lot to boot."[26]

In Texas, the comments were greeted with a—well, with a snort, is probably the word. It was just Perry running his mouth. Other Americans, however, were shocked, maybe because they're not used to hearing their governors allude to secession or sovereignty. After Perry joined the presidential race two years later, the faux pas was revived to much fanfare: How could the Texas governor offer himself as a candidate for president of the country when he was on the record saying his state was thinking about leaving the Union?

I am a product of Texas public schools, so it's possible that my reading skills are just stunted, but Perry's statements don't strike me as a call for secession. "We've got a great union" is the first clue. "There is absolutely no reason to dissolve it" is the second. When pressed for clarification, Perry has repeatedly said that he wasn't seriously suggesting secession. He's also indicated that he finds all the hand-wringing to be slightly hysterical, in both senses of the word. PolitiFact, a non-profit organization that rates the truth or falsity of various political statements, has sided with the governor on this, also repeatedly. There is no serious separatist movement in Texas. The most coherent separatist movement in the United States, I believe, can be found in Vermont, which likes to think of itself as also having once been an independent republic (it wasn't).

To be sure, there are a lot of Texans, including the governor, who seem to think that Texas *could* leave the Union if it wanted to, although it can't. (There's a consensus among constitutional scholars that the Civil War put that question to rest for every state.) A 2009 Rasmussen survey found that 31 percent of Texans believed their state had the right to secede.[27] Rather than this number being evidence of some rabid revolutionary groundswell, it might very well reflect a problem in the Texas schools—I remember learning in class that Texas has the right to leave and also that Texas is the only state that can fly its flag at the same level as the US flag. As it turns out, however, it's not just Texans who think their state can secede. A June 2012 Rasmussen poll found that 24 percent of all Americans think individual states have the right to come and go freely—not Texas, that is, but any state that wants to go.[28]

Only 18 percent of Texans in the 2009 survey, however, said they *wanted* to leave the Union; 75 percent wanted to stay. A Research

2000 poll, taken that same year for Daily Kos, found similar views around the country. Asked if their state would be better or worse off as a separate country, about 80 percent of Americans said the states were better off together. The South was the outlying region in that survey: only 61 percent of southerners were sure they wanted to stay in the Union, and 9 percent thought their state would be better off as an independent country. The rest, 30 percent, weren't sure, which sounds about right. A Republic of Alabama would have some problems. Texans are more confident about their ability to go it alone, even if they're nonetheless pro-Union.[29]

Still, the belief that Perry was calling for secession has been incredibly persistent. I suspect some Democrats are trying to gin up outrage for political purposes. In June 2012, Martin O'Malley, the governor of Maryland, told reporters that Republican governors were threatening as much in response to the Supreme Court's decision to uphold the health-care reform bill. "Some of our colleagues would like to get out of being members of the union," O'Malley said. "And by that, I mean the United States, so I think, who can predict what some of the ewoks on their side of the aisle will chase, I don't know." He didn't call Perry out by name, but he might as well have. Catherine Frazier, the governor's press secretary, had said that Perry "has absolutely no interest in accelerating the implementation of Obamacare." By the going evidentiary standards, that's basically proof that Perry was holed up in the Texas capitol jumping on his desk and firing pistols in the air.

Many Americans, however, were probably sincere in their belief that Perry was threatening to secede. The idea that Texas wants to secede seems to have taken root. After the 2012 elections, hundreds of thousands of disgruntled Americans signed online petitions on a White House website calling for their respective states to be allowed to secede. Almost every state was represented, but the fact that the Texas petition had more signatures than any other touched off a new round of chatter from outside observers, even though Texas's petition was bound to have the most signatures, given how many people the state has, and even though a genuine secessionist would scoff at the idea of signing an online petition on a White House website.[30] A troubling possibility is that all the discussion about secession is creating confusion rather than clarity. The June 2012 Rasmussen survey, recall, found that 24 percent of Americans believed that individual states have the right to secede. In June 2011, a Rasmussen poll on the subject had found that slightly fewer Americans, 21 percent, held that belief.

That brings us to the crux of the issue. While Texas has primary responsibility for its own reputation, the state does seem to induce a sort of collective confusion, like a political version of body dysmorphia disorder, that isn't doing either the state or the country any favors. I ran into this phenomenon in July 2012 when the *New York Times* asked me to review a new book about Texas by Gail Collins, one of the paper's in-house op-ed columnists.[31] She opens her book with an account of that same April day I described above. In it, she mentions that Perry quoted Sam Houston: "Texas has yet to learn submission to any oppression, come from what source it may." For Collins, this was evidence that Texans might actually be in favor of secession. "When Houston made that remark," she writes, "he was definitely attempting to break away from the country to which Texas was then attached."

Houston made that claim in an 1850 speech to the US Senate about the US Army's occupation of Santa Fe, in the New Mexico territory, following the Mexican-American War. The borders of Texas were a catch-as-catch-can affair at that point. Houston thought part of the New Mexico territory should go to Texas, but his main point was that Texas's concerns should be addressed before, say, California's, as Texas had been annexed earlier and had been waiting to settle its borders for several years. So Houston wasn't threatening to break away from the United States; quite the opposite. He was arguing that Texas had rights because it was part of the United States.

And as we know, Houston's commitment to the Union didn't stop there. As the speech went on (and on), he shifted gears to address issues closer to home for the assembled senators. This was July 1850, and the month before, delegates from nine slaveholding states—not including Texas—had met in Nashville to try to figure out what they would do if the federal government decided to ban slavery in the new western territories. The Nashville convention, Houston said, was unconstitutional; the states weren't allowed to make deals among themselves without congressional approval, so the whole thing was "ridiculous flummery." For his part, he added, he was committed to the Union, and Texans felt the same way: "Think you, sir, that after all the difficulties they have encountered to get into the Union, that you can ever whip them out of it? No, sir. . . . We shed our blood to get into it, and we have now no arms to turn against it."

"But we have not looked for aggression upon us from the Union," Houston continued, coming back to the matter at hand. "We have looked to the Union of these States and its noble course to vindicate our rights, and to accord to us what in justice we claim—what we have ever claimed—and less than which we can never claim."

It's easy to see how this particular misunderstanding could arise. There's no reason a person from Ohio or Washington would have a sideline in this particular subject, and Lord knows Texans spin their own history enough that the water is pretty muddy. Texas did secede, and Texans do talk big.

That last may be a cultural thing—Texans tolerate this sort of bluster and sometimes even take pleasure in it as a sort of sport. "It's a long-held theory of mine that politicians should provide public entertainment," wrote Molly Ivins in *Shrub*, her book about George W. Bush, and she gave him high marks in that respect at least. Other public figures provide similarly good value. In 2012, Drake, a Canadian rapper, shared a personal experience on Twitter: "The first million is the hardest." He was summarily retweeted by T. Boone Pickens, the oilman from Amarillo, who appended his rejoinder: "The first billion is a helluva lot harder." For that matter, Texans sometimes scold other people for being overly polite or chicken. Here's Perry again, on the

2010 sinking of South Korea's *Cheonan*: "The United Nations responded with its characteristic force, passing yet another resolution expressing displeasure."[32]

This approach has its pros and cons. Texans are not, for example, passive-aggressive, and surely part of the reason Texans don't mind tough talk is that Texans sometimes are tough. Lyndon Johnson, to take one, was a notorious bully. On a personal level, he bullied his wife, bullied his staff, and even, in an extraordinary recorded phone call, bullied Haggar Slacks into custom-tailoring a pair of pants to leave more room "down where your nuts hang."[33] Politically, he bullied America into tragedy in Vietnam, and he bullied Congress into passing voting rights, civil rights, and the Great Society reforms.

On the other hand, Texans occasionally go so far that even Texans are offended. In 1990, Democrat Ann Richards famously got a boost in her bid to become governor after the Republican nominee, Claytie Williams, compared rape to bad weather: "If it's inevitable, just relax and enjoy it." That wasn't a flippant response to a question about sexual violence, by the way. He had some reporters out to his ranch, and it was fixing to rain, which reminded him of his favorite rape joke.

Richards herself was no knuckle-dragger, but she did have a sharp tongue and got herself in some trouble over it for good measure. Her jabs about the George Bushes—"He was born on third base and thought he hit a triple" (about George W. Bush), and "He was born with a silver foot in his mouth" (about his father)—were treasured by Democrats. When the comparatively mild W. beat her in the 1994 gubernatorial election, however, some pundits admitted that the ridicule might have been a factor in turning voters off.

And if Texas pols manage to offend Texans, it's no surprise that national audiences sometimes find their style repugnant. In 2011, while running for the Republican presidential nomination, Perry said that if Ben Bernanke came to Texas, he would be treated "pretty ugly." That was a boorish thing to say, and silly; whatever your feelings about quantitative easing and monetary policy, neither was "almost treason-ous," as Perry also put it.

Still, I was surprised to see that pundits took the remark as a threat to *lynch* Bernanke. That seemed like a real anthropological non sequitur, not to mention somewhat unfair to Perry, who signed a hate-crimes law in 2001 and who managed, in any case, to leave Bernanke in peace after that.

If outsiders have a hard time discerning the cultural factors behind Texan behavior, Texans can't necessarily see what outsiders are seeing either. That same year, I wrote a piece for the *New Republic* about Perry's rhetoric. When the editor sent back his changes, he had added a clause pointing out that it was extremely insensitive of Perry to bring up secession, given that such language would remind people of the racial strife and suffering that had precipitated the Civil War. The change was wrong, and I took it out. When Texans talk about being independent and not needing Washington, they're always referring to the Republic of Texas. That's where the state directs its romantic yearning. It's never to the Confederacy.

But the edit did make an impression on me. It had seriously never crossed my mind that the people upset about Perry's secession com-ments thought it was a crypto-Confederate thing. Ivins, for that mat-ter, had reported a similar experience in the wake of the September 11 terrorist attacks, when Bush started talking about smoking Osama bin Laden out of his hole and so on. "I am such a Texan that . . . it was 'Sign me up for the posse, sheriff' time for me," she wrote, in an update to her Bush biography after W's first term in office. "It never occurred to me that was inappropriate language. When others pointed it out, I, like Bush, promptly became defensive."

In the arts, Texans are often depicted as loudmouthed, greedy, and somehow involved in oil, like JR from *Dallas*, the Rich Texan from *The Simpsons* ("If not for oil, you wouldn't have four-wheel drive!"), or Tex Richman, the villain in the most recent installment of *The Muppets*

(2011), who buys the old Muppets theater because he wants to get at the oil underneath.

Sometimes the critique is subtle. A friend bought a beautiful book for her infant son, *This Is Texas*, part of a 1960s children's series by Czech illustrator Miroslav Sasek that includes *This Is Paris* and *This Is New York*. We leafed through it one night over a glass of wine. "Leonard's Subway, the only privately owned subway in the world, takes you from the parking lot to Leonard's Department Store," Sasek wrote. "No charge. It is also the only subway in Texas where passengers might drown in oil." We puzzled over this. "There's a certain *tone*," my friend concluded, "that isn't in the other books."

The sneering reached a new high when George W. Bush emerged on the national stage, speaking English the way he does. "Such frank boobery would seem to represent a culmination of the long, strange history of anti-intellectualism in America," writes Mark Crispin Miller, who was moved to write a whole book on the subject of Bush 43's syntax and diction.[34] "Certainly George W. Bush has always postured as a good ole boy, who don't go in fer usin' them five-dollar words like 'snippy' and 'insurance.'" Over the course of this nuanced critique, Bush is compared unfavorably to, well, lots of people, but I am particularly moved by Miller's wistful comment that, unlike President Bush, Franklin Pierce "was fluent in Greek and Latin, like so many of his peers." Yes, the good old days of antebellum America. Black people were held as slaves, women couldn't vote, and the American buffalo was on the verge of extinction, but at least the affluent white men of America's political elite spoke Greek so that we didn't have to be so ashamed of our boobery. More problematically, Americans sometimes exult when Texans fail. Look back on the commentary surrounding Enron, in which you could cut the schadenfreude with a knife, or after the 2011 wildfires that destroyed hundreds of homes in central Texas, when lots of people thought of the same joke: Texans should have prayed harder for rain.

This is not very neighborly, even if Texas has a lot to answer for. I'm not sure how often Floridians are scolded for the fact that their state single-handedly screwed up the 2000 presidential election, Iowans held personally responsible for agricultural subsidies that exacerbate food insecurity around the world, or New Jerseyans asked to explain their idiosyncrasies, some of which are charming. Texans, however, are routinely asked to account for guns, the death penalty, the prison-industrial complex, the savings and loan crisis, George W. Bush, Karl Rove, Enron, Halliburton, Tom DeLay, Rick Perry, the Confederacy, the Republican Party, the religious right, the war in Iraq, the war in Afghanistan, war in general, stupidity in general, and the fact that Texans ride horses to school.

Some of these charges have the sting of truth, but Texas isn't really as horrible as everyone thinks. If you just look back at how far it has come to get to where it is today, you would be hard-pressed to consider it crazy. Texas spent its first forty years grappling with its own revolution, the Mexican-American War, the Civil War, and Reconstruction: that's why Texans aren't big on government. Its next thirty years, however, brought the rise of the cattle industry and the discovery of oil—two phenomena that solidified Texas's love of the private sector.

5

LAND AND CATTLE

IN 2010, GLOBAL UTMANING, a Swedish think tank, issued a report entitled "The Nordic Way" about, essentially, how great Scandinavia is: rich, free, peaceful, egalitarian. And not only that, the authors argued, the Nordic countries are, contrary to what you might have heard, bastions of individualism. Think of Pippi Longstocking, the mischievous redheaded girl, as a case in point—the character is a cultural icon in Sweden and not someone who likes being told what to do. "Statist individualism" is the phrase the authors used to indicate that the government's role in Scandinavia is to foster the conditions that allow people as much freedom as possible. A strong social safety net supports people. Women, for example, don't have to be dependent on men; subsidized child care helps a woman raise her children without the economic support of a husband.

The authors asked readers to consider a triangle. At one vertex is the government, at the second is the individual, and at the third are hierarchical institutions "such as the traditional patriarchal family and demeaning charitable organizations in civil society." Looking at three modern welfare states—Sweden, Germany, and the United States—the authors observed that each approaches the triangle differently.

Sweden, for example, is wary of the third vertex—private organizations such as families, churches, and charities. That's why in that country individuals are allied with the government, yielding the statist individualism previously described. The German state, by contrast, is less concerned with individualism; it allies itself with families and other civil society groups. The triangle doesn't specifically mention corporations, but one example of Germany's commitment to group cohesion would be the work-sharing policy called *Kurzarbeit* that Germany adopted during the recession: if participating companies agreed to reduce workers' hours, rather than lay people off, the government would help supplement the wages to make up the difference.

The United States, meanwhile, has historically been skeptical of government. Individuals are more likely to draw their support from other institutions—family, church, charity. Even when they engage with the government via politics, Americans are liable to ask the government to limit itself. "In the U.S.," wrote the authors, "individual (rights) and family (values) trump the state (always seen as a threat to liberty)."

The triangle is a little simplistic, perhaps, but as a heuristic, it's not bad. The United States is clearly a small-government country when compared to its peers in Europe, and Americans are more likely to turn to their families or private groups for support. That's partly a matter of necessity, given that this country's safety net is smaller than Sweden's, but there's also a cultural dimension: it would never occur to an American to breezily summarize charities as "demeaning."

And Texas, with its suspicion of government and its devotion to the private sector, isn't wholly out of sync with American tradition. It does, however, take both phenomena further than most states do. One woman learned that the hard way: Oprah Winfrey.

"THIRTEEN YEARS AGO," wrote Oprah Winfrey in the March 2011 edition of her monthly column, "What I Know for Sure," "I was on trial in Amarillo, Texas, for defaming a burger."[1]

In 1996, that is, she had invited a representative from the Humane Society to appear on her show. Mad cow disease was the disease of the moment, and her guest explained that every year thousands of American cows drop dead overnight, at which point they are ground up and fed to other cows. If any of the dead cows died of mad cow, then other cows could get mad cow too.

Hearing about these encephalitic, cannibalistic cows, Oprah announced that she would never eat another burger. When cattle prices plummeted shortly thereafter, ranchers were outraged. So they sued.

They eventually lost, and things worked out for Oprah: "I learned a lot about myself," she avowed. But it was a revealing episode. You would think that Texas, as free and proudly belligerent as it is, would be the ideal place to defame a hamburger. For goodness' sake, Texan politicians are always thundering on about frivolous lawsuits; tort reform is one of the things Rick Perry includes in his recipe for economic success—a recipe, remember, that has only *four* ingredients.

But as we've seen before, and as Oprah's experience made clear, Texas looks out for its businesses. Incentives and subsidies help them along their way. A minimalist approach to taxes and regulations anticipates their needs. And if you mess with Texas business, you might get in trouble for it. In most states the ranchers wouldn't even have been able to sue. Texas, however, is one of about a dozen states with a law against food defamation.

The fact that the majority of Texans are okay with the state's fealty to business interests strikes national Democrats as incomprehensible. Most Texans, after all, aren't rich. Many of them are flat poor. And yet over and over again they elect leaders whose governing principle seems to be Fat Cats First. In this, they are like middle- and working-class Republicans around the country. The phenomenon is so widespread, and so bizarre, that in 2004 progressive journalist Thomas Frank wrote an entire book about it, *What's the Matter with Kansas?* In response to the titular question, he concluded that millions and millions of Americans are simply "deranged." The Republican Party's power brokers, Frank argued, realized that they could win over a healthy swathe of the electorate by making a big fuss over social issues like abortion and gay marriage—issues that are so emotive that voters will prioritize them, even if the party with their preferred views has an economic agenda inimical to their interests.

The triangle that Global Utmaning presented points to an alternative explanation. Americans are bullish on the idea of free enterprise because the system historically worked for them. In Texas, at least, they see the private sector as a crucial part of the safety net. If that's the case, Texans are hardly crazy. If you look at the history of the state, it's a reasonable perspective.

AT THE END OF THE CIVL WAR, Texas was in a slightly different situation from that of the other former Confederate states. Not having much wealth or infrastructure in the first place, Texas hadn't been devastated by the war in quite the same way. Thousands of its men had died in the war, but no cities had been burned to the ground; there was nothing to rebuild. There wasn't much appetite for the Reconstruction that followed, either. The effort in Texas was overseen by General Philip Sheridan, who clashed with the locals immediately and continuously and wasn't one to suffer in silence. "If I owned hell and Texas," he told a reporter in Galveston in 1866, "I would rent Texas out and live in hell."[2]

Sheridan wasn't the only person who felt that way. The Indians may have known Texas as "the happy hunting ground"—that is, heaven—but later arrivals tended to see Texas as a more infernal sort of place. Texans, of course, think this is funny. One of the state's folk songs tells the story of how the Devil created Texas, with its blazing sun and stinging insects, as the land where he would feel most perfectly at home.

One thing Texas always had going for it was land, and lots of it. In east Texas, some of it was even fertile. Historian H. W. Brands observed that Texas has existed in a state of seclusion imposed by the land and its climate. Unlike many states, it doesn't have a dominant river; rather, the state is striped with several smallish ones, running from the northwest toward the Gulf of Mexico. "In the age before motorised land travel, rivers were the key to crossing continents," he wrote. "With no large rivers, Texas held the key to nothing besides itself."[3] But those dinky little rivers, dawdling through the hills, hardly had the strength to push their silt out to sea. They just piled their treasure along their own banks.

Strong homestead policies, an inheritance from Spanish and Mexican law, meant that the land was accessible to anyone with a little bit of money. Before the revolution, undeveloped land in Texas went for a few cents an acre; throughout the rest of the official United States, an acre was more than a dollar.[4] So it was that at the time Texas became a state in 1845, most of its people were small farmers—25,000 of the 43,000 employed in the state, according to the 1850 US Census. The land was good for sugar cane and sweet potatoes, but cotton was the main cash crop.

It was a tough and monotonous life: tearing down and rebuilding fences, plowing, plowing, planting, plowing, hoeing, planting, hoeing. Maybe, once in a while, killing "a beef." One farmer's journal, from 1848, takes a dark turn in the first week of November: "We had a light frost the first this year." Three days later: "We had frost quite heavy." Two days after that: "Very heavy frost the sugar cane was Killed on the fourth of November." This wasn't a plantation economy; the aforementioned census found 21,878 slaveholders in Texas, more than half of whom had five slaves or fewer.

Still, it was a living, and a broadly accessible one. By the end of Reconstruction, Texas had become America's biggest cotton state. Even today it produces about a quarter of America's cotton, which is now shipped to Bangladesh to be spun into yarn, then to Vietnam to become a T-shirt, and then back to Texas to be sold at Wal-Mart.

Texas also had cattle, another legacy of the Spanish empire. People had been herding cattle in Spain for hundreds of years, and when the conquistadores came to the Americas, they brought the cows and the knowledge with them. The Mexicans then invented ranching; they learned how to ride horses from the Indians and developed the tools they needed to control cattle on the open range—the spurs, the lassos, the brands. That's why so many cowboying words (lasso, corral, rodeo, ranch, stampede) are drawn from Spanish.

The Anglo settlers weren't so successful as ranchers to start with. Some of the east Texas settlers kept small herds and sold them at the stockyards in New Orleans. Others hunted wild cattle for meat. But with the size of the territory, a lack of fencing, and Comanche and Apache raids, the whole business was initially more trouble than it was worth. Locally, there wasn't much demand. Cows were easier to come by than currency in those times, and in the Texas stockyards beef was selling for just a few cents per pound.

After the war, though, Texans saw an opportunity. Left unattended, the descendants of the Spanish cattle had multiplied and became feral. There were millions of cows and calves roaming east Texas, most of them unbranded and more or less there for the taking. The South was too impoverished and devastated by the war to be a viable market, but America's northern cities had an appetite for meat and the dollars to pay for it. Best of all, the federal government was building transcontinental railroads. If Texans could drive their cattle up to Kansas, they could load them onto the trains at Abilene.

The result was the birth of the Texas cowboy. "With peace established," wrote Texas folklorist J. Frank Dobie in 1941, "the catching and branding of these cattle became in some regions almost the sole occupation of the returned men and developing youth."[5]

The wild cattle were known as mavericks—an Anglo-Texan contribution to the English language. Their namesake, Sam Maverick, a lawyer from South Carolina, had at various points tried to run a gold mine in Georgia and a plantation in Alabama, but without much success. He eventually turned up in Texas just before the revolution with the idea of becoming a land baron like Stephen F. Austin. He also became one of the men who signed the state's declaration of independence from Mexico. He is best remembered as one of the state's first cattle barons, although he never really had many cows and it was an accident that he had any at all. In 1845, a neighbor owed him money and tried to pay him back with four hundred cows. Maverick didn't have any interest in that line of work, but the neighbor didn't have anything else to offer. Because cash was in short supply, a cow and a calf together were worth about $10.[6] So Maverick just took them and left them to wander around under the loose supervision of a slave family.

That was about it until 1856, when Maverick decided that he might as well sell them. But there was a complication. His herd, most of them at least, had never been branded. On the open range, there was no other way to keep track of which cow belonged to whom. Maverick found a buyer who was willing to take a risk: he would pay for four hundred cattle, and that would entitle him to all the local cows that might have belonged to the herd, whether that ended up being more or fewer.

The apocryphal version of the story holds that the deal was actually a ruse on Maverick's part. If everyone was using brands to mark cattle, he could declare that his brand was no brand and that any unbranded cattle must be his. In reality, Maverick probably didn't care enough to concoct such a scheme; he seemed sincerely bored by the cow business, and unbranded cattle were an easy target for cattle rustlers, so this idea wouldn't have worked anyway. Texans had already developed the habit, though, of never letting the facts stand in the way of a good story, so soon enough lone cows were called mavericks.

Today, of course, the word "maverick" is used to describe somebody who makes his own rules. "According to an old saying representing a common belief, all it took to make a cowman—an owner—was 'a rope, nerve to use it and a branding iron,'" Dobie explained. "It took more than that. When mavericks were thickest, markets were remote and uncertain. Any man who developed a fortune on the open range was masterful enough to control his part of it and to

maintain ownership of stock widely scattered and always being further scattered unless the scatterers were held down."[7]

Catching the animals was only the first task. Driving a herd of
longhorns up to Abilene could take several months, and the journey
was a hard one. The cowboys had to keep an eye out for rustlers and
raiders. All the while they were vulnerable to storms and heat, snakes
and coyotes. "Herds would always drift before a storm and we would
have to follow them for miles, while vivid lightning and crashing peals
of thunder made our work awesome and dangerous," recollected one
cowboy years later. "Sometimes several head of cattle or horses were
killed by one stroke of the lightning, and many of the cowboys met
their death in the same manner."[8]

The biggest headache came from the cattle themselves. It's strange
that today's Texas politicians claim they don't believe in evolution,
because Texan farmers and ranchers got a firsthand look at the process
in action. The descendants of Spanish cattle quickly transformed into
a new breed. Foraging in the wild over several generations, longhorns
had become tall, tough, and leggy.[9] They could run for miles and were
hardy in the face of hunger and thirst. They were also well suited to
traveling together. In a herd, a social order would naturally emerge.
The cattle who took the lead tended to stay there for the whole drive.
The weak or lazy ones made up the rear. Most of them seemed to find
a best friend. According to Dobie, "When in any kind of mix-up these
pardners became separated, they would go bawling until they found
each other."[10]

But under certain conditions, these traits made them hard to
handle. These cows were ferocious, fast, suspicious, and self-reliant.
Chroniclers of the era rarely resisted the parallel between the head-
strong longhorns and the Texans who were trying to control them.

"It is the domestic animal run wild, changed in some of his habits
and characteristics by generations of freedom and self-care," observed
Richard I. Dodge, a midwestern army officer. "Texas was a new country then, and certainly an aggressive country. Every bush had its thorn;

every animal, reptile, or insect had its horn, tooth, or sting; every male human his revolver; and each was ready to use his weapon of offense on any unfortunate sojourner, on the smallest, or even without the smallest, provocation."[11]

That was why stampedes were a constant danger. The slightest surprise—a sudden noise, an unexpected animal—could send the entire herd careening. Even if the whole herd was asleep, if any individual animal sensed a disturbance, they all might leap to their feet and bolt before the cowboys realized that there had been any disturbance at all.

Despite the difficulties of life on the trail, people were drawn to the work. All a person needed was grit and determination, and although women liked cowboys well enough, it was men who fell in love with the business. They enjoyed the pride of hardship, the intimacy that arose among men living without women, the exclusivity of their private knowledge.

And for those who had the mettle, the opportunity was real, at least during the early days. A young man could make a living doing general cow work, catching mavericks and branding them for owners, getting paid by the head. But more importantly, he could go into business for himself. Some ranchers paid their cowhands in cattle, and an enterprising individual could also catch mavericks on his own time. "Today many of the richest and greatest men of Texas were cowboys," wrote Charles Goodnight, the founding owner of the JA Ranch, in the state's northern panhandle, which is still in operation today. "Of the hands I employed there are now at least three millionaires. Fewer cowboys have been tried for crimes than any other class of men."[12]

One of the first labor disputes in Texas arose because cowboys felt their economic rights were being abridged. At the beginning of the 1880s, big businessmen from the Northeast and Europe decided they wanted to get in on the beef bonanza. They bought up large swathes of Texas land and fenced it with barbed wire, a relatively recent technological innovation. And they wanted their ranch hands to work for wages. Any mavericks, they decreed, would belong to the company.[13]

In response, in 1883, several hundred cowboys went on strike. They were worn down quickly. There were plenty of able-bodied men around to be hired in their stead. But the protest said something about Texas values that persists today. In 2008, John Cornyn, a Republican senator from Texas and not in most cases a man to sympathize with organized labor, wrote a column (he writes an occasional column about Texas history and current events) to commemorate the cowboy strike and praise the strikers' actions: "At stake was their chance to claim a part of the American dream."[14]

The cowboys were self-reliant, but with a voluntarist side; they were willing to help each other. "A man walking needs some explanation," noted Frank Hastings, a rancher, "although he is always fed without question."[15] That helped mitigate some, though far from all, of the hardships on the frontier.

Meanwhile, the state's easy openness, reinforced in both culture and lack of law, attracted outsiders. In 1860, Texas had about 604,000 people. By 1870, the figure had jumped to some 818,000. And ten years later, it had roughly doubled, to nearly 1.6 million. Most of those migrants were people looking to make a living. If anyone had asked them the modern question—but are they *good* jobs?—the answer probably would have been "good enough for now or better than what I had before."

Then, as now, people were ultimately on their own. There was certainly no recourse to government, with barely any government to appeal to. One man struck out with little more than a couple of ponies, two blankets, a skillet for cornbread, and a can for boiling coffee. Within six weeks, he had branded about 250 cattle, a reasonable little herd. But he didn't realize he had to register his brand until a friend loped by and happened to mention it. The next morning, when he turned up at the county courthouse, the clerk told him that someone else had just recorded that brand as his own. None of the cattle were legally his. There was nothing anyone could do about it.[16]

The safety net was so threadbare, in fact, that alternatives took root. Cowboys developed their own code. "With us of the Plain country, a man's word was his bond," said rancher J. Frank Norfleet. "Our cattle deals, our land sales—transactions running into many thousands, frequently—were often completed 'sight unseen.' . . . We never doubted each other; in fact, no graver insult could have been passed upon a neighbor than to demand legal formalities in dealing with him." Explaining why it was no wonder he had fallen for a con, he reasoned, "If I was gullible, I was simply following the reasoning habits I had acquired in my lifetime of experience."[17]

The cowboys also occasionally called on the Texas Rangers—an informal policing force that had been gathered, subject to funds and availability, since before the revolution. They were famous for being tough and lethal. Equipped with little more than horses and guns, Rangers tracked hostile Indians or Mexicans or outlaws over hundreds of miles and provided an early iteration of Texas justice.

The dangers of living at the mercy of a brutal and half-wild paramilitary force were evident, and the abuses of the Rangers became impossible to ignore after the Mexican Revolution began in 1910. The Rangers were under instruction to keep Mexican soldiers from crossing into Texas, a task that they pursued with too much enthusiasm, as in 1918 when they massacred fifteen Mexican American men and boys at the tiny border town of Porvenir. This triggered an investigation in the state legislature, with the result that the force was officially merged into the state's public safety bureaucracy.

Nevertheless, during the cowboy heyday, the Rangers had been regarded as among the state's few effective quasi-public servants. Historian T. R. Fehrenbach would later described them as "one of the most colorful, efficient and deadly bands of irregular partisans on the side of law and order the world has ever seen."[18]

Remnants of cowboy culture persist in modern Texas. For most residents it's little more than a matter of public self-image, although some pockets of the state are still rife with cowboys, or at least people who do cowboy kinds of things. The west Texas town of Sweetwater, for example, has hosted an annual rattlesnake roundup since 1958. Participants in this event win prizes for bringing in the most snakes, the biggest snake, and so on. The year I went, there were tens of thousands of rattlesnakes in pens, slithering and rattling. A handler wrapped a four-foot snake around my neck. In the air, the sour smell of the live snakes mixed with the savory smell of dead snakes being fried as snacks. The whole event had a slightly festive feeling, between the patriotic country music and cavorting teenagers, but the larger purpose was very serious. Rattlesnakes are a legitimate pest, liable to kill cows, dogs, and people, and the people of Sweetwater prided themselves on catching as many snakes as possible. Knowing how to catch a rattlesnake, ride a horse, and shoot a gun may no longer be critical life skills for most Texans, but we're not so far removed from the era when they were.

THE CATTLE KINGDOM was destined to be short-lived. By the 1880s, overgrazing had made it harder to drive cattle over the great distances of the Chisholm Trail, as did a severe winter in 1886–1887. The development of barbed wire meant that ranchers could keep their cattle hemmed in on ranches on the plains—no need to fetch them from as far away as Texas—and on top of all that, the demand for beef withered as a result of a national economic downturn.

In just a few decades, however, the individualistic and proto-libertarian ethos symbolized by the cowboys had seeped into Texas's character. The private sector was already emerging as a substitute for government, even when it came to the provision of public services. And Texans were starting to believe in their ability to bootstrap themselves as long as they were willing to work hard.

This hasn't been a wholly positive state of affairs for everyday Texans. After all, hard work can take a person only so far. That much was clear even in the 1880s. "Cattlemen have always been subject to disasters beyond their control," observed Texan journalist S. C. Gwynne in November 2012, adding that ranching has always been "a tough, almost comically cruel business."[19] No matter how tough a person was, no one could control everything. When the beef boom collapsed toward the end of that decade, the cowboys were out of luck. No amount of hard work and sheer will could have saved them from the drought and depression that ensued.

And as the cowboy strike suggested, people are inevitably affected by other people; that's why some observers have always thought that the cattle kingdom's ethos of self-reliance was a mirage. "The real-life cattle baron was and is about as democratic as a feudal baron," wrote novelist and essayist Wallace Stegner. "The cowboy in practice was and is an overworked, underpaid hireling, almost as homeless and dispossessed as a modern crop worker, and his fabled independence was and is chiefly the privilege of quitting his job in order to go looking for another just as bad."[20]

But humility would have to wait. Texas was about to discover that it was richer than anyone could possibly have imagined.

6

BLACK GOLD

AMERICANS TEND TO BELIEVE in economic mobility, in the idea that people can get ahead through talent and hard work. This belief persists in spite of the fact that in some respects the United States is less mobile than other rich countries.[1] The question of whether Americans are correct to feel that way, of course, is different from the question of whether they do.

Texans, are, if anything, even more committed to this belief than other Americans. Don't take my word for it, though; take it from a young Democrat: "Now, in Texas, we believe in the rugged individual," said Julián Castro, the mayor of San Antonio, in his keynote speech at the 2012 Democratic National Convention in North Carolina. "Texas may be the one place where people actually still have bootstraps, and we expect folks to pull themselves up by them."

I had made a similar observation several months earlier to Mark Strama, a Democratic state representative from Austin. He agreed immediately: "That's the oil industry." It was the state's oil industry, in other words, with its wildcatters and speculators, that had fueled the typical Texan's belief that he too can make it big.

At the beginning of the nineteenth century, few could have imagined that oil would one day become a hugely valuable resource. Wood was America's preferred fuel source, and it would remain so until 1885, when it was overtaken by coal.[2] Oil, when encountered by Indians or settlers, was occasionally used as a cure-all or as grease for the axles of a wagon. A few enterprising quacks had been bottling it up and selling it as medicine—three teaspoons a day was the recommended dose for a variety of minor complaints. But it didn't seem to have any large-scale commercial potential.

In fact, oil was widely seen as a nuisance. The really valuable commodity in the nineteenth century was salt, an object of elaborate, dangerous, and arduous mining operations. Oil was often found near salt mines—an inconvenience, because it fouled up the salt wells and had to be refined out of the salt water. When drillers seeking salt accidentally tapped an oil well, they would often simply abandon the site and start over from scratch somewhere else.

Things started to change in the 1850s, as chemists developed techniques for refining oil into kerosene, meaning that it could be readily used as fuel. In 1854, a Canadian chemist patented his technique for doing so, and the North American Gas Light Company was formed that year as a result. The market for the new product was still small, but its prospects were tempting. If drillers could get their hands on a large quantity of oil—rather than just the burbles that came up from the salt mines or the slicks that pooled at the top of some lakes—there might be some profit to it.

In 1858, the Seneca Oil Company—which had been incorporated four years earlier as the Pennsylvania Rock Oil Company by a pair of businessmen acting on a hunch—was the first American company to try to drill an oil well on purpose. The man they sent to the fields of western Pennsylvania, Edwin Drake, had no experience with oil or with drilling. He had previously worked as a train conductor, but he was looking to try something new. In 1859, after struggling for a few months as the locals grew increasingly amused by his efforts, he hit an oil well, thus ushering in the age of American oil exploration and production.

This boom was slow to reach Texas, even though everyone who arrived in the state, from the Spanish onward, knew that there had to be some oil there. Greasy lakes, rivers that smelled like sulfur, ponds that bubbled more than could be considered strictly normal, all hinted at a surfeit of the stuff underground. By the 1880s, a handful of landowners had started looking for oil, although none of them were producing it in quantity or expecting to make much money that way. In most cases they simply used the oil as fuel on their own farms or sold sloshes of it as lubricant for the few industrial operations, such as lumber mills, that had emerged.[3]

One Texan who took a different view was Patillo Higgins, an eccentric from the east Texas town of Beaumont. That stretch of the state, approaching the gulf, was dotted with so many peculiar little hills that it was known as the "pimpled plain." Noting the devilish, sulfurous smell that pervaded the area, many locals figured there might be oil there. Higgins had a big imagination, and by the early 1890s he had managed to raise enough money for two drilling attempts just outside Beaumont.

He had his eye on a site that was sometimes called Big Hill. Its other name, Spindletop, would one day be famous around the world. But not yet: both of Higgins's first attempts, in 1892 and 1893, failed. Once the workers he hired got below the surface, they found themselves trying to drill through several hundred feet of quicksand. This was a geological feature of Texas's Gulf Coast that the Pennsylvania drillers hadn't experienced. Few businessmen were anxious to push on with such a tricky technical assignment. Drillers in north Texas were starting to pull up oil in modestly good quantities, but they didn't have to go through all that quicksand to get it, and even so, the oil they were finding was of poor quality. The oil in the Pennsylvania fields was relatively high in paraffin, meaning it could be refined into kerosene, which was at that time the major commercial product for which oil was used. The Texas oil was more sulfurous; it couldn't be refined into kerosene, and it therefore wasn't anything to get unusually excited over.[4]

More to the point, the experts still didn't think there was oil in east Texas. In 1895, the Texas Geological Survey sent a surveyor to east Texas in response to Higgins's appeals, but the bureaucrat in question was unimpressed. He reported that there was no evidence of any oil in east Texas. Anyone who said otherwise, he added, was suffering from "idle dreams or insane notions."[5]

Even though Higgins refused to be deterred by evidence or the absence thereof, his friends and backers in the area were losing interest. To fund further attempts, in their view, would just be throwing good money after bad. In 1898, Higgins, as a last resort, took out an ad in a mining journal. Only one man responded.

Anthony F. Lucas had been born in Dalmatia and trained as an engineer before immigrating to the United States. He grew up in a salt-producing area in Europe, knew the techniques for mining it, and specialized in salt exploration after moving to the US. He had been working as a mining engineer along the Gulf Coast, mostly in Louisiana and Texas, when Higgins's ad caught his attention.

Once Lucas saw the pimpled plain, he agreed with Higgins that it looked promising. The mounds, Lucas knew, were covering salt domes. When trapped far underground, salt tends to push toward the surface of the earth. If the subsurface salt was flowing upward, something might rush in to fill the caverns it created. And given the slow, heavy, sulfurous air, the something in question might well be oil, just as Higgins had long suspected.

The drilling began in 1900. Lucas ran into the same quicksand that had stymied Higgins's previous attempts, but he had known to expect it. He had his contractors drill and case the well in sections, using five concentric rings of piping, as in a collapsible telescope. After three months, and 1,160 feet below the surface, they were finally able to report a success of sorts: the water used to clear the pipes flushed out some seashells. That would be the top of the salt dome. Just a little farther, then.

They kept drilling and cracked into rock. At the wellhead, water and drilling mud started gurgling up. Curt Hamill, a worker perched on the top of the derrick, leaped down as fast as he could. Moments later, the innermost pipe, about six tons of steel, shot into the air, blowing off the top of the derrick. A torrent of gas, oil, and rock followed closely behind. The workers, scrambling to respond, built a levee to surround the oil; it was overflowed by the end of the day. They built a second one and it overflowed and a third one and it overflowed. By the third day, officials estimated the flow at 75,000 barrels a day—more than 3 million gallons. "Probably I had been too conservative in my previous estimates," reflected Lucas later.

It was quickly apparent that this first well was the biggest in America. Almost overnight, the Beaumont region exploded. Still, experts remained skeptical. The man who had originally adjudged the field a lost cause, William Kennedy, teamed up with another geologist, C. W. Hayes, to publish a report in 1903, asserting, "No rational theory . . . connects [these oil fields] in any way with deep-seated commercial deposits of oil or gas, and experience has shown that they have no connection with such deposits."[6]

But there were plenty of chancers who didn't need a rational theory. They could see the gushers soaring into the sky—whenever someone struck oil, it was common practice to let the oil gush for a few minutes, for public-relations reasons. By the middle of that year, there were more than two hundred wells on the Spindletop Hill. The derricks were built so close together that sometimes workers would build planks between them at the upper levels in case there was a blowout and someone needed to escape.[7] And these wells were productive. In 1901, according to the Energy Information Administration, the United States produced 69.3 million barrels of oil.[8] Nearly a quarter of it came from the wells that had just been built in Texas.[9]

ECONOMISTS HAVE LONG OBSERVED that natural resources may be a curse as well as a blessing. An abundance of one resource may lead a state or country to focus on exploiting that resource rather than laying the groundwork for a more diversified economy. The effects are exacerbated if an outside actor develops the resource in question, as the state's resource wealth is spirited out of the area of origin altogether. Even in the United States, where we're supposedly all in this together, states have suffered from their mineral wealth. Kentucky and West Virginia, for example, are poor states today partly because they have so much coal.

Texas, similarly, could easily have become a banana republic of the wealthy, industrialized Northeast. It was a poor state with minimal capital, laughable infrastructure, and limited government. So it was a bit of luck—for Texas, at least—that by the time Lucas brought in that first gusher, skepticism about big business, and about the northeastern oil industry in particular, was already on the rise.

Since 1859, when Edwin Drake had proved that oil could be extracted in great volumes, easterners and midwesterners had poured into the Pennsylvania fields. "Fortune was running fleet-footed across the country, and at her garment men clutched," reported Ida Minerva Tarbell,[10] a muckraking journalist. Among these men was John D. Rockefeller. Today he's remembered for his philanthropic endeavors and his palatable iteration of Republicanism, but he began as an oilman and a clever plutocrat. His company, Standard Oil, started out as a small producer and grew into the colossal urmonopoly of its time. It could easily have become the dominant oil interest in Texas—there was simply no person or corporation in Texas big enough or rich enough to compete with it—if not for a timely dose of government intervention.

That is, in fact, the great and mostly unappreciated irony of Texas's oil and gas industry. Texas discovered oil at precisely the moment—the *only* moment in state history—when populists had the upper hand in government. This was an accident of history that would prove to have enduring consequences for both Texas and the United States.

Populism as a movement emerged in the United States at the end of the nineteenth century, for reasons that are too complicated to detail here. But we can quickly summarize by saying that in the years after the Civil War, American agriculture was almost completely reorganized. In the South, the end of slavery meant that the plantation system gave way to sharecropping and tenant farming. Having few assets, these farmers wanted access to credit. Concurrently, millions of Americans were striking out for a new life in the western territories. Those faraway farmers needed a way to transport their crops to market. By the 1880s, then, American small farmers needed banks and railroads—and the banks and railroads were big enough, and consolidated enough, to squash the small farmers.

Texas was a natural breeding ground for the ensuing agrarian revolt. In addition to being affected by both of these regional issues, the state, having joined the national economy relatively late in the game, had always been wary of the big businesses that had already taken root in the United States. Its first state constitution, in 1845, declared that "monopolies are contrary to the genius of a free government, and shall never be allowed." The events of the subsequent decades only reinforced that feeling. Agriculture (including ranching) was the state's biggest industry—its only industry, really—throughout the nineteenth century.

Farmers were, as a result, Texas's most powerful interest group, and northeastern monopolies were one of their greatest grievances. The banks and the railroads weren't even the only industrial interests that had made life harder in Texas. In the 1880s, for example, cordage companies had banded together to goose the price of binder twine—a serious blow to small farmers, who needed the twine to tie up cotton bales.

In 1889, Texas became the second state, after Kansas, to pass an antitrust law—a law that included an exemption for agriculture, which confirms that it was indeed the farm lobby that had led the quest for the law. The next year, Texas elected a new governor, James Stephen Hogg, a populist who campaigned on a promise to ensure more state oversight of the (national) railroads. The agency he created, the Texas Railroad Commission, would eventually take on oversight of the state's oil industry too, meaning that it was soon to become the most important state regulatory agency in the history of state regulatory agencies. But more on that in a minute.

The immediate result of the populist surge was that when the Spindletop gusher came in, in 1901, Texans—prone to be hostile to outside interference under any circumstances—already had an antitrust law that gave them the capacity to keep outside businessmen at bay. Actually, Texas had started its fight with Big Oil years before, as soon as it got the law. In 1894, the state indicted Rockefeller and the other directors of Standard Oil for antitrust violations; there was little oil activity in Texas at the time, but Standard was controlling what there was. A lawyer for the company protested that the Texas antitrust law might not be constitutional, and in any case Standard Oil wasn't doing hardly anything in Texas. Even so, the state took the case all the way to the Supreme Court, and in 1895 Texas won.

The result was that at first, at least, Standard Oil backed away from Texas, and other national oil companies were similarly dissuaded from setting up in-state operations. "Texas politicians had demonstrated to 'foreign' capitalists that they could exercise a large measure of control over business activity in the state, if they were so minded," writes Roger Olien, a Texan historian who has specialized in the state's oil industry.[11] "At the very least they could create exceptional impediments for a firm based outside the state."

This was blatant protectionism, of course. But Texans didn't really pretend otherwise, even at the time. "Shall Texas or the trusts control?" Hogg had asked in 1900. It was a rhetorical question. Then, as now, Texas was probusiness. But it was even more pro-Texas. As the oil industry grew, the state's parochialism would pay off—for Texas.

Other Americans didn't realize the same gains, and as Texas became richer, they occasionally felt that it was at their expense.

Writers and historians have also debated the extent to which the state's growing oil industry was good for everyday Texans, as opposed to Texas as a state. "No other industry in American history has ever been quite so democratic," writes Robert Bryce in *Cronies*, his 2004 book about the political influence of the Texas plutocracy—a book that is, as you might guess from the title, largely critical of the men behind the curtain. Olien thinks that Texans did better for themselves than they might have: "Keeping political power in their own hands, Texans accepted capital from outsiders, but strictly on their own highly advantageous terms."[12] Journalist Bryan Burrough, who traced the rise of four Texas oil families in his 2008 book, *The Big Rich*, strikes a slightly different note: "If Spindletop created an oil industry for Texas, little of it ended up controlled by Texans. The big money at Spindletop was initially split between groups of powerful Texas businessmen and seasoned oilmen from back east."

As these comments suggest, the supposed egalitarianism of the oil industry is at least partly a matter of perspective. If the oil industry was more democratic than any other in American history, as Bryce says, that wouldn't necessarily make it democratic in any objective sense. And as Burrough points out, the huge profits were going to businessmen, even if they were Texan businessmen.

On the other hand, the oil brought wealth to many Texans for the first time—not just the lucky wildcatters. Landowners could make some money by selling or leasing. Young men could find work in the oil fields so long as they were willing to deal with rough, occasionally fatal conditions. At the time, for example, there was no equipment to indicate when they were breathing too much poisonous, sulfurous gas. It was up to the workers to gauge their own exposure. "They knew when they were breathing gas, and they knew about how much they could stand," reported Charlie Jeffries, who worked on a rig at Sour Lake, near Spindletop, in 1903. "When one felt that he was getting too much, he would go away a short distance and breathe fresh air till refreshed. Still, sometimes, in spite of every precaution, one would be overcome, and if help were not at hand, his life would be the forfeit."[13] Other risks included being maimed, trampled, blinded, or murdered. The early oil industry wasn't, in other words, a crazy boondoggle for everyone.

What's clear, though, is that the discovery of oil was a good thing for many Texans, and a great thing for *some* Texans, enough of them that it made an impression on their peers and thereby helped cement the belief that Texas was a place where bootstrapping was possible. This belief had arisen early, because entrepreneurs did build this state, often with very little help from the government. Those first *empresarios*, like Stephen F. Austin, were basically government contractors, paid in land to take on a task that the Republic of Mexico didn't have the capacity to do directly.

It's a wonderful historical irony that oil, which turned out to be the most important industry in Texas history, is extremely difficult to manage without the sort of centralized planning that only government, even in Texas, can provide. In fact, as Professor David F. Prindle observes in his 1981 history of the TRC, the oil industry is strikingly unresponsive to the "invisible hand" that classical economists describe, for two reasons.[14] First, oil can't be made; it has to be discovered. Second, Prindle explains, "in a society recognizing the private ownership of property, the unusual physical qualities of oil introduce a dynamic that leads to both economic and physical irrationality." In other words, oil flows in response to pressure. If one person starts drilling, his neighbor has a reason to do the same; otherwise the oil in the reservoir is going to flow away from his property. But if lots of people start producing oil, then the pressure in the reservoir will drop, so the remaining oil becomes too sluggish to flow. An unregulated oil market would produce too much at first, and exhaust itself too quickly; the market would be flooded, and then the fields would run dry.

book but that one
was on back order.
Ok — now to the
dénoument :
Book #2 finally
got here & is
enclosed.

Happy Birthday!

Boria

Gloria Wilner

Paul, I bet you don't
remember this—
On a visit here (last
summer?) you spotted
a book (paperback)
that I said not to
read then, because
I was saving it for
your birthday. You
objected to having to
wait so long so we
agreed you could have
it then. I have no
memory of title or
author. At that
time I also said
I'd ordered another

Texans realized that in the first decades of the twentieth century, as drillers jostled alongside each other to get the oil while the getting was good. The TRC was tasked with regulating oil pipelines in 1917, on the reasoning that pipelines are also a form of transportation, and shortly thereafter it was asked to oversee other aspects of Texas's oil production, including production quotas.

In 1935, the TRC got a boost from government intervention at the federal level. While Congress couldn't regulate any state's oil production, it could pass a law giving the federal government the authority to crack down on efforts to skirt state production quotas by sneaking oil across state lines. Given that Texas was producing nearly half of the nation's oil at that point, the new law reinforced the state's tremendous influence over the nation's oil production—and by extension, the nation's oil prices—until the 1970s, when the Organization of Petroleum Exporting Countries (OPEC) started to throw its more considerable weight around. OPEC, incidentally, was partly modeled on the TRC.

The regulators, however, never got as much hold on the popular imagination as the wildcatters. And so the lesson Texans took from the oil industry was that capitalism creates opportunities; they remained wary of government, as they are today. That doesn't mean they were or are right, necessarily—but given other experiences Texans have had with government, or the lack thereof, it's not that hard to understand.

7

THE UNGOVERNED

TEXAS TODAY IS A STATE that prefers limited government. Even its Democrats are more conservative in that sense than their national counterparts. As with so many aspects of the state's culture, the small-government stance took root long ago. The reason for that wasn't just that Texans had a history of conflict with the various governments they happened to be held under at the time. They also never developed the habit of expecting much from their government.

After annexation, for example, Texas had serious public health problems. Its citizens were riddled with such diseases as malaria, cholera, yellow fever, dysentery, and gonorrhea. The public sector had few resources for sanitation or other public health interventions. It was hard to recruit doctors to the frontier, anyway, because so many settlers had no way to pay them other than in cows, pigs, and chickens. The government, fragile as it was, could do little other than pressure the newspapers not to write stories about the various outbreaks of disease; if word got out, then it would be even harder to get doctors to come to Texas. People got used to making do on their own.

They might have developed a different view, but they never really had a chance. In 1876, in the wake of Reconstruction, Texas wrote a

new constitution that has effectively guaranteed a limited government ever since. Barring some kind of overhaul—which has been
attempted several times, never successfully—the state's role is bound
to be a small one.

Texas is one of only four states, for example, that doesn't have a
personal income tax. Creating one would require an amendment to
the state constitution, which would have to be passed by a two-
thirds majority in both houses of the legislature and then approved
by a majority of voters.[1] Another unusual thing about Texas is that
its legislature meets for only 140 days, every *other* year. This creates
problems because the legislature does have some responsibilities,
such as writing the budget for the following two-year span. In January 2011, the state comptroller told legislators they would have
$72.2 billion to spend in the 2012–2013 biennium. The projection
resulted in harsh budget cuts, and turned out to be too low, by
nearly $20 billion.

One way to interpret the Texas constitution is that the delegates
who wrote it had nothing but contempt for the government. That's
why they took care to limit it in perpetuity. That is, in fact, pretty
much what happened. The state's current constitution was written in
1876, less than a decade after the state had been taken over by Radical Republicans, who had saddled the state, during the Reconstruction, with a government that was much bigger than Texans were used
to or wanted. The 1876 delegates were determined to keep politicians from having so much power ever again. They largely succeeded, because even though the anger of that era has abated, the
document it gave rise to continues to hold sway. In a superficial
respect, of course, the delegates' plan failed, because the Texas Capitol has once again been infiltrated by Radical Republicans, but we'll
come back to that later.

WHEN THE CIVIL WAR came to an ignominious end, all of the Confederate states understood their defeat as a military failure rather than a

moral one. Texans, in addition, liked to tell themselves that their state was unique. This was a preoccupation that had obviously preceded that war. Among the grievances listed in Texas's secession ordinance, for example, was that the federal government had failed to protect Texan settlers from Indian attacks on the frontier.

This attitude was clearly self-serving. Slavery had been the cause of secession in Texas as in every other Confederate state. Although there were relatively few slaves in the poor and sparsely populated Republic of Texas—that is, between 1836 and 1845—the state's population had grown steadily since annexation, and slavery had taken root firmly by the time of the Civil War. The 1850 US Census counted 58,161 slaves in Texas and an overall population of 212,592. By 1860, the state's population had nearly tripled and included 182,566 slaves.

Still, Texas had lost less than many states during the war, largely because it had had less to lose. Being at the western edge of the Confederacy, the state had seen minimal fighting. Also, the abolition of slavery didn't threaten Texas's future the way that it did the other formerly slaveholding states. Despite the growth of slavery in the antebellum era, Texas was the whitest state in the Confederacy, and after the Civil War about 30 percent of its people were freedmen. In Mississippi, by contrast, the 1860 Census had counted about 354,000 white people and about 437,000 slaves. African Americans were also the majority in South Carolina, which went into the war with 291,000 whites and some 402,000 slaves. Emancipation in those states posed a potentially existential threat to white supremacy. White Texans didn't like the end of slavery, but they had less reason to fear it.[2]

In the aftermath of the Civil War, then, Texas was resigned to being readmitted to the Union under the lenient terms that Abraham Lincoln had set out. Andrew Johnson, the Southern Democrat who ascended to the presidency after Lincoln was assassinated in 1865, planned to follow his predecessor's plan, after declaring the insurrection over in August 1866.[3]

What followed would be a crucial chapter in the development of Texas's political identity. By 1867, Republicans in Congress had realized they didn't like President Johnson and they didn't need him either. Annoyed by his magnanimity to the beaten Southerners, the Republicans preferred to reconstruct the South according to their own specifications. They swiftly passed a series of acts, overriding Johnson's veto, that took a harder line. The advent of Radical Reconstruction put most of the former Confederacy under military control. Texas was lumped into a district with Louisiana. Anyone who had done anything in public life on behalf of the Confederacy was barred from future public service, from serving on a jury to holding office. Whites could be disenfranchised for disloyalty, and many were. Meanwhile, the freedmen would have full civil rights, including the right to vote.

Besides being a tremendous blow to the ego of Texans, Reconstruction also threatened to upend the political order. By 1868, Texas had about 100,000 registered voters, lower than might be expected given that the 1870 Census would find that Texas had about 800,000 people. Anglos maintained a whopping majority in terms of population, but they had been whittled to a narrow majority of the electorate, because the Republicans had been busily registering the freed slaves and summarily dismissing thousands of white voters. Partisan affiliation fell mostly along racial lines, but given how small the white majority was, and the ban against former Confederates holding office, Texas Democrats were thoroughly driven from power. In 1869, they were so discouraged they didn't even have a candidate for governor; a Republican, E. J. Davis, won the office.[4]

Having asserted unprecedented power in the state, Republicans sought to put their stamp on Texas. As the majority party at the state constitutional convention called in 1869, they drew up a constitution that reflected a governing vision unlike anything Texas had seen before. The document favored centralized authority for the first time in Texas's history. It brought public schools under state, rather than local, purview; introduced several new tax streams; and expanded the governor's role.

The message was clear enough: national Republicans weren't even going to bother reconstructing Texas as it had been before the war. They wanted to raze the state's political infrastructure, such as it was, and build it from scratch—effectively by force but with the humiliation of democratic pretense.

Resentment was mounting. White Texans felt they were being subdued for political reasons, which of course they were; the carpetbaggers were attempting to remediate the condition of the freedmen, no small task given that white Texans would have been happy for African Americans to be second-class citizens indefinitely. During the previous constitutional convention, in 1866—after the passage of the Thirteenth Amendment but before the insurrection in Texas had officially ended—delegates had abolished slavery, and authorized some economic rights for the freedmen, but they had also barred African Americans from voting or holding office.

When Texas was readmitted to the Union in 1870, it was still in effect an occupied state under Republican rule. Even Texans who had opposed secession to begin with were becoming far less sympathetic to the national government. The policies and tactics of the Reconstruction government were unpopular with everyone except the Republicans who had written and enforced them. Texas being Texas, the very idea of having a superempowered governor, an elaborate school bureaucracy, and occasional and arbitrary imposition of martial law was a bridge too far.

In 1872, Democrats finally mustered enough seats in the legislature to force a gubernatorial election. The following year Democrat Richard Coke, a former Confederate officer, won the governorship.

The Republicans did not take the results gracefully. Governor Davis outright declined to accept that he had lost. Republicans locked the Democratic legislators out of the capitol and stationed guards around the first floor so that they couldn't sneak back in to vote.[5] But the Democrats out-tricked them by sneaking into the second floor of the legislature, where they were able to quickly count the votes and announce that Richard Coke was indeed the new governor.[6]

The new administration set to work summarily undoing the previous one. In 1875, a new constitutional convention met. The document its delegates produced limited the state government severely. It also bolstered individual rights. The writ of habeas corpus was reaffirmed, as were due process, the right to bear arms, the right to free speech, the right to free religious expression, and the separation of church and state. All in all, more than two dozen rights were detailed in the first article of the constitution, including a metaright: "To guard against transgressions of the high powers herein delegated, we declare that everything in this 'Bill of Rights' is excepted out of the general powers of government, and shall forever remain inviolate, and all laws contrary thereto, or to the following provisions, shall be void."

The convention delegates whittled away the governor's job description until his office was one of the weakest in the country. The legislature, they decided, needed to meet only once every two years (under Reconstruction, it had been convened annually). Most of the public sector took a salary cut, including the delegates themselves, who slashed their per diem at the start of the discussions.[7] Joe B. Frantz, a former head of the Texas State Historical Association, notes that the delegates were so hostile to government and public administration that they didn't even hire a stenographer—a real disservice to the future heads of the state's historical associations, because it meant there were no official records of the deliberations.[8]

Perhaps most significantly, the delegates severely limited the state's authority to borrow, tax, and spend. Though this might sound appealing to today's Republican Party, many scholars, not to mention Texans themselves, would come to regret that the delegates went to such lengths to tie their own hands. They had come up with dozens of tax rules, most of them concentrated in one article, others jammed haphazardly throughout the document. Some of these were in direct contradiction with each other, and none of them showed much thought, foresight, or even awareness of what other parts of the constitution were saying about the state's responsibility to its citizens.

In Article 7, for example, the constitution tasks the legislature with finding out a way to create and support an efficient system of free public schools ("a general diffusion of knowledge," it explains, is "essential to the preservation of the liberties and rights of the people").[9] This is a worthy standard, which Texas can hardly meet. Schools cost money, and the constitution didn't provide for a state-level income tax or sales tax or property tax, which are the usual ways that states raise money.

"In a state constitution there is no need to mention any power to tax," sighed George Braden, a constitutional law expert, in a 1976 analysis. "The legislature has all the taxing power anybody can dream up."[10] Similarly, he observed, there was no need for a state constitution to explicitly limit both taxing and spending; a limit on the former was bound to achieve the latter. His advice came one hundred years too late. The whole thing was a "mess," concluded Braden, having attempted to explain the matter in nearly one hundred pages of Talmudic detail.

Texans were so upset by the federal government, in other words, that they took out their frustration on the state. Counterintuitive, perhaps; maybe they would have done better to create a stronger state, so as to guard against encroachment by the feds. But the feeling seemed to be that government was government. If the federal government could commandeer the state government, as it had during Reconstruction, the difference was immaterial. "In almost every way possible they indicated that public administrators were a nuisance who needed to be turned out almost as quickly as they assumed office," concluded state historian Joe Frantz. "The system provided for little continuity or time for planning, and Texas has suffered from it for a century."[11] The new constitution became the law of the land on February 15, 1876. And with that, Texas's hostility to government—its own and everyone else's—became a self-fulfilling prophecy.

THERE WERE SEVERAL MOVEMENTS in subsequent years to replace the 1876 constitution, none of them successful. The most sustained effort came in 1974 when the legislature set out to replace the old constitution with one that would be less erratic and less restrictive. "Its members repeated all the old mistakes and added a few new ones," according to Frantz.

The US Constitution works, in part, because of its elasticity. The Texas legislature, and the lobbyists, took the opposite tack; they tried to preempt future interpretations the state might come up with by detailing their specific preferences on the issues of the day. By the time they were through, the legislature itself didn't even approve its own document. The next year, the state went to the voters directly and offered them eight propositions that had been suggested during the drafting attempt; the voters rejected all of them. The result, Frantz concluded, was that "Texas lumbers along with a constitution that was written for a horse-and-buggy age."

Individualist, small-government ideology can't explain this much commitment to the old constitution, especially considering how ideologically impure Texans are in practice when government is able to provide something they want. Throughout the twentieth century, for example, Texans were receptive to government spending and occasionally pursued it with ardor. Nor does an explanation lie in a solemn respect for tradition. Texans are fond of tradition, but they fiddle with the constitution all the time. As of 2012, voters had considered 653 amendments to it and approved more than two-thirds of them.[12]

Here's another way of looking at the matter: it might be that Texans believe in small government because their government is small. In 2010, computer scientist Jaron Lanier published *You Are Not a Gadget*, a jeremiad against the unanticipated consequences of technological design. The details of any new device or system, he explained, reflect any number of factors—the designer's conscious decisions, of course, but also the designer's unexplored assumptions and habits, the technological constraints of the time, the materials available, and so on. Regardless of whether these constraints are deliberate, users often receive them as such. The tools teach the user how they should be used. "We tinker with your philosophy by direct manipulation of your cognitive experience, not indirectly, through argument," Lanier asserted.[13]

This might apply to the political habits in Texas. The delegates who wrote the 1876 constitution clearly intended to limit the government forever. Certainly, they hamstrung the state with arbitrary restraints that made governing difficult. But, as Lanier argued, the effects of a design may start to seem normal, even right. The governor can hardly do anything, so no one expects much from him. The legislature isn't even there most of the time. The state agencies don't have much room for encroachment. There aren't that many regulations, which is lucky, because there aren't that many regulators. The State Board of Education can't even force its local counterparts to teach kids that premarital sex is a sin. Some aspects of the Texas constitution were clearly intentional and would be included if the document were rewritten today. Other aspects, though, are bugs. One of Texas's problems is that it's not entirely clear which is which.

The best example of this dilemma is probably the state's skimpy legislative schedule. The framers of the Texas constitution clearly didn't want state legislators to do much; the only task they are required to tackle is drawing up a state budget. Given that they have only four months every other year to manage that, the budget does end up subsuming much of the legislature's time. In theory, a small-government conservative might think that's a fine idea. In practice, however, even Texas's small-government conservatives sometimes complain. It's hard to write a good budget that spans two years, takes effect more than a year later, and is largely based on projections about how much money the somewhat unpredictable sales tax is going to bring in.

THERE HAVE, OF COURSE, always been Texans who wanted a more active government. That's one of the major points made by Jim Hightower, a Democrat who served as agriculture commissioner of Texas from 1982 to 1990 before losing that office to Rick Perry, then a little-known state representative who snuck up with a propesticide platform.

Today, Hightower is one of America's most high-profile populist—on the left, at least. One of his themes is that the parties have been co-opted and the people misled (unlike Thomas Frank, he thinks this is true of Democrats as well as Republicans). In his view, Texas is a Republican state because the people have gotten so discouraged that they don't bother to vote. If they did vote, the Democrats—the progressive Democrats—would surely take control. After all, he observes, there was a time when Texas was America's populist states.

That's true, but there are complications in the picture. One is that Texas's populists were actually relatively conservative. They even had a big hand in writing the superstrict 1876 constitution. About half of the delegates were affiliated with the Grange, one of the farmers' coalitions. (The state has big tax exemptions for agricultural interests even today, when it isn't just lowly farmers who get to take advantage of them. Michael Dell, the founder and CEO of Dell, is one of the beneficiaries; Rick Perry is another. Put up a few birdfeeders, house a roadside zoo, and, presto, your land is farmland.)

The version of populism that flourished in Texas wasn't strictly a philosophical indictment of big business or a vote in favor of a robust public sector. It was a reaction to the big business interests that already existed and were making it harder for Texas businesses to get big.

Texas's populist politicians, in fact, talked up the virtues of free enterprise. In 1895, when James Hogg (who was then attorney general) went to the legislature to promote the antitrust law, he made the case that it would be good for business: "The contention that this anti-trust law is a menace to prosperity and will deter capital from investing in this State, is, logically, to insist that the way to induce the investment of capital, and to promote prosperity, is to welcome monopoly and legalize trusts—to substitute combination to fetter trade for competition to give it freedom."[14]

By the late 1800s, the aspirational ideal of success through entrepreneurship had already taken hold. Even before the oil strike at Spindletop, Texans had gotten the idea that any of them could become entrepreneurs. They saw themselves as workers allied against bosses, but also, importantly, as potential bosses allied against the established, moneyed bosses of the North. Regardless of whether it was true, that belief would prove salient.

You can see the tension if you compare the 1892 Omaha Platform of the national populist movement with the Texas party's version. Both documents argued that the working people of the United States, particularly farmers, were being systemically disadvantaged by federal policies that favored established moneyed interests—bankers, corporations, etc. They called for many of the same things—a graduated income tax, free silver, labor protections, electoral reforms—and the Texas platform specifically endorsed the populist platforms presented elsewhere, including Omaha.

The Omaha Platform, however, called for a more robust government to step in. "We believe that the power of government—in other words, of the people—should be expanded (as in the case of the postal service) as rapidly and as far as the good sense of an intelligent people and the teachings of experience shall justify, to the end that oppression, injustice, and poverty shall eventually cease in the land." With regard to the railroads, a major issue at the time, the national populists wanted a government takeover: "Transportation being a means of exchange and a public necessity, the government should own and operate the railroads in the interest of the people. The telegraph, telephone, like the post-office system, being a necessity for the transmission of news, should be owned and operated by the government in the interest of the people."

The Texas platform preferred a smaller role for government: "We demand that all revenues—national, state, or county—shall be limited to the necessary expenses of the government, economically and honestly administered." It advocated more government oversight of certain industries, but government takeover only as a last resort: "We demand the most rigid, honest, and just national control and supervision of the means of public communication and transportation, and if this control and supervision does not remove the abuses now existing, we demand the government ownership of such means of communication and transportation."

It's as if the national populists saw the political system as a potential bulwark against private greed, whereas Texas populists still thought the political system was part of the problem. "The fruits of the toil of millions are boldly stolen to build up colossal fortunes for a few, unprecedented in the history of mankind," said the national platform, "and the possessors of those, in turn, despise the republic and endanger liberty." The Texas take was this: "[Politicians] have snatched our government from the hands of the economy and now a billion dollars is spent by a single Congress, both parties vieing with each other in making big appropriations for rivers, harbors, public buildings, extravagances of officials, congressmen, the pensioning of rich widows, burying dead congressmen, etc."

Accordingly, the national platform called for government to have a broader mandate so that it could help more people. The Texas platform called for government to do more in some respects—one of its complaints was that the state had failed to provide effective schools, as the state constitution required—but it also suggested that government be reined in, or at least subject to more oversight by the people.

The Texan skepticism about government would be reinforced, at times, by bad government. James "Pa" Ferguson, who served as governor from 1915 to 1917, had some progressive inclinations. "Let us have more business and less talk," he announced in his first guber-natorial platform, in 1914. "Instead of wrangling over the question of whether man shall drink, let us consider for a time how he and his loved ones may get something to eat and to wear." He was also a crook; the legislature impeached him in 1917 after a Travis County jury indicted him on nine charges, including embezzlement.

In 1924, his wife, Miriam (or "Ma") Ferguson, ran for office as a proxy for her husband. She was the first woman to be elected governor of Texas (and one of the first in the United States; on November 4, 1924, Wyoming also elected a woman, Nellie Tayloe Ross, who was inaugurated two weeks before Ferguson, in January 1925). In Ma Ferguson's case, though, a heavy asterisk must be applied, since there was never any question who was calling the shots. "Two governors for the price of one" was her campaign promise, which exaggerated how much governing she was fixing to do.

After such experiences with government, the Texas framing might start to seem logical. If government is inept, making it bigger and more powerful might not be the best idea.

HOW DO TODAY'S TEXANS FEEL about their feeble government?

The fact that the state has long posted some of the lowest voter turnout rates in the country has sometimes been considered a sign of voter disgust, if not suppression.[15] Utah, however, also has low voter turnout, and rarely is it dinged for bad government; that state is run with Mormon discipline.

Another possibility, then, is that Texans have been happy enough with the status quo. The government might not do much, but at the same time it doesn't meddle with people that much, nor does it ask for much in terms of taxes. That has apparently been an acceptable deal for most Texans, particularly because the people have been able to look elsewhere for the services the government can't provide or won't provide or both.

Lobbyists, for example, are happy to take on some of the legislative opportunities and responsibilities that in a normal state would be handled by legislators. The media, state and national, occasionally provide oversight. Churches and charities supplement the threadbare safety net, and the private sector provides a considerable number of public goods. Not the most elegant system, perhaps—but it hasn't failed hard enough to compel real change.

8

THE SHADOW STATE

IN 1976, *TEXAS MONTHLY*, the monthly magazine about Texas, published a long article asking why Dolph Briscoe, then the incumbent governor, even wanted the job. He was apparently spending as little time in Austin as possible, preferring to decamp to his ranch in Uvalde, but the details of his schedule were a bit vague, given that Briscoe's office had repeatedly declined or ignored requests to tell the press how the governor was spending his time, leaving reporters to try to puzzle it out by looking at scraps of evidence such as the state payroll records for "acting governors." (Whenever a governor leaves Texas, the state has to hire a substitute.) The few comments Briscoe had offered were not reassuring; he had said, for example, that he didn't even keep an agenda himself, preferring to rely on what his secretary told him. The article's writer, Griffin Smith Jr., noted that this kind of thing would never happen if Texas had a CEO: "If a corporation ran its headquarters with the same haphazard unaccountability, it would be out of business in six months."[1] Two years later, the state elected its first Republican governor since Reconstruction: Bill Clements, a businessman from Dallas.

At times, Texans have seemed to trust businessmen more than their own government. On a steamy morning in April 1947, for example, there was a fire on board the French vessel SS *Grandcamp*. The ship had pulled into the port of Texas City, just inland from Galveston Island, the night before, and when the fire triggered an explosion—the *Grandcamp* was carrying more than 2,000 tons of ammonium nitrate in its cargo hold—much of the town was flattened. Nearly 600 people were killed; some 5,000 were injured, in many cases gruesomely; and about 2,000 more were left homeless. It was, and remains, the most deadly industrial accident in American history.

People in Texas City felt that government was to blame: no one had warned them of the explosive potential of ammonium nitrate, and after the catastrophe, the federal government was disinclined to pitch in. "Two weeks after the explosion, the small-town mayor flew to Washington to appear before the House Appropriations Committee, to beg them to approve a measure allocating a mere $15m to repair Texas City," wrote Texan journalist Bill Minutaglio. "The money [would] never come."[2]

The next year, the widows of Texas City became the first Americans to sue the federal government under the Federal Tort Claims Act of 1948—a new law that gave Americans, for the first time, the right to hold the federal government liable for certain damages. A district court ruled in their favor. In 1953, however, the US Supreme Court turned them down, reasoning that people didn't have the right to sue the government over things that had happened during the normal business of governing.[3] Europe had been devastated by World War II. Rebuilding it was in the interests of the United States. Fertilizer would help. And so the ammonium nitrate shipments were a national security issue. Sorry, widows.

Luckily, Texas City had some help from the private sector. Within days of the explosion, the people got what they considered to be good news. Monsanto, one of the biggest employers in the city, announced that it would resume operations as soon as possible. It would build a new chemical plant even bigger than the old one, which had burned down. "In Texas City, if there is resistance to the idea of Monsanto rebuilding its massive chemical plant, not a word is uttered publicly," explained Minutaglio. "There is, instead, widespread relief. It is saluted as industry's instant belief in the future of Texas City. There will be jobs again. Someone, at least, thinks that the city is worth reclaiming."[4] Charities also helped with the rebuilding. Sam Maceo, a businessman and mobster from Galveston, launched the Texas City Relief Fund and arranged for Frank Sinatra to sing at a benefit concert.

It seemed like a clear-cut case: in the absence of a strong, or even adequate, public sector, alternatives emerged. Business was the big one. Texans were used to taking care of themselves and happy enough about doing so if they could. In 1946, William Ransom Hogan, a historian based at Tulane University, noted that Texans had adopted this attitude by the time of the republic. "While citizens of the Republic demanded that their government see that 'all start fair,' they were perfectly willing to maintain freedom on a competitive basis," he wrote, "and the pressures of potential insecurity were never so great that they drove the people to any form of collective or utopian experiment."[5]

This wasn't to say that Texans were heartless, Hogan added: they were quick to volunteer for militia duty, warmly welcomed newcomers to the state, and were happy to pitch in if a neighbor or traveling stranger needed food or a place to lay a bedroll for the night.

As time went on, the private sector started taking an increasingly active role in public policy. Industry lobbied on behalf of its immediate interests, but it also took up more far-ranging priorities, such as education and infrastructure. Its motives were far from altruistic. By promoting universities or supporting the arts or lobbying in support of a sales tax, these businesses were contributing to the state's economic development. "It was the business community that went to the legislature and said, you know, this is something that we need for revenue, to fund schools, to fund roads," notes Don Baylor, an analyst with the Center on Public Policy Priorities in Austin, with regard to the state sales tax, which was created in 1961. "The business community is absolutely essential for providing cover and credibility to the legislature."[6]

The need for public services also gave rise to two of the epiphenomena that Texas is famous for: Bible-thumpers and vigilantes.

IN 1972, TEXAS POLICE set up a sting operation outside a plain-looking house in La Grange, a small town in east Texas. Over the course of two days, they counted almost 500 visitors, most of whom were men. That was all the evidence the state needed to prove the house was a brothel. Actually, it was more than the state needed: the Chicken Ranch, the operation in question, had been in business since 1905, and everyone knew about it. Given its longevity, it was practically a civic institution. When the brothel was shut down (by Briscoe, as it happened) people around the country were sympathetic—to the brothel. ZZ Top wrote a song about it, and the controversy became the basis for 1982's *The Best Little Whorehouse in Texas*, starring Dolly Parton and Burt Reynolds. "Don't feel sorry for me," says Parton's character, a plucky madam. "I started out poor, and I worked my way up to outcast."

The Chicken Ranch was no anomaly. Texas had a history of cheerfully licentious behavior dating back to the frontier days. The Anglo settlers of Texas were cheerfully godless. "We hear no ravings, and see no rompings, or indecorous and indecent exhibitions under the cloak of a religious assemblage," reported one settler in 1830, approvingly.[7]

One of Texas's problems with Mexico, in fact, was the latter's rule that all newcomers had to be (or become) Catholic, although that complaint should be classed as a pretext. Most of the Texians simply ignored it. Some went out of their way to promote other religions—not out of piety, but in an effort to attract American attention. "I regret that the Methodist church, which, with its excellent itinerant system, has hitherto sent pioneers of the Gospel into almost every destitute portion of the globe, should have neglected so long this interesting country," wrote William Barret Travis, the hero of the Alamo, in an 1835 letter to a New York paper.

Travis, recall, had set out for Texas because he was facing jail time over his staggering debts and had left his pregnant wife and young son behind in Arkansas. He was a man who possibly could have used some pastoral care, in other words, but no one, at the time or since, has ever thought he was sincerely hoping to get it. Historians have argued that it was effectively an economic development gambit.[8] If Texans feigned an interest in religion, it must have been because they knew that civilized countries—rich countries—needed to have churches.

The Republic of Texas had no state religion. It didn't have many saints either. Hogan suggested that most people didn't see a need; they were happy enough drinking, fighting, and enjoying the heady fruits of the freedom they had just achieved. He went on to remark, "With all of its immense power for good, denominational religion, bolstered by dogmatic authority, tended to offer certainty and provide a refuge for the timorous—qualities that did not attract many self-reliant frontier individualists, so resentful of authority."[9]

That resentment helps explain why the state's constitution is in some ways more explicit in guarding government from the influence of the church than the US Constitution is. It technically disallows atheists from holding public office, stipulating that no candidate should be subject to a religious test "provided he acknowledge the existence of a Supreme Being." But the state constitution does assert the right to religious freedom and separates church and state operationally:

All men have a natural and indefeasible right to worship Almighty God according to the dictates of their own consciences. No man shall be compelled to attend, erect or support any place of worship, or to maintain any ministry against his consent. No human authority ought, in any case whatever, to control or interfere with the rights of conscience in matters of religion, and no preference shall ever be given by law to any religious society or mode of worship. But it shall be the duty of the Legislature to pass such laws as may be necessary to protect equally every religious denomination in the peaceable enjoyment of its own mode of public worship.

. . . No money shall be appropriated, or drawn from the Treasury for the benefit of any sect, or religious society, theological or religious seminary; nor shall property belonging to the State be appropriated for any such purposes.[10]

But freedom of religion, in Texas as in the rest of the United States, has never meant freedom from religion. As people poured into the state, God inevitably followed.

Texas became a state during the Second Great Awakening, the Christian revival movement that began at the end of the eighteenth century and took off around 1820. The First Great Awakening, which preceded the American Revolution, had been a highbrow and didactic affair. Think of those charming puritanical sermons you read in high school history class: "The God that holds you over the Pit of Hell, much as one holds a Spider, or some loathsome Insect, over the Fire, abhors you, and is dreadfully provoked; his Wrath towards you burns like Fire; he looks upon you as worthy of nothing else, but to be cast into the Fire; he is of purer eyes than to bear to have you in his Sight; you are ten thousand Times so abominable in his Eyes as the most hateful and venomous Serpent is in ours," and so on.[11] The preachers of the First Great Awakening were, in other words, bossy and judgmental.

The Second Great Awakening was, by comparison, populist, decentralized, and individualistic. Denominations proliferated; religious visionaries were common. Joseph Smith, who brought out the Book of Mormon in 1830, would prove to be the most influential of these self-appointed prophets, but he was hardly the only one. And mainline Protestants, as Travis indicated in his letter in 1835, had started sending missionaries to the frontier in droves.

The circuit preachers made their pitches at rowdy tent revivals. Those who tackled the task of civilizing the Texans were predominantly Methodists, followed by Baptists. The two denominations had previously battled for souls in Appalachia and the South. Both churches, as a theological matter, professed that the common man could receive salvation through faith alone. This proved to be a more palatable message than the deterministic, authoritarian preaching that had cowed New England one hundred years before. Still, the clergy must have felt themselves forsaken. As Hogan put it in his history of the Texas Republic, "Privations and poverty, loneliness, conflict with an unconquered wilderness and with ribald degenerates—such was the lot of the frontier preacher."[12]

Drunkenness, in particular, was rampant, even among the upper strata of the nascent pseudosociety. "There is scarcely to be found a man of distinction, scarcely an individual holding offices of honor, who is not a *slave*, more or less, to intemperance," thundered one believer in 1843.[13] Judges were falling asleep on the bench; legislators were lolling around the streets of Austin.

During the early years, the churches of Texas never commanded majority support among the people. At the time of annexation, perhaps 15 percent of the Anglo settlers were churchgoers, and many of those were still dancing and carousing.[14] Civilization was so haphazard, though, that the church was able to make some inroads by offering public services—the kinds of services that might have been offered by the government if the republic had been bigger, wealthier, or otherwise more well situated to do so.

The Methodists in particular were preoccupied with social progress. In addition to temperance, the biggest issue of the olden days, preachers scolded their flock about the need to educate their children, to stay out of debt, not to kill or even fight, and so on. In some cases, they volunteered themselves as an ad hoc judiciary. The only punishment they could really mete out was throwing someone off the church rolls, but it wasn't as if there were many rival institutions up for the job. Religious organizations became a part of civil society in Texas by offering themselves as a bulwark against the shortcomings of the state. In the late 1930s, when the Franklin Roosevelt administration sent writers and researchers around the country to produce a series of historical and cultural guides to the states, the writers who ended up in Texas observed that the state had a long tradition of "what might be called emergency religion." For example, "a frontier character known as 'the Ring-Tailed Panther' forced a missionary at the point of a pistol to hold services for his dead dog."[15]

Texas's early churches, then, were meddlesome, action oriented, and not particularly theological. "The frosty certainty with which early church leaders viewed their right to schoolmarm over the lives of followers and others was rooted more in the unlettered Second Great Awakening than it was in any biblical warrant," writes James L. Haley, another historian of Texas's formative years. "Nevertheless, it was the cornerstone upon which the evangelical church in Texas was built, and it influenced—and sometimes actuated—every subsequent moral debate in the state."[16]

Texas churches can still be quite prescriptive. One dramatic illustration of this came in 2008 when Mike Huckabee, a Baptist preacher and former governor of Arkansas, agreed to do a bit of guest preaching at the Cornerstone Church in San Antonio. Cornerstone is an evangelical megachurch, nondenominational but with a Pentecostal flavor. As megachurches go, it is modestly sized, drawing about 8,000 worshippers weekly. Its head, John Hagee, is the kind of evangelical who makes people wary: old, judgmental, and sonorous like Foghorn Leghorn. And there's plenty to dislike about his ministry. In 2003, the *San Antonio Express-News* revealed that his work—in addition to his daily responsibilities, he is the president and CEO of John Hagee Ministries—had earned him a cool $1.25 million the year before. That was far more than any other "nonprofit" director in the city had made and about nine times as much as Billy Graham had. When questioned, Hagee pointed out that Graham's house was already paid for.

Technically speaking, this wasn't a political event, but it was part of a campaign swing. Huckabee was running for president, and he had notched a few victories in the southern states. Texas, with its socially conservative and populist elements, must have seemed like the logical next step. It would turn out to be fruitless; by the time the Texas primary rolled around in March, John McCain had already locked up the Republican nomination. But Huckabee's scrappy underdog campaign had been punching above its weight in terms of entertainment value; action star Chuck Norris had joined him on the trail, as had the Duggar family—Jim Bob and Michelle and the eighteen kids they had at the time.

I had turned up early, for some reason anticipating that there would be tremendous public demand for this kind of sermon, and so I arrived in time for adult Sunday school. It turned out the church was in the middle of a multiweek session on deliverance. Ushers handed out a set of PowerPoint slides. The day's topic was "The Nature & Activity of Demons." Satan, according to the slides, is engaged in guerrilla warfare against the world. His minions look innocent, but they systematically invade the people and the government and infect us with their ideologies. They tempt, defy, intimidate, and enslave their victims. These demons do not value life. They don't negotiate, and they don't operate under the accepted rules of war.

The most practical part of the discussion covered the symptoms of the demonized ("demonized" in this context meaning that there is a demon inside you, not that other people are judging you unfairly). People with indwelling demons may experience some or all of the following problems: fear, rage, pride, religious pride, dysfunctional family relationships, stubborn habits, "bitter memories that will not go away even after forgiving," "no abundance of life or peace," and—this one is a dead giveaway—"unreasonable anger or fear of a Pastor or a Spiritual Authority." It sounds pretty heady, but note the emphasis on empowering the worshipper to diagnose and cure demonization. A worthwhile public service, given how few Texans have health insurance.

As they did in the early days, Texas churches still play a prominent role in civic life. That's why one of George W. Bush's first moves as president was to create a White House office of faith-based and community initiatives. (Bill Clinton had had a similar idea as president, and of course Clinton was the former governor of Arkansas, also a state with lots of room for church charity.)[17] Though churches are more or less involved in these issues throughout the United States, the phenomenon is apparently more pronounced, or at least more visible, in states where the government doesn't provide extensive social services. And that's one area where Texas is at the head of the pack; the state spends less money per capita than all but two others (Nevada and Florida).

This may also have something to do with Texans' high rate of charitable giving. In 2008, according to an analysis from the *Chronicle of Philanthropy*, Texans gave $10.7 billion to charity (including churches). In terms of median contributions from discretionary income, Texas ranked second.[18] The authors of the report noted that the data were necessarily limited. They analyzed only charitable contributions from households with more than $50,000 in annual income. Still, the report revealed a striking pattern: the red states were, on average, more charitable than the blue ones.[19]

It was an unpopular finding. The *Chronicle of Philanthropy* drew the same conclusion I would: "The reasons for the discrepancies among states, cities, neighborhoods are rooted in part in each area's political philosophy about the role of government versus charity."[20] Upset that the blue states were being called out as misers, or that the red ones were being lionized, Democratic readers were quick to point out that most red states were religious and that most of their giving was to churches and religious charities.[21] If you looked strictly at giving to secular charities, then all the states were pretty stingy, but New England was somewhat less thrifty than the other regions.

That critique, however, makes sense only if you don't consider religious giving to be a legitimate form of charity. Most Americans do, as do the Constitution, the law, and the IRS. It's one of the ways that we differ from, say, Britain, where the Church of England is sanctioned by the state yet (perhaps not coincidentally) quite mild-mannered, as noted by Eddie Izzard: "Do come in, you're the only one today! Now the sermon today is taken from a magazine that I found in a hedge."[22]

A church's projects may not be to everyone's taste, but then again neither are PETA's. Even the Bill and Melinda Gates Foundation catches heat from time to time.[23] The relevant question is whether a faith-based charity's methods are constitutional, and that depends on the context. When evangelicals proselytize in the streets, that's their right. When they proselytize in the public schools, that's a problem, because it violates the establishment clause.

Fortunately, religious groups do occasionally take up worthy causes—causes that are worthy even from a secular perspective, I mean. In Texas, one of the evangelical priorities has been prison ministry. In 2008, I drove out to Cleveland, in east Texas, to spend an evening at the nonprofit Prison Entrepreneurship Program (PEP). Its founder, Catherine Rohr, had been working in venture capital in New York before she got religion and started volunteering with Chuck Colson's Prison Fellowship.[24] In 2004, she packed it all in to start the program, which took a few dozen prisoners each cycle, paired them with volunteer mentors, and set them to work writing business plans and practicing their interview skills and etiquette. "They're not in here because they were bad businessmen," she told me, an insight that was also central to the plot of the cable TV series *The Wire*. After the offenders were released, the program kept an eye on them as they navigated reentry. The state of Texas has never excelled in that area—the standing offer is $100 and a bus ticket to Dallas or Houston—and some of them, in any case, had been inside so long that they didn't know how to use cell phones.

The program has gotten results. Since it began, less than 5 percent of its participants have gone on to reoffend in the next three years; around the state the figure is closer to 25 percent. In 2011, according to PEP's most recent annual report, 100 percent of the ex-offenders who had been out for twelve months were employed. That is higher than the national average, although their average wage was $9.87/hour, so the jobs they were getting weren't the best.[25]

It's a labor-intensive scheme, and probably not a scalable one. The program also has a pretty stringent application process, so its success might be the result of picking up the offenders who are unusually sincere about wanting to change. After my visit, on the other hand, I received a nice thank-you note from one of the inmates, who apologized for being nervous when we met and explained that he hadn't talked to many women since being convicted of aggravated assault for pistol-whipping his girlfriend some years before.

This is the kind of faith-based charity even an atheist would probably approve of and representative of how the church has stepped up in the absence of the state government. The fact that it involves the prison system is particularly apt—after all, meting out justice is another function that the private sector has frequently assumed from the beginning of Texas history.

THERE IS A WIDESPREAD BELIEF among the American public, fueled by the state's high incarceration rate and reruns of *Walker, Texas Ranger*, that Texans are big on law and order. This is only half true. They do like order, but they've never had a particular talent for law.

Maybe that's because so many of them have found themselves on the wrong side of it. All the political leaders of the Texas Republic were criminals by the standards of the Mexican government. Before the revolution even began, Stephen F. Austin had, as mentioned, been imprisoned in Mexico and William Barrett Travis had been locked in a brick kiln. Travis, for that matter, was among the many settlers who had scooted to Texas after running into legal trouble elsewhere.

Order, on the other hand—Texans needed that. Mexico had opened its borders to Anglo settlement partly because it figured the newcomers could guard the sprawling, rugged territory themselves. After becoming independent in 1821, Mexico was a poor, fragile, and physically huge country. It couldn't afford to send armies to its faraway borders. Settlers on the northern frontier, however, could help defend the more densely populated states of northern Mexico.

After the revolution, the Anglo-Texans, in turn, were desperate for protection—from Indians, from Mexicans, and from each other. None was forthcoming from the government. This spurred the settlers to organize themselves into voluntary, informal bands of rangers. The title became official in 1835, formally adopted by the body that declared itself the government of Texas (although since the government of Texas itself wasn't official at that point, we're getting into metaphysical territory here).

Even after Texas became a legal entity, the Rangers remained somewhat mutable. They were officially a paramilitary force that the state could summon or disband at will. But because Texas rarely had the means to maintain continuous law enforcement, or the capacity to make the Rangers behave, they often functioned outside the government. When officially disbanded—that is, when the government couldn't afford to keep paying them—the Rangers would nevertheless organize themselves to go out on patrol, fight baddies, demand payment in kind from other settlers, and so on.

It was the young republic of Texas, in fact, that drove the growth of America's handgun market. In 1838, Samuel Colt, a gun maker from New Jersey, developed a revolving pistol that could shoot a number of bullets before being reloaded. Back East, this innovation simply wasn't that popular. It would seem that for easterners, brawls and disputes proceeded with such thoughtful deliberation that if a man needed an additional bullet, he could simply retire to his quarters, drink a snifter of brandy, have the valet polish his monocle, and reload at his leisure.

Not so in Texas. The Rangers, darting around on horseback as they were, immediately saw a use for the new six-shooters.[26]

The Rangers were brutal even by the standards of American law enforcement. The regular soldiers who came to Texas after 1845 in the form of the US Army sharply disapproved of the Rangers' practices. Even so, Texans—or Anglo Texans, at least—were grateful to have the Rangers. There were plenty of other self-appointed enforcers in Texas who caused even more trouble. In 1844, Sam Houston, during one of his stints as president, had to send the Texas militia into Shelby County, in east Texas, to dismantle a pair of rival gangs that were feuding with each other and terrorizing their neighbors. One of the gangs, presciently, was called the Regulators. The other was called the Moderators.[27] Both had started out, in 1839, as groups of local men who were trying to keep each other from cattle rustling and land swindling, although by the time Houston sent in the militia, the situation had devolved into an all-purpose feud.[28]

In those days, even traditional law enforcement had a tendency to go rogue; the government was so scattershot that accountability was minimal. "One day while I was alone the Confederate soldiers came around gathering up horses," reported one Texan, reminiscing about his childhood during the Civil War. "They threatened to take mine and had me scared to death. I begged hard for my horse and I told them I needed him to get supplies with. After frightening me real good they told me I could keep my horse. I was the only one they left with a horse around that neighborhood."[29]

A cowboy described how one morning, while breaking camp, an officer came up and pistol-whipped him and accused him of stealing hogs. He tried to explain that it was a false charge—"The boys, in a spirit of fun, caught two or three hogs that were foraging about the camp and the squeals of the swine led the settlers to believe that we were stealing the hogs"—but the officer wouldn't let the herd proceed until the cowboys emptied out the chuck wagon to prove there were no hogs on it.[30]

Texans, then, were inclined to take a balanced view of the Rangers; they did some bad things, but they also did some good things, and the early Texans often needed the help. Stegner asks readers to consider Larry McMurtry's western epic *Lonesome Dove*. The novel, which George W. Bush would one day cite as his all-time favorite, follows two former Texas Rangers. "They kill more people than all the outlaws in that book put together do, but their killings are *right*," Stegner notes. "Their lawlessness is justified by the lack of any competing socialized law, and by a supreme confidence in themselves, as if every judgment of theirs could be checked back to Coke and Blackstone, if not to Leviticus."[31]

The deficiencies of socialized law didn't only justify individual initiative; they also encouraged it. Early Texans were quick to think that criminals forfeited their rights, even to life: "When a cutthroat died in a clash with a reputable citizen, the general feeling was that justice had been meted out, however informally."[32] People weren't particularly moved by the idea that a punishment should be commensurate to the crime. In a contemporaneous poem, Luther A. Lawhon, a cowboy, waxed sentimental about cowboys:

> *He'd stand up—drunk or sober—'gin a thousand fer his rights;*
> *He'd sometimes close an argument by shootin' out the lights;*
> *An' when there was a killin', by the quickest on the draw,*
> *He wern't disposed to quibble 'bout the majesty uv law.*[33]

Early courts, similarly, were hardly credible. One account explained that in the frontier towns of the Panhandle, there were hardly any people available for jury duty, because the law stipulated that only landowners could serve. Those who were available were, inevitably, connected to the accuser or the accused (if not both) by blood, marriage, commerce, or friendship. The same could be said of the judges and the lawyers. Justice was literally a joke: "From these conditions there arose a disregard for the law and a levity toward its administration that made the term of court not a serious time for the adjustment of the difficulties of the people but a festive occasion like a county fair."[34]

Most of the Texans were tough-minded themselves, or at least learned to cultivate a degree of detachment. A cowboy named Branch Isbell would later recall that in his time on the Chisholm Trail, it was common practice to kill any calves that were born along the way, as letting them live would have slowed down the whole herd. "I had a pistol and it was my duty to murder the innocents each morning while their pitiful mothers were ruthlessly driven on. . . . Being the executioner so disgusted me with six-shooters that I have never owned—much less used one from that time to this."

As disgusted as he was, though, Isbell wasn't quite like Ferdinand the Bull, in the old children's story, who sits around eating flowers and refuses to face the matador. He went on to say that he didn't regret killing the calves; in fact, he reasoned that it was the reason he lived long enough to write down his memories. "It is likely, too, that not being a gun-man during the following five or six years kept me from becoming involved in several shooting tragedies that I saw enacted. Unpreparedness has kept me peacefully inclined."[35] It was a hard life on the frontier. Sensitive souls were poorly suited to it—so poorly suited, perhaps, that they knew to steer clear.

In the twentieth century, Texas's ideas about justice have become more normal, but it's a long road.

ALL OF THIS VOLUNTARY ACTIVITY became self-perpetuating over time. If a nongovernmental actor did a better job at providing a public good than the government did itself, then people would turn to that actor the next time around. And if people weren't particularly confident about their government, they wouldn't be hugely excited about paying taxes or voting or running for office—leaving the government to become even broker and weirder over time.

The virtues and the flaws of this approach are straightforward. There is the classically liberal argument that a smaller government maximizes the freedom of its citizens; the less money people have to turn over in taxes, the more they have left to spend or allocate as they please, as it is generally considered their right to do. More pragmatically, nongovernmental actors have certain strengths relative to the public sector. A corporation, for example, has an incentive to perform well. If it doesn't, it will eventually fail—in theory, at least, although in practice it might be bailed out or nationalized or otherwise propped up. As Smith noted in his critique of Briscoe, government doesn't work that way. Politicians are accountable to the voters insofar as they have to stand for elections, but the metrics on which their performance is assessed are often vague.

On the other hand, the public sector has strengths relative to the patchwork system of corporations, churches, charities, and so on. Private actors are unreliable partners. In some cases, their resources may be harnessed, or carefully steered, in response to political finessing or public clamor. But the state can't guarantee that the private sector or civil society will take up key public priorities. The state's oversight of private actors is limited. And the overarching problem is that for a private actor, the public good is not necessarily the top priority. A private prison company, for example—and Texas has contracts with several of those—makes its money by leasing prison beds to the state.

But the private sector has long been the most important part of Texas's supplemental or shadow state, and even if the state does become Democratic, that's not likely to change. After all, the last time Democrats dominated Texas—and it wasn't that long ago—they were probusiness too.

9

DEMOCRATIC TEXAS

"**YOU'RE NOT CONSIDERED ONE** of the battleground states, although that's going to be changing soon," said Barack Obama in June 2012 while fund-raising in San Antonio. The next month, the Democrats announced that Julián Castro, the mayor of that city, would give the keynote speech at this year's nominating convention—the same show-case that had made Obama's name in 2004. For several years, Democrats had been eyeing Texas and looking forward to the day when they could bring it over to their column.

At first, that sounds crazy. Texas is by far the biggest and most powerful of America's red states. It has 26 million people, 36 seats in the United States House of Representatives, and 38 electoral votes. For twelve of the twenty years between 1988 and 2008, a Texan was in the White House—first George H. W. Bush and then his son, George W. Texas also produced Phil Gramm, a leader in the push for financial deregulation, and Tom DeLay, the former House majority leader.

Not content to command high office, Texas Republicans often try to foist their ideas on the rest of the country through other channels. The state has been the testing ground for a variety of right-wing reforms in education, criminal justice, and financial and environmental regulation. Texans have bankrolled Republican candidates and conservative PACs around the country.

The state has helped provided the intellectual underpinnings for the religious right. In the small town of Aledo, outside Fort Worth, self-proclaimed historian David Barton publishes scores of books and tracts arguing that America has always been conceived of as a Christian nation. The Tea Party also has a connection to Texas. That movement's avuncular godfather, Ron Paul, was the longtime congressman from Lake Jackson, a leafy exurb of Houston.

Within the state, Republican hegemony is unquestioned. The GOP controls every statewide office in Texas and both houses of the legislature. In the state House of Representatives, Republicans have a supermajority. Democrats have not won a statewide election since 1994. In 2010, they didn't even come up with a candidate for the Comptroller's Office—a noticeable gap in a state with only seven statewide executive offices.

Given the sheer redness of Texas, it's easy to lose sight of the fact that fifty years ago Democrats were just as dominant in Texas as Republicans are today. For decades, Texas was one of the most influential Democratic states in the country. Dozens of congressmen have their offices in a building named for Sam Rayburn, the Texan who spent about half a century in Congress, including seventeen years as Speaker of the House, longer than anyone else in that chamber's history. The first American president from Texas, Lyndon Johnson, made civil rights his first priority, and when today's Democrats go to battle over the proper role of government, many of the programs they're defending were created by Johnson as part of his Great Society.

In other words, Texas used to be plenty Democratic. So before we ask when the state will turn blue, we should ask another question: How did it get so red?

TEXAS, LIKE THE OTHER former Confederate states, was Democratic before the Civil War, and it stayed that way for almost a century once it expelled the carpetbagging Republicans of the Reconstruction era. Between 1883 and 1960, Texas sent only five Republicans to the US House of Representatives and none to the Senate.[1] During the same period, all of its governors were Democrats, every one of its lieutenant governors was a Democrat, and the Democratic Party continuously controlled both houses of the state legislature.

The Republicans could usually manage to field a candidate, at least for statewide offices, but their candidates weren't seriously competitive. When historians focused on that period refer to winning "the election," the referent is typically the Democratic primary—the general election was a foregone conclusion. Only during presidential election years did more voters turn out for the general election than for the biennial primaries, and it wasn't uncommon for a Democratic runner-up to net more votes in the primary than the Republican nominee in the general. In 1912 and 1914, even the Socialist candidates got more votes than the Republicans.

The 1952 elections dramatized the state of play with unusual clarity.

Allan Shivers, the sitting Democratic governor, was up for reelection. He had ascended to the office in 1949 after the incumbent, Beauford Jester, died of a heart attack while traveling via train to Galveston with his girlfriend. Shivers's succession presented the party with a problem. Jester had been part of the party establishment, and in Texas terms he was a moderate. He favored spending more on public schools, made no move to stop the University of Texas (UT) as it inched toward integration, and even toyed with the idea of repealing the poll tax.[2] But like most Texas Democrats, he kept his liberal impulses in check.

On integration, for example, it had been Jester's position that the University of Texas's medical branch was obligated to admit black students as long as they were qualified. The Supreme Court had already ruled, in 1950's *Sweatt v. Painter*, that the University of Texas Law School had to admit black students. The state had tried to skirt the

Fourteenth Amendment by announcing plans for a second, blacks-only law school—its constitution already called for a separate-but-equal system of public schools—but the Court was unimpressed, given that UT was bound to be the better of the two. In the words of the Court, "It is difficult to believe that one who had a free choice between these law schools would consider the question close." Jester, accordingly, argued that the only alternative to integrating the medical school would be to provide a second, equally good one for black students, but because building a second medical school was clearly out of the state's price range, UT would have to be integrated. Once Jester put the matter that way, the legislature grudgingly acquiesced.

Shivers, his successor, was less diplomatic, and he didn't hesitate to wade into the biggest fight available, which was with the federal government.

When Texas joined the Union in 1845, among its terms was that the state's rights should extend into the Gulf of Mexico for nine nautical miles. Other states got only three. Texas's reasoning was that it was, at the time of the annexation agreement, a sovereign country. The United States had already set a precedent by recognizing Mexico's ownership over its near-shore waters for nine nautical miles. For the better part of a century the issue rarely came up, and when it did, the country was happy to humor Texas on this point. It was just another piece of pointless Texas vanity. "Nobody cared. Who cares? [You] want to keep the muddy, sandy bottom in the Gulf of Mexico, set your hair on fire," explained Jerry Patterson, the Republican land commissioner, in 2008. "But then when offshore production of oil and gas became a reality, all of a sudden, the federal government cared."[3]

Those submerged tidelands added up to some 4 million acres, and they were probably bursting with accessible oil. The Truman administration figured the riches should go to the United States, and in 1950 the Supreme Court ruled against Texas's claim to these "marginal waters." That sent Shivers on a crusade. In 1951, he signed a law that allowed candidates for office to file for more than one party, which

Democrats took as a sign that he was angry enough about Harry Truman and the tidelands to switch parties over it.

The result was that Shivers ran against himself for reelection as the nominee for both the Democratic and the Republican parties. He won it for the Democrats, with 1,375,547 votes. The Republican version of Shivers pulled only about a third that number.

This wasn't just a fluke. The same year, Price Daniel, who was in his third term as the Texas attorney general, ran against himself for Senate. He, too, won as a Democrat. Daniel's vote haul and his margin of victory against the Republican version of himself were almost exactly the same as Shivers's had been: 1,425,007 to 469,494. (Daniel also, inexplicably, received 591 write-in votes.)[4] In other words, when asked to choose between two eerily similar candidates, about three-quarters of Texans opted for the one denominated as a Democrat.

But the election also suggested that party identification was largely meaningless, or at least that it didn't have the same meaning in Texas as it did in the states with distinguishable parties. The fact was that being a Democrat in Texas did not imply being progressive or left wing; it could mean quite the opposite. Then as now, Texans believed in small government, limited spending, and low taxes. That was all their constitution allowed them to have, and the people were satisfied enough with it. They usually recognized the existence of certain public goods—infrastructure, schools, public safety—but their willingness to pay for those things was haphazard, and they looked on other projects with skepticism. They were in favor of business and not predisposed toward labor. Most Texans were supportive of the New Deal, at least to the extent that it benefited them—a kind of pragmatic (if not quite hypocritical) self-interest has been a recurring phenomenon in American politics and persists to the present day. But Texas Democrats were generally in the small-government, antielitist Jacksonian tradition. Historian H. W. Brands, author of books about both Andrew Jackson and the Texas revolution, muses that one of the reasons the state is distinctive is precisely because it came into being alongside Jacksonian democracy; indeed, one of its most important leaders, Sam Houston, was Jackson's acolyte and personal legatee.[5]

Even as it remained Democratic, Texas was emerging as one of America's more conservative states. John Nance Garner, for example, served two terms as Franklin Roosevelt's vice president. Once he came back to Texas, he denounced New Deal spending at every opportunity. In 1944, conservative Democrats formed a group, the Texas Regulars, that meant to block FDR's reelection. If they could get to the nominating convention, they figured, they could throw a wrench in the gears and maybe send the nominating process to the US House, where the conservative wing of the party was more influential. "The Texas type of conservatism seems more virulent and entrenched than most other strains," wrote George Norris Green in his 1979 study of the state's political establishment at midcentury—a period he dubbed "the primitive years."[6]

Most Southern Democrats, of course, were conservative, and Texas was Southern then—or, at least, more Southern than it is now, politically speaking. (Today, when asked which region Texas belongs to, some Americans would say the South, some would say the West, and some would say the Southwest; the best answer is all of the above or none of the above.) During the first half of the twentieth century, though, the question was simpler. Texas was clearly more affiliated with the South than with any other region, even though Texas's politics had never fully mapped onto that of its former Confederates, and over the years, the state occasionally broke with the region.[7] (In 1928, for example, Texas supported Herbert Hoover for president, even though six southern states backed the Democrat, Al Smith.)

A hundred years after the annexation, however, Texas politics in many respects matched what would be expected from a southern state. Like the rest of the former Confederate states, Texas was still working through the ruination of the Civil War and Reconstruction. The state's alternative regional identities were as yet inchoate, and the nation as a whole was already uneasy about Texas, reasons already mentioned. The state was considered part of the South, and relations between the

South and the rest of the country were somewhat strained; in addition to the resentments that persisted in the wake of the nineteenth century, the South was still segregating African Americans and abusing them. Beyond that, there were idiosyncrasies particular to Texas, such as the fact that the state's oil industry had emerged as a force in American politics, and outsiders were wary of that lobby. Texan politicians couldn't get very far on their own; it was by affiliating with the southern bloc in Congress that they had their best shot at power.

Texas's southern side helps explain its conservative attitude toward labor. America's organized labor movement had taken shape at the beginning of the twentieth century in response to grim working conditions in plants and factories at the time. The movement got less traction in the South. The region was not heavily industrialized then, and a cheap workforce was one of the South's competitive advantages, as it is today. Accordingly, the prospect of reform didn't hold quite the same urgency. This is why most southern politicians were opposed to initiatives such as Franklin Roosevelt's 1938 Fair Labor Standards Act, which outlawed most child labor, established a minimum wage, and set a standard forty-five-hour workweek, among other things.

Texas, with its populist tradition, was surprisingly friendly to organized labor at the beginning of the century. In 1920, according to historians George Norris Green and Michael R. Botson Jr., "Texas workers were protected by laws that rivaled or surpassed those in more industrialized states"—including provisions for a minimum wage and workers' comp, and regulations on child labor.[8] But support for organized labor was offset by the broader support for business, even among relatively progressive Democrats. Lyndon Johnson, for example, came from a cotton and cattle family, rode to school on a donkey, and never forgot how it felt to be poor. "I know that as a farm boy I did not feel secure," he would say later, looking back on those early years.[9] Classmates have recalled how the young Johnson thought it was outrageous that a man could lose his farm when the price of cotton lurched from forty cents a bale to four.[10] He was one of a handful of southern congressmen who had supported the Fair Labor Standards Act (Sam Rayburn, his great mentor, was another). However, in spite of these progressive leanings, Johnson shared in the broader Texan suspicion of unions. In 1945, electrical workers with the Lower Colorado River Authority walked off the job, warning that they would interrupt power and electricity if the bosses refused to think about letting them bargain collectively. Johnson was livid. "The sick in hospitals are endangered. Farm products will spoil," he scolded. "Texans will not tolerate this stoppage or sabotage."

The Anglo majority also opposed civil rights. In the 1920s, Texas had barred African Americans from voting in the Democratic primary, which was tantamount to barring them from voting at all, given that the winner of the Democratic primary invariably won the election. (This "white primary" statute was overturned by the Supreme Court in 1944's *Smith v. Allwright*; Thurgood Marshall, later appointed by Johnson as the Supreme Court's first black justice, successfully argued the case.)[11] Texas was also the last state to get rid of the poll tax, which it did in 1962. While the tax was in effect, politicians had taken the opportunity to secure the minority vote by offering to pay people's poll taxes for them. Voters took the usual opportunities to resist civil rights; in the 1950s they backed referendums calling for segregated schools and against intermarriage.

At the same time, the issue of civil rights wasn't quite as polarizing in Texas as in other southern states. Plenty of Texas Democrats were Dixiecrats, particularly in east Texas, which has witnessed the worst racial abuses and is still the only place in Texas that could be mistaken for Louisiana. But the Dixiecrats never dominated the party, and it was rare for statewide elections to hinge on civil rights. In 1948, South Carolina's Strom Thurmond won four southern states as a third-party candidate for president. Revealingly, he pulled only about 9 percent of the vote in Texas, which went for Harry Truman.[12]

It's not particularly surprising that Texas voted for Lyndon Johnson in 1964. He was a Texan. No matter that he had already begun his push for civil rights. But in 1968, even with Johnson out of the running, Texas went Democratic again. It was one of only thirteen states to support Democratic nominee Hubert Humphrey, while five southern states, including neighboring Louisiana and Arkansas, went for George Wallace, the former governor of Alabama running as an independent on behalf of segregation.

There were, it seemed, issues much more important to Texas than race. Texans may have been bigots, but they weren't completely stupid, and, characteristically, they rarely lost sight of their self-interest. As in most matters, they were pragmatic rather than ideological. This had already become clear in 1952, the Shivers (D) versus Shivers (R) year. At the beginning of that year's presidential race, Democratic nominee Adlai Stevenson had been polling comfortably ahead of Republican nominee Dwight Eisenhower in Texas. But Shivers had resolved to make Texas's ownership of offshore oil a defining issue. He had pressed the point with both candidates. Stevenson told Shivers that he wouldn't restore Texas's claim to the tidelands. Eisenhower said that he would. So Shivers endorsed Eisenhower, and plenty of Texas Democrats followed his lead, giving Ike the win.

Texas's electoral votes didn't end up making much difference, considering the landslide victory Eisenhower ended up winning. Even so, he kept his promise to Shivers and signed a law giving Texas its nine nautical miles in 1953—a law that has since contributed several billion dollars to Texas coffers. "All because of the guy who was governor, who decided that his state was more important than his party," reflected Jerry Patterson. Texas also backed Eisenhower's reelection in 1956.

There's a pattern here: Texans have a tendency to set aside partisanship, biases, even their stated views, when economic goals are at stake. This longstanding phenomenon is still in effect today. It helps explain why contemporary Texas Republicans have a robust, albeit tacit, industrial policy. It also helps explain why they've never launched a crusade against unauthorized immigration like their counterparts in other states have. While unauthorized immigrants might put an extra burden on, for example, public schools, they also represent a large pool of low-wage labor.

Similarly, Texas's leaders have been surprisingly accommodating about letting people pursue their own economic goals, and most of the state's concessions toward civil rights and women's rights have concerned access to employment and other economic resources. In Texas, the right to pursue money is extended not just to plutocrats and cronies, but also to the people whom the state and the country as a whole have been slow to recognize as such—women, black people, unauthorized immigrants, and so on. Texans have been, perhaps, so obsessed with profit that they would consider it unfair to deny anyone a chance at the same, and whenever Texas does something unusually egalitarian, that's usually the explanation.

Consider, for example, Texas's slightly confusing attitude toward the legal rights of women. In 1972, it added an equal rights amendment (ERA) to the state constitution (to date, only twenty states have done so); the next year, it went to the Supreme Court to defend the state's draconian abortion laws, in *Roe v Wade*; the year after that, the state ERA was invoked, for the first time, to repeal a statute that limited the number of hours women could work.[13] That looks like an inconsistent approach to women's rights, but when reframed in terms of the *type* of rights in question, the inconsistency diminishes.

The recognition of economic rights has even influenced the all-important relationship between Texas and sports. This book has gone for a long time without talking about football, but no longer: in 1969, the Texas Longhorns were the last football team to win the national championship with an all-white roster.[14] Some professional sports, however, had been ordered to integrate years before, because they were a form of work. In 1954, Texas desegregated professional boxing after a black boxer, I. H. "Sporty" Harvey, sued for the right to fight white boxers too. A state court agreed that the ban violated the Fourteenth Amendment. The explanation didn't hinge on an ethical commitment to racial justice. Professional boxing, the judge wrote, was "a lawful calling in this State"; therefore, black boxers had to be allowed to compete for prize money as freely as white ones.[15]

WITH ALL OF THAT SAID, there have been pockets of progressive activity in Texas. Of all Texas cities, San Antonio has had the most significant sideline in leftist politics. Its demographics and economy have historically set it apart from the rest of the state.

The city's political evolution began around seventy-five years ago. About half the city's population was Hispanic, many earning about five cents an hour working as pecan shellers in what was the city's biggest industry at that time. Living conditions were grim. San Antonio's Mexican Americans were about six times more likely to die from tuberculosis as Anglos and more than twice as likely as African Americans.[16]

The city's political life had effectively been controlled by an Anglo machine for generations—until things began to change in the 1930s. In 1934, Maury Maverick, an outspoken liberal (and descendant of Sam Maverick, the accidental cattle baron), was elected to Congress. Following in his grandfather's linguistic footsteps, Maury is credited with another contribution to American English: the word "gobbledygook," inspired by his frustration with his fellow congressmen, who were, he said, "always gobbledy gobbling" like turkeys.

Maverick lost the primary in 1938 after conservative Democrats realized how liberal he actually was. He had supported the creation of a federal welfare department, denounced fellow Democrats for trampling on civil liberties, and joined Rayburn and Johnson in backing the Fair Labor Standards Act.[17] In San Antonio, the latter issue was especially charged. At the beginning of that same year, Mexican American pecan shellers had gone on strike in response to a wage cut that would have whittled their pay to even less than five cents an hour. City police had responded by beating and jailing thousands of people. Before the year was out, and in spite of having lost his congressional primary, Maverick became the first person in modern history elected mayor of San Antonio with significant support from the city's Mexican American voters.

In 1956, San Antonio sent Henry B. Gonzalez to the state senate; he was the first Mexican American to serve in that body since annexation. Over the next year, Gonzalez spent twenty-two hours filibustering and helping to ultimately defeat a number of segregationist bills.[18] He was elected to the US House in 1961, and stayed there until 1999.

A boxer and a polymath, Gonzalez acquired something of a national reputation as an uncompromising idealist—a trait that occasionally led him in unpredictable directions, as when he opposed the Voting Rights Act, reasoning that special legal protection would only aggravate the separation between ethnic minorities and America's Anglo majority. In 1986, at age seventy, someone called him a communist. In response, he punched the man in the face, which he later described as a measured response: "If I had acted out of passion, that fellow would still not be able to eat chalupas."

Maury Maverick's son, Maury Maverick Jr., upheld the city's progressive tradition when he represented San Antonio in the Texas legislature from 1951 to 1955. In the 1950s when legislators mulled a bill that would have made membership in the Communist Party an offense punishable by death, he deftly thwarted it by offering an additional suggestion: that anyone *suspected* of communism should get life in prison.[19] Maverick Jr. was also the lawyer who represented Sporty Harvey in his bid to desegregate boxing.

By 1974, San Antonio's left was further energized by community organizers. Ernesto Cortes Jr., a San Antonian who had trained at the Alinsky Institute in Chicago, came back to his hometown and started Communities Organized for Public Service,[20] the first Texas chapter of the Industrial Areas Foundation (the network of community organizers founded in 1940 by influential radical Saul Alinsky).

Still, for most of the twentieth century, in most of Texas, conservative Democrats still had the upper hand over moderates and moderates had it over liberals. In 1956, for example, Price Daniel—the moderate who had won all those write-in votes in his 1952 Senate campaign—became governor after defeating Ralph Yarborough, a progressive, in a closely contested primary runoff. In 1958, the *Victoria Advocate* reported that Governor Daniel was cruising toward reelection, but campaigning nonetheless—"not only on his own behalf, but to ensure that the liberal wing Democrats of Texas do not take control of the state's Democratic party of which he is titular head."[21] In 1962, a conservative Democrat, John Connally, decided to run for governor. He attacked Daniel, still the incumbent, for having supported an increase in the sales tax, and Connally thereby prevailed.

There were additional confounding variables, though. One was that by midcentury Texans had developed the habit of ignoring the political sphere. If politicians didn't cause that much trouble once elected—"politics simply did not impinge heavily on private life," as historian T. R. Fehrenbach put it—there wasn't much reason to get all het up about who was going to office in the first place.[22] General uninterest among voters enabled horse-trading, deal-making, and worse. This explains the 1948 Senate election that pitted Lyndon Johnson, then a congressman, against Coke Stevenson, then a popular former governor.[23] Johnson was less liberal then than he would be later, but he was also less conservative than Stevenson. Johnson campaigned doggedly and viciously. When he eventually won, by an 87-vote margin, people suspected he had done more than that, and for years he was dogged with a pointed nickname: Landslide Lyndon.[24] All these years later, it's commonly accepted that the election was stolen by low-tech strategies such as stuffing the ballot box, although there is some debate, given that such mischief was fairly common, over whether Johnson merely "outfrauded" Stevenson.[25]

A politician's personal appeal or connections could also trump his platform or ideology. So in 1957, even after losing the gubernatorial runoff to Daniel, Yarborough was elected to take over Daniel's old Senate seat in a special election. Yarborough hadn't got any less liberal in the intervening months, but he had been around for long enough that people were used to him.

More important, perhaps, was that by 1958 Yarborough happened to have help in the right places, which he hadn't before. In a 1992 obituary of Ed Clark, a longtime political fixer, *Texas Monthly*'s Robert Draper recalled a chance encounter between Clark and Yarborough in the 1980s. Having run across Yarborough on Congress Avenue in downtown Austin, Clark couldn't resist a taunt: "You know how you used to always say that the '56 election got stolen away from you? Well guess what. So was the '54 election."[26]

In 1958, by contrast, Yarborough had picked up some crucial support from popular leaders. The special Senate election was an open, winner-takes-all affair, and among the declared candidates was a Republican, Thad Hutcheson. Rayburn and Johnson thought Hutcheson had a chance at winning because he was closer to the Texas mainstream than Yarborough was. Not a big chance, maybe, but it would have been a problem given the R after Hutcheson's name. Johnson had just become the Senate majority leader, and neither he nor Rayburn, then Speaker of the House, could afford to lose a Democratic senator. They threw their support behind Yarborough, who won with a plurality after Hutcheson and another Democrat, Martin Dies, split the conservative vote. If there had been only one conservative in the race, that person would likely have won. But once Yarborough got into the Senate, he managed to stay there for a while, since he wasn't impinging on anybody's private life or anything; he was elected for a full term in 1958.

Given all of that, it's not surprising that Texas Democrats kept their hold on power for so many years even after it was clear that they weren't fully aligned with the national party. Most of the state's politicians were Democrats, so the party had cornered the market on talent. In addition, the Democratic Party infrastructure was strong enough to support vulnerable Democrats like Yarborough. At the presidential level, however, those factors didn't apply, which is why Republicans had an opening there.

That was one of the reasons John Kennedy wanted Lyndon Johnson as his running mate. Having him on the ticket might help shore up support in the southern states, where Democrats were wary of a Catholic liberal from Massachusetts, and it would definitely get him Texas. This was sound thinking. Kennedy did carry Texas in 1960, and it's safe to say that with a different running mate, he might not have. Johnson hadn't wanted to risk losing his powerful post in the Senate, and the state had tweaked its election rules to allow Johnson to run for both senator and vice president; he won the Senate reelection with a wider margin than the Kennedy-Johnson ticket mustered. Texas's loyalty to Johnson, that is, didn't extend to a more general embrace of Kennedy's vision for America. In 1961, after a special election to fill the Senate seat Johnson had vacated by becoming vice president, John Tower became Texas's first Republican senator since Reconstruction.

But the party identity of the state hadn't switched over yet. The Democrats were still conservative, and they were still the default party of Texas. The 1970 Senate election made both of those facts clear. Yarborough may have been the incumbent, but he was still vulnerable. He had been one of the few southern Democrats to vote for the Civil Rights Act and the Voting Rights Act, and he had vocally opposed the war in Vietnam. He was, in other words, still out of line with majority opinion. He had won reelection in 1964 against a fairly well-liked Republican, George H. W. Bush, but that had been a landslide year for Democrats, not least in Texas. This time around, LBJ wasn't going to be at the top of the ticket. Bush, who had been elected to Congress in 1966, decided to try again.

Bush's chances were scuttled, however, by another Democrat. Lloyd Bentsen, a moderate congressman from the Rio Grande Valley, defeated Yarborough in the primary. In the general election, pundits observed that the two candidates, Bush and Bentsen, were eerily similar. "The only evident difference between them, judging from their own TV spots, seemed to be that Bush loosened his tie a little more and kept one hand in his pocket while strolling," recalled Al Reinert for *Texas Monthly* in 1974.[27] It was like Shivers versus Shivers all over again, and as in 1952, the tie went to the Democrat, Bentsen.

But the Democratic establishment was in decline, and 1972 proved to be a critical inflection point. Connally, the popular former governor, had returned to politics as the head of Democrats for Nixon, a national organization. Texans, who had voted against Nixon in 1968, chose him over George McGovern the second time around. Tower won reelection to the Senate; Yarborough had tried to stage a comeback, but he didn't even win the Democratic primary. Democrats managed to win the gubernatorial election, but it was messy. They had started the race with two heavy-hitting candidates, both of whom were part of the Democratic establishment—Preston Smith, the incumbent governor, and Ben Barnes, the incumbent lieutenant governor. In 1970, the suggestion that neither would win would have been unthinkable. In 1971, a scandal changed everything. Frank Sharp, a Houston banker and developer, had arrived at an understanding with various legislators. He would loan them hundreds of thousands of dollars, which they would use to buy stock in one of his companies and they could then sell for a profit, so long as they dealt with some legislation that would benefit the company in question in the interim. Even by Texas's standards, it was blatant fraud. Federal regulators noticed and intervened. Although neither Smith nor Barnes was among the high-ranking officials who ended up facing charges, they did end up so covered in mud that when the primary rolled around, neither of them even made the runoff.

The Democrats' choice came down to Sissy Farenthold, a fairly liberal state representative, and Dolph Briscoe, the former state representative and rancher from Uvalde. Both had campaigned as outsiders, a message that proved effective against Smith and Barnes, both consummate insiders, although it didn't work so well against each other.

Briscoe, the more conservative of the two, won the runoff. His victory in the general election was relatively narrow, all things considered. The Republican candidate, Henry Grover, came within 100,000 votes of winning. He might have won altogether if not for the fact that Tower, by then a popular and influential senator, clearly preferred Briscoe.

It would be one of the last times that a Texas Republican crossed party lines to help a Democrat get elected. Texas's political realignment was afoot. And when the Republicans got power, they would prove to be partisans of a different stripe than the Democrats had been.

10

THE RISE OF THE RIGHT

AFTER LYNDON JOHNSON SIGNED the Civil Rights Act of 1964, he turned to his aide and remarked, "I think we just delivered the South to the Republican Party for a long time to come." Just a few months later, it looked like Johnson's comment would prove prophetic.

In the 1964 elections, the Deep South flipped from Democratic to Republican. The Republican presidential candidate, Barry Goldwater, carried just six states—Louisiana, Mississippi, Alabama, Georgia, South Carolina, and his home state of Arizona. Four years later, in 1968, the Dixie bloc went against the Democrats again, although in that case four of them went for George Wallace.

In 1972, Richard Nixon swept the entire South, along with most of the other states, in his landslide victory against George McGovern. In 1976, Jimmy Carter reclaimed the South for the Democrats, but in 1980 he won only his home state of Georgia. Since then, the region has heavily favored Republicans in presidential elections, although Bill Clinton, who is from Arkansas, carried some southern states in 1992 and 1996, and Barack Obama won Florida, Virginia, and North Carolina in 2008.

Yet, as we've seen, Texas wasn't quite part of the Deep South bloc. The state had broken with Dixie on a couple of occasions before the civil rights era. It naturally went for Johnson in 1964 and stayed Democratic, voting for Hubert Humphrey, in 1968. Carter carried the state in 1976, but narrowly, and since then Texas has given its electoral votes to the Republicans in every presidential election. It would have done so even if four of those elections hadn't had Texans (George H. W. Bush and George W. Bush) at the top of the ticket.

So Texas turned red after Johnson signed the Civil Rights Act, but not simply because of it. A number of other factors were at work. The first was that Texas Democrats were running out of steam. After they had dominated state politics for about a century, the bench was running thin, and the leadership was losing its way; the Sharpstown scandal had showed as much. Democrats started losing elections and Republicans started winning them.

Texan Democrats increasingly felt, too, that their contributions to the national party had been underappreciated. At the time of his death in 1973, Johnson considered himself a failure, as did most Americans, largely due to the trauma of Vietnam. In Texas, however, he retained his loyalists, who were bitterly disappointed when subsequent Democrats tried to distance themselves from Johnson. They saw civil rights, the Great Society, and the war on poverty as part of Johnson's record, not just JFK's. The fact that outsiders saw it differently made some Texans irritable.

Things came to a head in 1976 when Jimmy Carter, the Democratic presidential candidate, sat for an interview with *Playboy* magazine. Nationally, the interview was notorious because it made Carter seem odd. "I've committed adultery in my heart many times," he revealed. Texans, however, were more shocked by a comment Carter made at the end of the interview, bundling Johnson with the post-Watergate Nixon and dismissing them both as liars and crooks.

Newspapers reported that Lady Bird Johnson, the president's beloved widow, was surprised (which everyone took to mean that she was furious, but too gracious, as usual, to say so). Former governor John Connally was more vocal in his disapproval. He had been an inconstant ally over the years, a protégé of Johnson's who turned against the older man as his own political fortunes rose and Johnson's seemed to recede. On that 1963 day in Dallas, Connally had barely even bothered to acknowledge the vice president. In 1972, he had become the head of Democrats for Nixon, a national organization. But when the *Playboy* interview hit the newsstands, Connally wheeled around and thundered that Texas Democrats should vote for Gerald Ford. Carter did carry Texas's electoral votes, but by a narrow, 3-point margin.

Texas's realignment also had an ideological dimension. At the national level, both parties were changing: the Republicans emerged as the conservative party, the Democrats as the liberal one. Texas Democrats, as discussed, tended to be conservative. By the 1970s, the disjunct between Texas Democrats and the national party was becoming harder to ignore, especially because as the southern states turned Republican, the southern bloc in Congress, with which Texan politicians had been affiliated, was losing its influence. Northern Democrats had less reason to compromise with their counterparts elsewhere. It became clear that Texas Democrats were, in national terms, more like Republicans than Democrats. It was no surprise that Texas would back Ronald Reagan over Jimmy Carter. His socially moderate supply-side conservatism resonated with Texans, as did his running mate, George H. W. Bush. Republicans were about to retake the state.

AS TEXAS DEMOCRATS started to lose their grip, Republicans were working to win. They had started to organize at the grassroots level, specifically in the churches. The religious right, a national phenomenon, arose largely in response to the social changes of the 1960s and 1970s—"social changes" being a euphemism for feminism. In 1960, the pill debuted. In 1973, *Roe v. Wade* established the legal right to abortion. In 1975, South Dakota became the first state to outlaw marital rape. These kinds of radical changes were eroding the historical role of women as the long-suffering stewards of national morality, and religious conservatives soon organized to fight back. Focus on the Family was founded in 1977, followed by the Moral Majority in 1979.

Despite being conservative, Texas hadn't been a particularly moralistic state. Sloth was the source of its classically liberal virtue: the government wasn't disposed to exert itself. The legislature had been socially moderate in the 1960s, when such issues arose, but by the 1980s the religious right had emerged as a force in Texas politics.

Such a quick transformation was odd. To get an explanation, I went to see Kathy Miller, the head of the Texas Freedom Network, an Austin-based nonprofit that works to keep the church and the state separate, as both God and Texas had intended. She argues that it was precisely because of Texas's slightly schizoid nature that the theocrats were able to muscle in. On the one hand, Texas is kind of southern, so it has a long tradition of action-oriented Protestantism. Similarly, Texas isn't northern. Those states have historically led the nation on church-state separation, because, among other reasons, they're the states that got most of America's Catholic immigrants. New England Protestants, as broad-minded as they were, didn't necessarily want their kids going to the parochial schools that were popping up.

At the same time, Miller continues, Texas has this western, libertarian, antigovernment side. The government itself is small and undernourished, and Texans don't pay much attention to it. The religious right figured that if it could get access to the levers of power, it could push its agenda without much interference. And the religious right wanted to test its ideas in Texas. For today's ideological crusaders, Texas is usually worth the trouble. The state is so big, and so diverse, that if you can get something done in Texas, you can probably scale it elsewhere.

All the elements for a takeover, in other words, were in place: means, motive, and opportunity. It would have been the perfect crime, except for one problem: Texans themselves. The voters had historically favored fiscal conservatives over social ones. The two aren't mutually exclusive, of course, but neither are they intrinsically connected. Miller, who spends much of her time trying to track what the far right is up to, is clear on this point: even if the religious right is getting stronger, it doesn't speak for a majority of the state. "I do feel, and I know, that Texans believe the separation of church and state is a foundational principle for our country," she says. "We've polled on that."

The leaders of the religious right probably knew that too. That's why targeting party infrastructure, rather than voters themselves, was a key factor in the religious right's rise to power. If Texas was becoming a one-party state, then the movement wouldn't need to compete at the polls anymore. It could compete at the precinct caucuses instead. If it won influence within the Republican Party, that was tantamount to getting influence in the state. It's also, surely, one of the reasons that strategists set their sights on the State Board of Education. Texans, like everyone else, believe in evolution and don't think abstinence-only sex education is effective. Minors, however, don't vote, and if they talked to their parents about sex, America wouldn't have such fraught debates about sex-ed curricula in the first place. Any concrete gains the religious right could achieve with regard to public education, then, would be less likely to elicit a backlash at the polls next time an election came around.

Migration to Texas may also have played a role in the state's partisan switch. During the 1970s, the population of Texas swelled by nearly 30 percent. It was a hard decade for most of the United States. Things were pretty good in Texas, though. Oil and agriculture were so dominant that the state's economy was countercyclical. Jobs were plentiful, and about 3 million people moved to Texas from other states. Many of the newcomers were northern and lacked the knee-jerk anti-Republicanism of the Old South. Even among Texas Democratic officials, party identification wasn't such a fiercely tribal matter. A number of legislators, including Rick Perry and Phil Gramm, joined the voters in switching sides.

In 1978, Texas elected a Republican, Bill Clements, as governor. It was the first time the state had sent a Republican to that office since Reconstruction. Democrats have taken back the governor's mansion twice since then—in 1982, with Mark White, and in 1990, with Ann Richards—but neither victory was resounding, and neither politician was reelected.

In 1999, Rick Perry became the first Republican ever to serve as lieutenant governor. The legislature was soon to follow. In 1997, the Texas Senate got a Republican majority for the first time ever. The Texas House of Representatives didn't get its first post-Reconstruction Republican majority until 2003.[1] Since then, however, there have been few moments of weakness for Republicans in Texas. In 2009, it looked like the House might become bipartisan again; the Republicans controlled it by the narrowest possible majority, 76–74. But the Democrats' hopes were quickly quashed; after the 2010 elections, Republicans returned with 101 state representatives to the Democrats' 49.

TWO ADDITIONAL ASPECTS of Texas's political realignment are worth noting. The first is that the nature of partisanship changed. Texas's leadership didn't just switch from Democratic to Republican. It became ideological in a way that it hadn't been before. The second is that Texans themselves, for the most part, didn't change. The electorate has remained much the same as ever: pragmatic, fiscally conservative, socially moderate, and slightly disengaged. The result is that the state's top political leaders are significantly more conservative than the electorate—which is surely an unstable equilibrium, even if Texas voters are apathetic.

How did this happen? Democrats had been partisan enough to side with fellow Democrats over Republicans in a pinch, the issues notwithstanding—as when Rayburn and Johnson stepped up their efforts for the liberal Ralph Yarborough. But the Democratic partisan identity had been somewhat amorphous. There were enough disputes among the liberal, moderate, and conservative factions to demonstrate that there were no holy cows in the party. The Texan affection for other Texans was also a factor. When Republicans did get into office, Democrats were happy enough to work with them; after all, they shared so many views. And Republicans, at times, showed the same sense of tribal (that is, Texan) loyalty. Before Bob Strauss moved to Washington to become treasurer of the Democratic National Committee, he met with a Dallas oilman, who took Strauss to his office and handed him $10,000 in $100 bills from a desk drawer. The oilman was a Republican. He knew the money was going to the national Democrats, who were hostile to his industry, but he just didn't want Strauss to go to Washington feeling naked.[2]

The next generation of Texas Republicans, who had cut their teeth in the 1970s and 1980s, felt no such compunction. Around the country, party labels were increasingly taken to indicate underlying substantive content. The people who switched parties now did so deliberately. Those like Perry and Gramm, who had been Democrats by birth, became Republicans by choice, and as they say, there's nothing as pure as a reformed whore. Once in power, Republicans pressed their advantage aggressively. One of the people working on Bill Clements's campaign for governor, for example, was Karl Rove, who would soon emerge as an assiduous and successful operative.

Perhaps the most aggressive move by the Republican partisans came in 2003. The US House of Representatives had a relatively narrow Republican majority at that point, 229 to 204. National figures—led by Tom DeLay, the House majority leader, a Republican from Sugar Land—wanted to pad their lead. At the time, Texas had 32 seats in the House of Representatives, 15 of which were held by Republicans. DeLay figured Republicans could do better than that. They had just got the majority in the Texas House of Representatives; they already controlled the Senate and every statewide office.

The Voting Rights Act would have blocked either party from any redistricting effort that was aimed at reducing minority representation, but it didn't prohibit discrimination for partisan reasons. Democrats were perfectly aware of that, having drawn the maps according to their own preferences back when they had control. As of 2003, the House delegation included 10 Anglo Democrats. All of them could be targeted without too much legal trouble. It was even possible, Republicans thought, to redraw the districts so that the Texas delegation could lose Democrats but gain a couple of minorities.

The Democrats in Austin were upset, but outnumbered. On the other hand, there were enough of them that if they left en masse, they could deny the Republicans the quorum they needed to hold the vote. In May of that year, 51 state representatives snuck away under the cover of night. They turned up in Oklahoma, outside the reach of the Texas authorities. It was almost the end of the regular session, so the idea was to stay in Oklahoma long enough to run out the clock, which they did. Then Perry (who had become governor) called a special session to force them to take up the issue. This attempt also failed, this time thanks to the Democratic senators who bolted to New Mexico.

The tactic was effective, but there was no sustainable strategy. "There were several possible scenarios that could have ended with a Democratic victory," noted Steve Bickerstaff, a professor of law at the University of Texas, in a 2007 study. "By the summer of 2003, however, none was realistic."[3] The Republicans had too much power, both in Texas and in Washington.

Significantly, too, the Democrats were losing on the public relations front. Their plight had brought them acclaim from national progressive groups such as MoveOn.org, but Texans were getting tired of the drama. The scheme hadn't been popular initially among Texas's moderate voters. Some of the Anglo Democrats targeted were fairly senior in Congress, and most of them were moderate; none of them were hugely controversial. But by the same token, Texans weren't rushing to man the barricades; a limited government tends to keep a low profile.

And the Democratic leaders in Texas were getting tired too. John Whitmire, a state senator from Houston, was the first to leave New Mexico. He told reporters he was homesick. Eventually, the Republicans were able to corral the requisite number of Democrats. They sat there stewing while Republicans tore up the old maps and then kept stewing through 2004 as Republicans picked up seven of the ten targeted districts. In 2002, Texas had 17 Democrats and 15 Republicans in the US House. In 2004, it had just 11 Democrats and 21 Republicans.

Not only that, the new maps took measures to ensure that the Republican gains would be resilient. Texas's demographics were changing more rapidly than anyone, even the demographers, had anticipated.[4] This motivated Texas Republicans to be less invidious about certain racially sensitive issues than some of their national counterparts were; it was in 2001 that Perry signed the Texas version of the DREAM Act, the measure that allows certain unauthorized immigrants to pay in-state tuition rates at Texas's public colleges and universities. But the expectation was still that African Americans and Hispanics would favor Democrats, and so in some cases Republicans drew Democratic districts in areas that were getting more Democratic anyway. "What can I say?" wrote Bickerstaff. "The partisan design was masterful." Ten years later, the Republican dominance is so thorough that Democrats sometimes look like a third party, after the right and the far right.

This brings us to the other interesting aspect of the situation. Despite the fact that Texas's government has become more conservative, Texans themselves haven't really changed. Neither has state policy, broadly defined.

In other words: an unstable equilibrium. Its political leadership is more conservative than its electorate, and if anything, the gap is growing. The Republicans are moving farther to the right, even as the people of Texas look less and less like the affluent, older Anglo men who are running the place.

And yet Texans haven't stopped electing Republicans. This point tends to cause national observers to conclude that Texas has gone crazy. But there's a much more compelling explanation. Forty years ago, for the reasons described, Texas voters started to give Republicans a chance, and thus far, they haven't been disappointed—or, at least, they haven't been disappointed enough to do anything about it. For decades, Republicans have had the edge in structure, in organization, in money, and in candidates, whereas Democrats are still trying to recover their footing.

Texans are, ultimately, a pragmatic people. Politicians and their excesses can be justified by the economy alone. And that's one area where no one's been disappointed. So maybe it doesn't matter if the state's leaders breathe fire, pray for rain, turn up at Tea Party rallies, and spend all day suing the federal government.

How crazy is that, really? Texas is a pretty good place to live; that's why several million people have moved here since the beginning of this century. There are plenty of areas where Texas lags behind the nation as a whole, but none of them are new, and in most of them—schools, criminal justice, poverty, quality of life—Texas is showing some improvement. What's new is that outsiders have started focusing on the state's shortcomings. That's a sign of progress, in a way, if it means the United States has higher expectations for Texas in this century than it did in the last one. Rightfully so. Twenty-first-century Texas is a better place than people expect and getting better all the time, even if it has its work cut out for it.

11

TWENTY-FIRST-CENTURY TEXAS

IN 1839, AN OHIO NEWSPAPER published a bit of doggerel about all the people who were trying their luck in Texas: "When every other land rejects us/This is the soil that freely takes us." The writer was making fun, but people didn't listen. In 1850 (the first year Texas was included in the US Census), there were some 213,000 people in the state—not even 1 percent of the total US population. By 1860, the state's population had nearly tripled, to 604,000. In every decade since, Texas has grown more quickly than the United States, sometimes to a stupidly disproportionate degree.[1] As of 2012, more than 26 million people live in Texas, making it second only to California (which has about 38 million) in terms of population. Between April 2010 and July 2011, Texas added 529,000 people, more than any other state during that time.[2]

With growth comes change, and Texas has seen that too.

The state has always, of course, been ethnically mixed. The word "Texas" itself is, fittingly, an Anglicization of a Spanish transliteration of an Indian word. When the Caddo Indians encountered the conquistadores, they called them *teychas*, meaning "friends" or "allies." (It wasn't an attempt, on their part, to be droll—the tribes of the Caddo confederacy were well established and fairly peaceful to the explorers, to their ultimate detriment. When they did fight, it was apparently with some reluctance. Fehrenbach, the historian, claims that white enemies usually had advance warning if they were in trouble "by the fact that the Caddos went into sobs and fits of weeping."[3] The conquistadores took that for the name of the place and started calling it *Tejas*. As the Spanish interchanged "x" and "j" sounds, the Anglos wrote the name down as Texas.[4] But the revolution established Anglos as the dominant tribe in Texas, politically and economically. They were also, by far, the largest.

That era has already ended. Demographers like to say that Texas today looks like the United States of twenty-five years from now. White people are still the majority in the United States; nearly two-thirds of Americans are non-Hispanic whites. Texas became a "majority-minority" state sometime around 2005—the exact year is hard to pin down because no one had quite projected how quickly the change would come. As of 2011, about 45 percent of Texans were Anglo. Nearly 40 percent were Hispanic, 12.2 percent were black, and about 4 percent were Asian.[5] Roughly 16 percent of people living in Texas were foreign born, compared to about 12.7 percent around the country.

In 2003, the state demographer's office projected that if Texas kept drawing as many migrants as it had in the 1990s, not even a quarter of the people in Texas would be Anglo in 2040.[6] As an aside, Texas is the only state where "Anglo" is in common usage. Steve Murdock, a longtime Texas state demographer who directed the 2010 US Census, says that even in other southwestern states he gets a puzzled look when he tries the word on an audience.[7] It's been used in Texas since the first American settlers started to turn up, and it used to be a linguistic/cultural/ethnic identifier: Anglos were the English-speaking Americans, as opposed to the Spanish, Mexicans, and Indians, although few of the Americans were Anglo in the sense of ethnically English. Today the linguistic connotation has fallen by the wayside (most Texas Hispanics do speak English and don't speak Spanish) and "Anglo" is an ethnic category. "White" doesn't always meet the occasion because so many Hispanics are also white and people get tired of saying "non-Hispanic white" after a while.

For that matter, Texas is the state that spurred the use of "Hispanic" as an American ethnic category. Anglo Texans had always conceived of Mexican Americans as part of a different racial group, but in 1952 the Texas Court of Criminal Appeals turned down an appeal from Pete Hernandez, a farmworker who had been convicted of murder and was appealing on the basis that everyone on the jury had been white. The Supreme Court had already ruled, more than seventy years previously, that states had to allow African Americans to serve as jurors under the equal protection clause of the Fourteenth Amendment, which disallows governmental discrimination on the basis of race. The Texas court found that Mexicans "are not a separate race but are white people of Spanish descent." In 1954's *Hernandez v. Texas*, the Supreme Court rejected that logic, noting that in Jackson County, where Hernandez had been tried, people of Mexican descent were barred from eating at certain restaurants, were directed to separate restrooms (separate from both the black and white facilities, that is), and had to send their kids to segregated schools.[8] In other words, "the Court established that Mexican-Americans constituted a protected class for equal protection purposes," writes Carlos Soltero, a professor of law at the University of Texas; it also "rejected Texas' limited biracial view of the Equal Protection Clause"—a view that most Americans shared at the time.[9]

Texas's ethnic diversity has allowed for recurrent and occasionally idiosyncratic racial tension and injustice. The state's first Republican governor, E. J. Davis, was a Unionist who, like Sam Houston, had opposed secession. When he was elected in 1870, he alienated many of his former confederates by supporting the rights of the freed slaves. Davis nevertheless clashed with Philip Sheridan, the Union general appointed to oversee Reconstruction in Texas—the one who had said that if he owned both hell and Texas, he would rent out Texas and live in hell. Their dispute was over Indian affairs. The federal government, seeking peace with the Indians, wanted Texas to parole a couple of Kiowa chiefs, Satanta and Big Tree, who had been imprisoned after a series of skirmishes in east Texas. Davis initially demurred, because Texans would have been outraged, but eventually agreed, because he wanted to placate the federal government. He nonetheless earned a rebuke from Sherman: "If they are to take scalps, I hope yours is the first."[10]

A more recent example would be Johnson's bewildering record on civil rights. As president, he did more to advance racial equality in the United States than anyone since Abraham Lincoln. Even his critics acknowledge that he genuinely cared about the plight of poor Hispanics in Texas. As a young man, he had worked as a schoolteacher in south Texas; most of the students were Mexican American, many of them spoke only Spanish, all of them were poor, and Johnson was, by all accounts, tireless on their behalf. Despite that, during his first two decades in the Senate, Johnson had a perfect record of opposing civil rights reforms—not just voting against these measures when they appeared, but also helping to keep them off the floor via procedural maneuvers. In 1957 and 1960, however, he wrestled two civil rights bills through the Senate, and when he became president, passage of the Civil Rights Act was his top priority.[11]

At the time, Johnson seemed to indicate that it was all a long game. "Well, what the hell's the presidency for?" he retorted, when an adviser warned him that pushing for the Civil Rights Act was not the best use of his time.[12] But LBJ also said that he hadn't realized the scope of the issue until the 1950s, when he asked Gene Williams, a black man who worked for the family, if he and his wife, Helen, would bring Beagle the dog with them as they drove from Washington back to Texas at the end of a congressional session. Williams agreed but seemed unhappy about it, and when pressed, he explained that it was hard enough for him and his family to drive through the South without having a dog in the car to boot. "And that for the first time really aroused in my consciousness the terrible injustice that we whites had perpetrated in a nation where men were supposed to be created equal for almost two centuries," Johnson said in 1972.[13]

Given that Johnson was a consummate politician, another possibility is that Johnson's stance moved in concert with public opinion. Robert A. Caro, Johnson's great biographer, describes how the president sat stone-faced in the presidential limo on March 14, 1965, as protesters, massed on the White House lawn, sang "We Shall Overcome." The next day, he went to Congress and announced that he wanted a voting rights act.[14]

Progressives, both then and now, have often taken that view—that Johnson, so long an opponent of civil rights, pushed for them only when it became politically advantageous to do so. In the fourth volume of Johnson's biography, Caro—by no means an apologist—argues against this cynical interpretation. "Although the cliché says that power always corrupts, what is seldom said, but what is equally true, is that power always *reveals*," he writes.

Today's Texas politicians, in any case, are more openly moderate.

For the hundreds who gathered on the grounds of the Texas capitol on March 29, 2012, for the unveiling of the state's new Tejano Monument, the event was long overdue. Spanish conquistadores, speakers noted, arrived in the territory a century before the Pilgrims landed on Plymouth Rock. Their descendants were among those who fought for independence from Mexico some three hundred years later, and it was the vaqueros, or cowboys, who equipped the American cattle industry with spurs, lassos, and distinctive hats. "If it wasn't for the Tejano heritage, Texas today would probably be Ohio," said Andrés Tijerina, a historian who served on the monument's board of directors.

The ceremony was bilingual and bipartisan. Many of the state's Republican leaders have tried to find common ground with Hispanic voters; the shared history is significant, and the demographics are not subtle. "*No hay nada que nosotros no podemos hacer,*" said Lieutenant Governor David Dewhurst, carefully.

Texas has, as you would expect, seldom elected people of color or women to high office. In 1977, a century after Reconstruction ended, every statewide officeholder in Texas was a white man, and if you wanted to tally exceptions among the politicians who could be classified as prominent, you would need, at most, one hand. That is changing. In 1995, Ron Kirk became the first black mayor of Dallas; Lee P. Brown was elected the first black mayor of Houston the next year. San Antonio had Hispanic mayors after it was first settled, but when Juan Seguin stepped down in 1842, he was the last Hispanic mayor of the Alamo City until Henry Cisneros was elected in 1981.

Ann Richards is the only woman to serve as governor other than Ma Ferguson. Kay Bailey Hutchison, who was elected in 1993, is still the only woman who has ever represented Texas in the US Senate. As in student councils around the country, women have a little more success when they run for treasurer. Carole Keeton Strayhorn held the powerful Comptroller's Office from 1999 to 2007, and Susan Combs has had it since.

Strayhorn was also the first woman elected as mayor of Austin, in 1977, back when she was known as Carole Keeton McClellan. In 1982, Kathryn Whitmire was the first woman to be elected mayor of Houston. Dallas followed suit in 1987 by electing Annette Strauss (another woman held the office for part of 1976, having succeeded a mayor who had stepped down to run for Congress).

At the same time, as all of these historic firsts suggest, Texas is changing. Belatedly and more slowly than it should be, to be sure, but changing even so. Julián Castro, now the mayor of San Antonio, is one of only two Hispanic mayors of America's twenty most populous cities. (The other is Antonio Villaraigosa, who is mayor of Los Angeles.) Annise Parker, who was elected mayor of Houston in 2009, is the only woman in that group and one of America's very few openly gay politicians.

The fact that Houston has a lesbian mayor is the single fact most likely to stop a progressive critic in his tracks. Chalk it up to two things. First, politics is still at least somewhat local. Before becoming mayor, Parker had been the city controller under Bill White—a worthwhile CV bullet in a year when everyone was panicky about the budget—and although she didn't begin the campaign as the frontrunner, her support steadily grew as she made the rounds of town halls, debates, and other forums.

Second, Houston is really not as redneck as people think. Bigots still exist, but they are no longer the bloc that they once were. "Houston's Choice for Mayor; Black Guy, Rich White Guy, Lesbian or Hispanic Republican," summarized the *Houston Press*, the local alt weekly, in October 2009. The author added that it was "the weirdest fricking mayor's race in years," although he considered the candidates themselves to be irredeemably dull.

THE GROWTH OF THE Hispanic population is not the only source of the demographic shift. Texas sometimes acts like, or sees itself as, a rural state. Small-town politicians punch above their weight in the state house, and Texas has more rural people than any other state—some 3.6 million. But it became an urban state, meaning that the majority of its people live in cities, around 1950; today the figure is about 80 percent. Six of America's twenty largest cities are in Texas—Houston, San Antonio, Dallas, Austin, Fort Worth, and El Paso, in that order. Every big city is growing, and so are some of the smaller ones. "As usual, Texas dominates our list of the fastest-growing cities, with Dallas–Fort Worth, Houston and San Antonio all in the top 10," announced *Forbes* in April 2012. Austin ranked first for the second year in a row.[15]

According to a 2012 study from Rice University, based on US Census data from 1990, 2000, and 2010, the Houston area is now the most ethnically diverse metropolitan area in the country. It is 40 percent

Anglo, compared to 48.9 percent for the New York City metropolitan area; its populations of Latinos grew by about two-thirds between 1990 and 2010, and the Asian share nearly doubled.

Some of the diversity is in pockets. About a third of the city's Asian population is Vietnamese, for example; Vietnamese fishermen are well represented along the Gulf Coast. There are more Norwegians around than you would think, unless you're thinking about oil, which is what they're doing there.

But much of the diversity is more or less sui generis. No one moves to Houston because it's fun. Even residents would agree: it's ugly, the weather is horrible, and it's a pain having to drive everywhere. Its assets are entirely practical: lots of land, low cost of living, a couple of universities, a bustling port, lots of trade, as ever, the economy. Everyone who's there is there for some practical reason. That makes it one of the country's least neurotic cities, but it also makes Houston a magnet for migrants from within the United States and without. And more than any other city in Texas—more than almost any other city in America—Houston has a distinctly global cast of mind. In the run-up to her first mayoral election, Annise Parker told me that she saw Houston as an international center, not a merely American one. Unlike Dallas, which is always angling to be a cultural city like Chicago, Houston wants a commerce-based empire of the sea.

On one trip I met my friend Laurent Tran, an aerospace engineer turned oil and gas consultant, for lunch at Hollywood Vietnamese. He had just come back from an assignment in Germany. There was, he said, a huge Korean population in Dusseldorf. He had dinner some nights at the Korean bar below his apartment, and there were always a lot of Koreans there, German Koreans. Ethnically Korean people speaking fluent, native-level German. That had surprised him, he said, although he felt stupid saying so, because it always annoyed him when people were surprised by his French accent. His parents, both of whom were born in Vietnam, had moved to Paris in the 1960s, where they lived until he was fifteen. France, they had concluded, still had a racial glass ceiling; the opportunities would be better for the children in the United States. So the family moved to Houston, and the parents opened a nail salon.

It wasn't the first time I had been to a Vietnamese restaurant with Laurent, and I had seen him slightly abashed on occasions when the waiter, assuming he was Vietnamese, addressed him in that language. On this day the waiter, who was a middle-aged Anglo with a thick southern accent, had heard Laurent field a quick call from his sister, in their native language, about his niece's flute recital that evening. "My lover is French," the waiter volunteered. "He was recently deported to Lyons." "Lyons, that's a nice city," said Laurent, proving that no matter where you come from, or the color of your skin, you can always count on men to be at least intermittently obtuse about matters of the heart.

TEXAS CITIES LACK THE DENSITY or the citified feeling of New York or Chicago or San Francisco; even downtown Dallas and Houston have a lot of elbow room. Most urban Texans depend on cars to get around, and houses are more common than high-rises, even in the close-in neighborhoods. In July 2012, the median price of a single-family home in Houston was $170,000—a record for that city,[16] which is the fourth largest in the United States. The national median price that month was $187,300.[17] But in recent years, Texans have taken a greater interest in walkability, arts districts, mixed-use developments, light rail, and similarly urbane initiatives. The change is visible in all of Texas's major cities.

In the 2012 edition of Rice University's long-running annual Houston area survey, to stay with that city, 51 percent of respondents said that they would prefer a smaller house in a more walkable neighborhood to a bigger house in an area that would necessitate driving everywhere. In 2008, 59 percent had preferred the McMansion.[18] The bad news for them is that their city famously has no zoning laws; neighborhood associations can occasionally throw a spanner in the works, but only in their little fiefdoms, which is why developers are currently planning a twenty-three-story high-rise on a busy downtown thoroughfare despite the objections of the Boulevard Oaks Civic Association *and* the Southampton Civic Club.[19] The good news is that the good Lord giveth different things depending on what the market demands. Houstonians are willing to pay for mixed-use developments and pedestrian-friendly neighborhoods, and so they're getting them.

Similar changes can be observed in San Antonio: downtown revitalization, art tours, light rail, renewable energy initiatives, and so on. Still, Texans were taken aback when Manny Fernandez, profiling Julián Castro in the *New York Times*, described the city as "a kind of Berkeley of the southwest, a progressive, economically vibrant and Democratic-leaning city of 1.3 million in Republican-dominated Texas."[20] San Antonio has about ten times as many people as Berkeley and covers more than twenty times as much land. It's also considerably less affluent than Berkeley—the median household income was about $20,000 lower in San Antonio than in its supposed California cousin—and, at least by one measure, more economically vibrant. At the time San Antonio's unemployment rate was 6.6 percent, a full 2 points lower than Berkeley's. The changes in San Antonio were driven by logic and predicated on projections of future growth.

The Texas city most inclined to progress for its own sake is Austin, which has a tradition of idiosyncrasy that predates its standing as the capital. In 1843, Angelina Eberly, an "innkeeper," fired a cannon at a couple of Rangers who were trying, at Sam Houston's behest, to move federal documents out of Austin for safekeeping.[21] The stated reason for the move was that Mexican troops might appear in Austin and commandeer the papers, thus destroying this crucial piece of proof that the Republic of Texas was real. Austinites, however, thought that this was an excuse and that Houston was trying to sneak the capital to east Texas.

Austin has been officially the capital since 1844, and in 1883 the main campus of the University of Texas was established there. Those two institutions, the state government and the university, have

historically been the city's biggest employers and most important economic engines. Both are, of course, somewhat insulated from the
cyclical economy; both, moreover, have always attracted a lot of
weirdos, so it's not really surprising that for much of the twentieth
century Austin seemed to be the only city in Texas where business
didn't reign. Janis Joplin, who was originally from Port Arthur, first
started to get noticed as a student at the university. By the time Stevie
Ray Vaughan and Willie Nelson turned up, about ten years later,
Austin was already known as a hippie enclave. The politicos weren't
prudes either. In 1961, Billy Lee Brammer's novel *The Gay Place*
painted a dramatic picture of the city's boozy, hands-on political culture; in 2009 his first wife confirmed, in her own memoirs, that
people had been doing a lot of partner-swapping back then.[22]

Recently, Michael Corcoran, the longtime music critic for the
Austin American-Statesman, decided that he had had enough and
unloaded on the city for its self-satisfied sloth: "A movie about the
Austin mindset was called 'Slacker' because 'Lazy and Full of Shit' was
too hard to market," and so on.[23] He had a point. Still, a lot of people
are moving to Austin for jobs, and even the ones who are just looking
for the easy life—cheap housing, cheap beer, and tacos for breakfast—
are helping to buoy the city's small businesses. And so it is that the old
juice bar has expanded to include two locations and a raw-food restaurant. Weirdness is now a cottage industry, literally; the slogan "Keep
Austin Weird" has been adopted by the Austin Independent Business
Alliance, and one man started a business, the long tail of the Texas
Miracle, selling bumper stickers to that effect.

Austin's politics have been fairly progressive, perhaps because half
the residents work in the public sector and the other half are in bands.
In 1988, advocates for the homeless staged the opposite of a hunger
strike: they acquired a goose, Homer, and announced that they would
kill and eat him unless city leaders agreed to meet. The leaders
acquiesed, and Homer's life was spared. He went to the Democratic
National Convention that year and returned to a mostly quiet life in

Austin. A few years ago, he fainted at a political rally, after which he retired to the Austin Zoo, where he was, last I heard, still alive.[24] In more recent years, Austin has become somewhat more centrist, so the old trope about it being a "blue oasis in a sea of red" is not a good summary. In reality, Texas's urban centers skew Democratic, as does the Rio Grande Valley. The state's rural areas are Republican, and elections are won and lost in the suburbs and exurbs.

Dallas and Fort Worth are the most conservative of Texas's big cities, but neither has distinguished itself as especially troglodyte lately. Fort Worth, which was built around its stockyards, still has cowboy elements; the last time I had dinner there, I ordered a chicken-fried steak, which the restaurant's menu categorized as being on "the lighter side." Dallas, meanwhile, retains its striver side. During the depths of the national recession, the local rich decided to raise some money to kit out the downtown with some new performing arts facilities. The project cost $354 million, all but $18 million of that coming from private donations. "Aesthetically it's stoic, even off-putting," explained a proud local at the Dee and Charles Wyly Theatre, leading a tour in 2009. At a public policy confab to commemorate the occasion, an immaculately Junior League–looking lady explained, "My next-door neighbors gave $42 million to the opera house."[25] It was the most Dallas-y thing I had ever heard until a couple of years later, when someone I know took to her Facebook page: "God truly answered some prayers today! Thank you father for loving us all!"—a comment that, according to geospatial tagging, was inspired at Neiman Marcus, and later described as an accident.

Is Texas getting highbrow? Those who say yes might also point to Marfa, a tiny town in west Texas. It used to be a sleepy ranching town, named at the behest of the wife of a traveling railroad engineer, who was reading *The Brothers Karamazov* when they passed through.[26] (The University of Texas–El Paso, about two hours west of Marfa, was designed to look Bhutanese because the wife of the school's first dean was reading an article about that kingdom in *National Geographic* in 1914 and put her husband up to it. Such are the tools by which women have wielded power.) In 1981, Donald Judd, a sculptor from New York, bought a bunch of land out there and plopped a foundation on it, triggering a minor cavalcade of arts-related activity, somewhat to the chagrin of the old-timers, who have objected to events such as the production of a Wallace Shawn play that included nudity. But over the next two decades, Marfa only got artsier; it now includes boutique hotels, vegan-friendly cafés, and a desolate pop-up Prada store.

Whether Texas is now sophisticated is, however, debatable because there have of course been cases where the Texas conception of refinement deviates from national norms; there was a plastic surgeon in Houston who built his swimming pool in the shape of an augmented boob (the areola was a hot tub). It's hard for me to arbitrate such claims, but from what I understand, sophistication is directly correlated with the number of utensils involved in a place setting. It therefore seems significant that almost all restaurants in Texas now encourage the use of forks, although they are often plastic, sometimes sporks, and in at least one barbecue spot—Kreuz Market in Lockhart—hard to find.

So when Tom Head, a judge in Lubbock County, said that he thought the city needed to raise taxes in light of the possibility that Barack Obama would be reelected, my feelings were bittersweet. His reasoning was that Obama would hand over control of the United States to the United Nations. ("And what is going to happen when that happens?" he mused. "I'm thinking the worst. Civil unrest, civil disobedience, civil war maybe.")[27] Bonkers, clearly, and any Texan would have to recognize the justice of the UN's perfectly passive-aggressive response: "It's absolutely ridiculous. . . . No one, not even the United Nations, would ever mess with Texas."[28] Still, Texas has few of Head's type these days, and fewer all the time.

But perhaps the preemptive nostalgia is unwarranted. For now, at least, Texas retains many vestigial parts.

12

VESTIGIAL PARTS

CONSIDER OAK HILLS, a San Antonio megachurch. The head pastor, Max Lucado, has written about twenty best-selling books, and he ministers to half a million followers on Twitter. "Guess who is thinking about u today? God is," and so on. Lucado trained in the Church of Christ, but Oaks Hills (like most megachurches) is nondenominational, and the approach is resolutely user friendly. In one typical message, Lucado explains grace by telling a story about how his puppy got in the trash and made a big mess. So he cleaned it up, and when he came back, the puppy was looking at him with a hangdog expression. But the puppy didn't need to be so worried because Lucado had already and implicitly forgiven the puppy for its misbehavior. For a heady, cerebral kind of Christian—an Episcopalian?—this kind of message might seem facile. Yet compared to Joel Osteen, who heads America's biggest megachurch and runs a spin-off self-help empire (*Your Best Life Now!*) in Houston, Lucado is practically St. Augustine.

In other words, while Texas occasionally produces a pastor like John Hagee, of the Cornerstone megachurch where I learned how to get rid of my demons, most of its religious leaders are temperate enough. Nor do the people seem overly zealous. On polling, Texans are generally in line with national opinion. The same is true in practice. The typical Texan doesn't, for example, seem unusually homophobic, even when you leave the liberal enclaves such as Austin. In 2011, cities guru Richard Florida ranked the greater San Antonio area as America's friendliest metro area for gay couples raising children. According to census data, fully one-third of same-sex couples there have children under eighteen; around the nation, the figure is slightly less than one in five. In August 2012, Mary Gonzalez, a Democratic state representative from El Paso who was the first lesbian to serve in the state legislature, announced that she was actually the first pansexual to have that job.

Even in the eastern part of the state, which is conservative and heavily religious, Texans have pushed back against the worst displays of bigotry. In 2012, the Westboro Baptist Church, a virulently homophobic group from Kansas, came to College Station to protest a funeral that was being held at Texas A&M University for a 1993 graduate, an Army officer, who had been killed in North Carolina. (The church has frequently protested at the funerals of soldiers; its reasoning, such as it is, is that soldiers support the United States, and the United States supports gays.) Some 650 Aggies gathered around the church, forming a human wall to keep the Westboro people away.[1] "In response to their signs of hate, we will wear maroon," wrote Ryan Slezia, the Aggie who coordinated the vigil. "In response to their mob anger, we will form a line, arm in arm." On that day, at least, the most deranged people in Texas were Kansans. Maybe Thomas Frank has a point?

At times, in fact, Texas's churches are more liberal than its politicians. In 2010, Andrew Doyle, the bishop of the state's Episcopal diocese, and James Baker, a former secretary of state, produced a "plan for unity" in response to growing internal debate over the church's teachings on homosexuality. After discussions in Houston, they agreed that the Texas diocese would allow its individual priests to decide whether to officiate gay unions.[2] The priests can't officiate gay marriages, though; the state doesn't allow those.

The strangest detail of all, however, is that if you want to get technical, Texas is *less* Protestant than the country as a whole. Nationally, according to the most recent American Religious Identification Survey, 50.9 percent of Americans were Christians other than Catholics. In Texas, non-Catholic Christians (including Mormons) were slightly less than half of the population.[3] Only one major religion was significantly overrepresented in Texas. About a third of Texans, 32 percent, were Catholics. Around the country, the figure was 25.1 percent. Texas's Catholic population is growing too; in 1990, the figure was just 23 percent. The reason, of course, is the growth in the state's Hispanic population.

And yet despite all of that, Texas has, as noted, proven to be an unusually happy hunting ground for the religious right. In 1995, for example, the state revised its education code to specify that schools should make it clear, in their sexuality education courses, that abstinence is best for teenagers. It's not a mandate, and the state has no way to force schools to comply; the local school boards still get to decide how this kind of guideline is carried out. But abstinence-only sex ed quickly became de facto policy across the state.

Several years ago, David Wiley and Kelly Wilson, both professors of health education at Texas State University in San Marcos, decided to figure out what exactly the schools were teaching teenagers about sex. Working in conjunction with the Texas Freedom Network (TFN), a nonprofit that works for church-state separation, they requested the relevant documents from all of Texas's school districts—the state has more than 1,000—and 990 replied.

Of these, only 4 percent provided anything like comprehensive sex education; 2 percent said they ignored the topic altogether, largely to avoid controversy, although one interim superintendent told the researchers that he figured most of the kids learned everything they needed to know from helping out with the farm animals. The vast majority of the school districts that provided the researchers with materials, 94 percent, were teaching kids only about abstinence.[4] And

those districts weren't necessarily confining themselves to the narrow
point that abstinence works when diligently pursued; a lot of them
were adding scare tactics and lies: condoms don't work, no one wants
to marry a slut, and so on. "We knew it was bad. We didn't know it
was this bad," said Wiley, who was at home recovering from knee sur-
gery when I called.

The problem, he said, was one of collective distraction and apathy.
Texas school districts are atomized; they're not under the control of the
counties. The superintendents knew what was going on, but they
wanted to steer well clear of politics. The teachers knew too, but some
of them were part of the problem, asking their pastor to come in for a
guest talk and so on. The parents, in too many cases, weren't paying
attention to what their children were supposed to be learning.

But when confronted with what the schools were teaching, Wiley
said, the parents took notice: "If they found out that the youth minis-
ter came up and said Jesus wants you to be abstinent or whatever—I
think parents are put out by that." Since Wiley and Wilson's report
was released, the issue has attracted more attention. In November
2011, TFN released a new survey: 25.4 percent of Texas school districts had started giving their students basic information about contraception;[5] "ignorance, it seems, remains a central pedagogical strategy
in Texas classrooms." Still, it was a lot better than the 4 percent from
three years before.

The religious right has caused other national controverseis. One of
the recurring myths about Texas is that the State Board of Education
has been taken over by creationists and ideologues who have devoted
themselves to rewriting the state's history and science textbooks
according to their preferred worldview. This is a national issue, the
critics say, because Texas textbooks effectively go national. About 10
percent of America's school-age children live in the state, so as a business matter textbook publishers are bound to make sure their books
conform to Texas standards. If the smaller states want to buy textbooks, they're stuck with the options approved for Texas.

There are a couple of problems with this line of critique. One is that the state of Texas isn't in the textbook business. The bigger issue, though, is that the religious activists don't have nearly as much power as you would think, given the hype. The activists have certainly *tried* to push their agenda through the schools, but as the old saying goes, trying ain't doing.

Consider the case of Bill Ames, who was appointed (by Don McLeroy, who was in turn appointed by Rick Perry) to the committee tasked with looking over Texas's social studies curriculum. When I ran into Ames, an older man with an egg-shaped head, he was at the state Republican convention, touting copies of his new book, *Texas Trounces the Left's War on History*.

Ames told me that there was a war on Christianity going on and that California was making children take part in Islamist role-play.[6] As for textbooks, he explained that his work was a necessary corrective to the left's efforts: "Frankly, the left doesn't want to celebrate things that make you feel patriotic." Instead, he continued, it is determined to convince children that America is historically and indelibly racist and imperialist. That "pushes the kids to a socialistic mind-set." I didn't see the connection, so Ames elucidated: if you can convince kids that America is racist, then they'll think that there is no real opportunity for individual greatness in America, so they'll want the government to take care of them, which would make them socialists.

That still didn't make any sense, really, but let's move on. Ames, who proudly noted that he was the only person on the committee who wasn't a teacher, explained that he had brought a list of dozens of suggested changes for the state's social studies curriculum. All of them failed, because all those teachers on the committee voted against them. But Ames was determined. When the committee produced its list of recommendations—which he wasn't impressed with—he tacked on all of his suggestions as amendments, as the committee rules allowed him to do. His suggestions were thereby passed on to the board, where they were once again rejected.

In other words, the Texas State Board of Education considered a lot of radical changes to the social studies curriculum and rejected them. The proposed changes, which were widely reported, never made it into the state curricular standards, much less the nation's textbook supply. As it stands, then, the national hand-wringing over Texas's textbooks is somewhat overwrought.

But if Texans as a group aren't actually as religious as state politics suggests, why hasn't there been a backlash?

Part of the answer, surely, is that most people don't vote on obscure social issues, minor policy changes, or pointless grandstanding. And to date, at least, most of the religious right's activity has fallen under that category. Perry is the most high-profile evangelical statewide leader in Texas, but mostly what he does is talk. In April 2011, with most of the state blanketed in severe drought, he issued an official proclamation: later that week, three days would be designated "Days of Prayer for Rain in the State of Texas."[7] That August, days before he announced that he would run for president, he held a prayer rally in Houston that drew some 30,000 people.[8]

Prayer is free, though, and Perry hadn't pushed for much more than that, although he'd had plenty of chances. That puts him in contrast to someone like Mike Huckabee, who has said that abortion is the most important political issue in the country. The reverend, for that matter, has always seemed to nurse a grudge against Perry; the likely cause is that in 2008, when Huckabee was still in the hunt, Perry endorsed Rudy Giuliani in the presidential primary. In 2009, the bad blood went public. The Texas governor's mansion was badly burned in what is still an unsolved act of arson, and the Perrys, being displaced, relocated to a rental in west Austin. Huckabee, brattishly, pointed out that when the Arkansas governor's mansion was being renovated, he and his family stayed in a triple-wide trailer on the capitol grounds. Perry's response was entirely fair: "Texas ain't Arkansas."

Perry goes to church; there's no reason to doubt that he's religious. If he's failed to advance the evangelical agenda, it's probably just because he's lazy. But the record is clear enough: as theocrats go, he's not an ambitious one. And that, in turn, helps explain why moderate Texans haven't raised a big fuss about it. Who cares if he's a creationist? He's not going to do anything about it. As far as he knows, or cares, the issue's already settled. In August 2011, campaigning in New Hampshire, he told a little boy (who had asked the question after being prompted by his mom) that Texas already does what the religious right wants it to do: "In Texas we teach both creationism and evolution in our public schools, because I figure you're smart enough to figure out which one is right."[9] That wasn't correct—Texas schools teach only evolution—but it did give some idea of how much energy Perry devotes to the issue.

Other evangelicals, however, aren't so desultory. That had become clear earlier in 2011, when the state passed a measure requiring women seeking an abortion to undergo a sonogram first—the most socially conservative new law in a decade. The legislature also decided to stop funding Planned Parenthood, which had been receiving state money as part of the Women's Health Program; the reasoning was that Planned Parenthood provides abortion services.

Both announcements were controversial, which points to a looming problem for the state GOP. Republicans have amassed so much power in Texas that the religious right is getting more ambitious—just as the moderates are becoming more skeptical. But we'll come back to that. Now, let's talk about guns.

IN 2011, TEXAS REPUBLICANS introduced a bill that would have allowed college students to carry concealed weapons on campus at the state's public colleges and universities as long as they were otherwise authorized to carry concealed weapons. For Texans, this wasn't an abstract issue. In 1966, a sniper had ascended the tower marking the center of the University of Texas's campus in Austin and opened fire, killing seventeen people and injuring thirty-one more. It was America's first mass school shooting and the worst until the 2007 attack at Virginia Tech.

At a Senate committee hearing on the campus carry law on March 22, Austin's police chief, Art Acevedo, pointed to a grim coincidence: earlier that school year, in September, a student had entered the University of Texas's main library with an assault rifle. It turned out that he was only planning to kill himself, which he did. This, Acevedo explained, was precisely why it was a bad idea to allow concealed weapons on campus: an armed student might well have tried to stop the guy with the rifle, triggering a crossfire situation.

A series of students, some of them distressed, also testified against the bill. They didn't like the idea of guns in their dorms and lecture halls. "I am sorry that it makes you feel uncomfortable, but comfort is not a right," said a witness on the other side, a student who identified himself as a veteran, a vegetarian, and not a hunter. Some of the witnesses in favor of the bill had an air of persecution, as if they were facing a war on guns, just as evangelicals sometimes complain about a supposed war on Christianity. On that point, the senators weren't hugely sympathetic. "I would argue that Texas is a pretty gun-friendly state," said John Whitmire, a Democratic state senator from Houston.

Even the Democrats, however, seemed to be resigned to the bill's passage. The state allows people to carry concealed weapons in most public spaces, and opponents were struggling to come up with an airtight case that a college campus is an intrinsically different sort of space. In primary schools, that is, concealed weapons are disallowed because those places are crawling with kids. One witness, a professor of biology, offered a similar argument, observing that major mental illnesses such as schizophrenia may not emerge until a person reaches the midtwenties. But the state already allows youngsters to have guns: at eighteen a kid can take up arms, and at twenty-one a young person can carry a concealed weapon. Eventually, however, the bill was undone by a different line of argument: allowing concealed weapons would be too expensive. The universities might have to pay more for their insurance.[10]

It wasn't the only time that Texas's hang 'em high tradition has been checked by fiscal conservatism. Texans are reluctant to bankrupt themselves even in the name of punishment. In 1876, delegates to the state constitutional convention argued for minor criminals to be punished at the whipping post rather than the penitentiary, because the cash-strapped state could barely afford its prisons.

Another check is Texas's pragmatic streak. That's why all Texas's major cities have sanctuary policies, meaning that police don't ask about someone's legal status unless it's directly related to the matter at hand. That way they don't spend all their time detaining and deporting people, and unauthorized immigrants, most of whom are lawabiding, can have at least some small measure of safety.

There's even evidence that Texas is getting more fair, although it has a long way to go. Since 1992, the Innocence Project, a nationwide legal organization, has helped forty-seven people (as of November 2012) get exonerated via postconviction DNA testing—including several men who had spent decades in jail for crimes they hadn't committed and several who were on death row.[11] Given how hard it is to get an exoneration after the fact, the real number of the wrongfully convicted has to be higher than that. In 2002, the Houston Police Department Crime Lab closed down its DNA lab altogether after investigators found that hundreds of cases had been bungled.[12]

In 2007, the legislature passed a new law, the Tim Cole Act, in response to one of these exonerations. Timothy Cole was a college student at Texas Tech University in Lubbock when he was charged with raping another student and sentenced to twenty-five years in prison. He maintained his innocence for years, turning down parole hearings because to have a chance at early release, he would have had to admit to a crime he had never committed. In 1999, he died in prison after a bout of asthma triggered a heart attack. Eight years later, when another man confessed to the crime, Cole was exonerated posthumously. The new law was intended to help the wrongfully convicted rebuild their lives once released. It provided for $80,000 in compensation for every year served, college tuition, and other forms support.[13] For once, no one tried to bluster through the issue and no one begrudged the expense.

Implementation has been tricky, however. In 2010, another man, Anthony Graves, was denied compensation after having served eighteen years. The issue was that he technically hadn't been exonerated—when he finally convinced the state to give him a new trial, the district attorney determined that the evidence against him was so flimsy he couldn't even be charged. He was presumed innocent, but not proven so. It took an additional year of wrangling before the state worked through the issue.

As for the death penalty, as mentioned before, a large majority of Texans still support it in concept, but over the past decade the number of death sentences issued in Texas has plummeted, for two specific reasons that no one would guess offhand. The first is that in 2005 Texas passed a law giving juries the option to sentence a murderer to life without parole; it was one of the last states to make such a provision. Life sentences were already an option, but due to the crowding in the prisons, parole was a distinct possibility. Once life without parole became an option, the number of death sentences handed down in Texas dropped overnight. In 2004, Texas juries issued twenty-three death sentences, according to the Death Penalty Information Center; in 2005, the number was fourteen; in 2006, it was eleven.[14] Jurors were less willing to send a killer to death if permanent incarceration could be genuinely guaranteed.

The second blow to Texas's death penalty pipeline came in February 2008, when Chuck Rosenthal, the Harris County district attorney, abruptly resigned. Rosenthal had been America's most ardent death penalty prosecutor. In an interview in 2007, Rosenthal had explained to me that his approach was simply to seek the death penalty whenever there was a chance the jury might go for it. His attitude about that was unusual, even among prosecutors. The law says that the death penalty is an option only if the murder was exacerbated by an additional factor (such as premeditation or rape) and there are no mitigating circumstances (such as youth or mental illness). In practice, most Texas district attorneys are more reluctant than Rosenthal was about asking for a death sentence. As a result, Rosenthal's office brought in more death sentences than any other county. Since 2001, when he took the job, Harris County alone had accounted for about a third of Texas's death sentences.

The events that prompted Rosenthal's resignation were unrelated to all of this. In 2002, Houston police had arrested a pair of brothers who were taking pictures of a drug raid happening to their neighbors and seized their film. The brothers had sued the city for the civil rights violations, and their lawyer, wanting to see what the district attorney's office was doing about the case, had subpoenaed Rosenthal's e-mails. Rosenthal deleted some 2,500 e-mails, a panicky move that drew public scrutiny to the e-mails he did turn over: chain e-mails that included racist jokes, and evidence of an extramarital affair—love notes to his secretary.[15] That the latter helped seal his downfall was a fine bit of irony; it was Rosenthal who had gone to the Supreme Court in 2003 to defend Texas's sodomy ban, which was declared unconstitutional in *Lawrence v. Texas*.

Since Rosenthal left, the number of capital sentences in Harris County has come down. Texas still has America's biggest death row and will no doubt lead the nation in executions for years to come, because there are so many people already on death row. But on the sentencing side, the change is clear. In recent years, Texas has become less draconian—not just in its use of the death penalty, but also in its approach to criminal justice more generally. It's just like the textbooks say: evolution happens, even if it doesn't happen overnight.

As for evolution, the United States has been getting safer since the 1990s, and Texas has seen the same trend. In 1996, according to data from the Texas Department of Public Safety, there were 1,476 murders in Texas—about 1 for every 13,000 people.[16] By 2010, the number of people in Texas had grown by about 5 million and the number of murders had dropped to 1,248. Only 1 in every 20,000 Texans was a victim of murder; the murder rate had dropped by slightly more than a third. The rate of rape had dropped by a third; of robbery, by a quarter.

The state's gun-slinging image, however, might not be going away. According to a 2012 study from the Law Center to Prevent Gun Violence, Texas has the thirty-fifth-weakest gun laws in the country.[17]

THE TRUEST STEREOTYPE about Texas is that the state is unusually friendly to business. The private sector is still seen as an ally of the people. As we've seen, that's where Texans have long looked for jobs, development, and, in many cases, core services. The preoccupation with economic opportunity is real; that was the only reason anyone came there in the first place.

Regardless of whether this confidence is misplaced, the result is that Texans often identify with business interests, sometimes in explicit opposition to their own government. When a conflict arises, the suspicion tends to fall on the politicians and regulators, rather than on the executives and entrepreneurs. This pro-business stance is so rooted and pervasive that most people would be politely confused if asked to justify it.

Even among public-sector workers, there are plenty who still depend heavily on the private side. State legislators, for example, earn a whopping $7,200 a year—less than almost any other state—so most of them need a day job. "Wentworth says he will quit lobbying," read a 2002 headline in the *San Antonio Express-News*, referring to a local Republican state senator.[18] Not knowing any better, you might assume that this Wentworth guy had just been elected. But no. He had held that office since 1993. It took him nearly ten years to conclude that this might be a problem.

If there's a way to do something privately, Texas will try; we've already made note of that, but examples keep pouring in. In 2012, an outfit called the Texas Central High-Speed Railway announced that it was going to build a bullet train between Dallas and Houston by 2020. They "sound very confident for a company expecting to succeed where scores of state planners, elected officials and private interests have failed," observed Aman Ratheja in the *Texas Tribune*.[19]

A related phenomenon is that Texas keeps trying to run public agencies like businesses. In 2011, the San Antonio Water System was looking for an additional 20,000 acre-feet of water and, to that end, issued a request for proposals.[20] In 2012, the University of Texas system approved incentive pay for its presidents and other officials pegged to graduation rates and other metrics.[21] In July 2012, the Texas Parks and Wildlife Department announced that it was seeking official corporate partners—ideally from a related category, like hotels or beverages, but "the opportunity is open to any interested company, and all business categories will be considered." The legislature had made it legal for Parks and Wildlife to do so the year before, a concession to the cash-strapped agency, which had been dealing with drought and other vaguely biblical weather events and was about to get its budget cut too.[22] A few months after that, a Republican legislator took me aside to explain his plan for how the state could spend less money: "Lean Six Sigma—ever heard of it?" referring to a fashionable management strategy meant to help whittle costs while maintaining quality.

It's not completely true that Texas businessmen can just do whatever they want. The people do sometimes push back. Take the Trans-Texas Corridor. This was a 2006 scheme, thought up by Rick Perry, to build a massive road that would run the length of the state, paralleling Interstate 35. Despite its lineage, the road wasn't a totally half-baked idea. The I-35, which runs right through San Antonio, Austin, and Dallas, is in many stretches stuffed like a goose, given the growth of those cities and the uptick in truck traffic since NAFTA was passed in

1995. There was a broad consensus that Texas could use more capacity there, but finding the money was going to be a hassle. The situation was so grave that one Republican—John Carona, a state senator from Dallas—even floated the idea of raising the gas tax.

Perry's idea was that the corridor could be a public-private toll road. Cintra, a Spanish freighting company, was lined up to do much of the work. Building it, however, would have required aggressive eminent domain actions, and Texans took vigorous exception to the idea that the state would commandeer private land on behalf of a company—a foreign company, no less. After about two years of public outcry, the state canceled the plan.

Apart from these exceptional cases, however, Texas has a presumption of goodwill and cooperation between the public and private sectors. Private citizens pour money into political campaigns. "Had I known you could raise $3 million, I'd have been here long ago," Mitt Romney said on a 2012 trip to Midland. Elected officials, in turn, are generally chummy with lobbyists. The exceptions are few enough to be enumerated. Sam Rayburn was one; at one point an oilman sent him a beautiful horse, and he sent it back. Ron Paul is another.

But even Texas liberals are more sanguine about lobbyists than you would think. For Molly Ivins, the criticisms leveled at the state on these grounds had an off-putting piety: "I know a number of pols I count as honest who never did anything in return for such favors. Is it any ranker than getting a large campaign contribution from someone with a special interest in legislation? For virtue, try Minnesota."[23]

That is a Texas tradition that isn't going to change any time soon. You have to dance with the one that brung you, I guess.

In fact, Texas Democrats even, on occasion, scold their national counterparts for letting down the cause. "If there was one thing that Texas Democrats did well in the '60s," wrote Ben Barnes, the former lieutenant governor, in his memoir, "—and one thing today's struggling Democratic party ought to emulate—it was creating this bridge between conservative business interests and progressive constituencies."[24] For

Barnes, it isn't just about tactics. He reminisces about the meetings Texas politicians used to have with business leaders who wanted to help raise money and bat ideas around: "They weren't afraid to take a hit now for improvement later, and their efforts are a big part of the reason why we were able to effect such dramatic improvement in the social and civic life of Texans."[25] Maybe Barnes would say that. He is, after all, a lobbyist now. On the other hand, maybe he is a lobbyist because he would say that.

Either way, Barnes was right in line with Texas Democratic tradition. That's worth keeping in mind as Texas turns blue: the Texas version of blue might not be quite the same as the national shade. Wait—is Texas turning blue?

13

TURNING TEXAS BLUE

A FEW WEEKS BEFORE HIS SPEECH at the Democratic Party's national convention, Julián Castro had given the keynote address at the 2012 Texas Democratic Party convention. It didn't make as much of an impression, though; the schedulers had screwed things up, so Castro went on past everyone's bedtime. The mayor himself was up early the next morning, however, for breakfast in the bustling hotel lobby. At some point his brother Joaquin, then a state representative from San Antonio, appeared and slid into the booth alongside him. Julián was wearing a suit and a wedding ring, and Joaquin was wearing jeans and bags under his eyes. The two are identical twins and have gone through life largely together: high school on San Antonio's west side, Stanford, Harvard Law, then private practice, then politics. Joaquin has never lost an election. Julián has, but it was partly Joaquin's fault. During his first campaign for mayor of San Antonio, in 2005, Joaquin offered to play Julián at one of the public events, and when they were discovered—because they went on a radio show and told everyone about it—the voters decided they were too young.

More recently, the brothers have been bemused at being described, in a mostly flattering account, as products of "an affair." That was true, they explained, in the sense that their father had indeed been married to someone else at the time. But he was separated, and their parents lived together until the twins were eight. Each brother took a packet of Equal and, in apparently unintentional synchronization, stirred it into his iced tea.

Joaquin, who stayed behind after his brother left, had the air of a man who has been jerked around a little too much for his liking. During his first year in the legislature, he was among the Democratic representatives who left the state under the cover of night for Oklahoma as part of a coordinated effort to break the quorum the Republicans needed to pass their ambitious new redistricting plan. At the time he was running for Congress; the district was a safely Democratic one, and the incumbent was retiring, and in November, he won. But for most of the preceding year, he had been forced to campaign for two different seats, since the district lines kept changing around him. In August he had moved out of his house and moved back in with his mom in order to be in the correct district. Only in May had he moved back. He had, he added incidentally, ignored his mother's advice not to buy a two-story house, and it turned out that he went upstairs in his house only once every few months.

The waiter came by with Castro's oatmeal and dressed it at the table with excruciating solicitousness: a spoonful of pecans, a spoonful of raisins, some berries. A delegate came over and apologized for interrupting but said that she just wanted to introduce herself: she had met Joaquin yesterday and wanted to meet his brother too. "I'm Joaquin," said Castro, smiling broadly. He had said, earlier in the conversation, that he had been ambivalent about going into politics in the first place. That morning, then, the Castro twins looked like a good stand-in for the Texas Democratic Party as a whole: half confident and ambitious, despite the hassles, half sick of the whole thing.

In recent years, national Democrats have started to talk openly about how Texas is becoming, or could become, a blue state. Their argument is simple: demographics. If the Latino population is surging, which it is, and if Hispanic voters tend to favor the Democratic Party by a whopping margin, which they do, it stands to reason that a majority-Hispanic Texas will be a Democratic one.

There is something inexorable about that logic, and Texas Republicans recognized it years ago. Like national Republicans, they argue that it shouldn't be that hard to bring some of these voters into the fold. Hispanics, they observe, tend to be socially conservative, hard-working, entrepreneurial, and family focused—values that map well onto the party's professed concerns.

Democrats are skeptical that the pitch will work because of the concurrent debate over unauthorized immigration. In recent years, a number of states, frustrated by federal inertia, have tried to take matters into their own hands. Republican-led legislatures in Arizona, Georgia, and Alabama have passed harsh new laws cracking down. The Republican primary electorate is more conservative on the issue of immigration than the country as a whole, particularly in early-voting states like South Carolina, where the concern about demographic change seems to outpace the change itself.

Texas Republicans haven't gone down that road, though; they haven't alienated Hispanic voters as assiduously as their national counterparts have. The result is that, although they usually lose the Hispanic vote, they don't lose it as badly as Mitt Romney. George W. Bush won his reelection as governor of Texas with 40 percent support among Texas Latinos, and in 2004 he pulled 44 percent of the national Hispanic vote. Perry was reelected governor in 2010 with 38 percent of the Hispanic vote. In the four-way race in 2006, he pulled 31 percent; if you add to that the 18 percent that went to Carole Keeton Strayhorn, the Republican who was running as an independent, the GOP won a narrow majority of Latino voters that year.[1] More recently, the Texas GOP has pinned its hopes on Ted Cruz, the new US senator, and another Bush, George P., who is the son of Jeb, nephew of W., grandson of H. W., and Hispanic; his mother was born in Mexico.

In the short term, though, this might not be crucial. Political change lags behind demographic change. Hispanics are 40 percent of the Texas population, but a much smaller share of the Texas electorate. In terms of voter registration and actual turnout, they badly lag behind Anglos. There are about 2.15 million Latinos in Texas who are eligible to vote but aren't registered.[2] The Democrats haven't proven effective at getting people registered, and Republicans, as you would imagine, haven't really tried.

Assuming it will take the Hispanic vote several cycles to catch up with the Hispanic population, then, Democrats are going to have to think of a different strategy. Because as the matter stands, Texas Republicans have another card up their sleeve, one that has rarely failed them: Texas Democrats.

The state Democratic Party's first mistake was to get complacent. Perry's happy-go-lucky career illustrates this well. Every step of his ascent was received as flukish. The closest race he ever faced was in 1998, when he ran for lieutenant governor; the Democratic candidate, John Sharp, the sitting comptroller, was demonstrably capable of winning statewide office.

The polls were tight for the better part of a year, but then Perry got a crucial assist from Karl Rove, who was by then working for George W. Bush. Bush was a safe bet for reelection, widely liked by the voters. But Rove wasn't content just to win the governor's race. He already had an eye on the 2000 presidential election, so he wanted a Republican as lieutenant governor, too. That would give Bush some breathing room if he ran for national office. It would insulate him from political battles that might pop up in the legislature, perhaps, and no one would be able to get a critical quote from the state's second-ranking official, an officeholder who was constitutionally more powerful, in some respects, than the governor himself.

And in Rove's assessment, Perry was a problem. He was unruly; he was planning to run a negative ad about Sharp, a high-risk strategy that could have backfired on all the Republicans on the ticket. The lore is that Rove offered Perry a deal: if Perry agreed not to go negative, he could get an endorsement from the governor's father, former president George H. W. Bush. It would be Rick Perry's narrowest victory ever—50 percent to 48 percent—and the common view among political pundits is that Perry resented Rove's interference. Setting that aside, as a result of having become lieutenant governor, Perry didn't have to do anything special to become governor; it was legally bound to happen when Bush was elected president.

So Perry had the unusual blessing of spending about twenty years in elected office without anyone taking him seriously. "Governor Goodhair, or the Ken Doll (see, all Texans use nicknames—it's not that odd), is not the sharpest knife in the drawer," wrote Molly Ivins in 2001.[3] One legislator, she noted, had already observed that Perry was "much more engaged" with the office than his predecessor had been, but she nonetheless summarized the common wisdom when she dismissed him as Bush's "exceedingly Lite Guv."

Democrats remained unimpressed when Perry was elected governor all by himself in 2002; it was inevitable given that the Democratic primary had mostly drawn headlines for scandal. Similarly, they were disappointed, but not surprised, when Perry was reelected in 2006. The Democratic candidate, Chris Bell, just wasn't very charismatic, and it had been hard to get the media to pay attention, what with Perry clowning around and Kinky Friedman, a Jewish cowboy comedian, carrying on a colorful third-party run.

Some were confident that Perry would lose in 2010. He had gotten only 39 percent of the vote in the 2006 election, which ended up being a four-way contest among the three candidates mentioned and Strayhorn, the former Republican comptroller who ran as an Independent. Perry had even suggested, as recently as 2009, that he might not run for reelection—no doubt a rare concession, on Perry's part, to political reality.

When he changed his mind and announced that he would run after all, the early polls showed him badly trailing Kay Bailey Hutchison, the longtime senator who had, for years, had higher approval ratings than any other statewide Republican. Democrats were even optimistic about winning the general election; their candidate was Bill White, who had twice been elected mayor of Houston, the largest city in Texas.

Perry won, of course. He clobbered Hutchison in the primary and trounced White in the general, although both of those verbs misleadingly suggest that the governor expended some significant effort, which he didn't. One of the few people who expected the campaign to be a cakewalk was Perry himself. I interviewed him at the beginning of the cycle, in his office in the state capitol. He said that he didn't even think Hutchison wanted to be governor and that she wasn't going to be a problem. Then he showed me a picture of some dachshunds that he had just posted on Twitter. As promised, he barely seemed to think about the election. He spent most of the year loafing around as usual—jogging, making bets with Bobby Jindal, sending out press releases about how Staples was going to relocate sixty jobs from California to Texas.

Both Hutchison and White seemed to be unnerved by this behavior and started to sputter during the primaries. White, an effective and no-nonsense technocrat, faced a largely self-funded opponent in Farouk Shami, a businessman from Palestine who had moved to Houston and started a successful line of frizz-fighting hair care products. Shami never had a prayer of winning, but he clearly loved campaigning. When they met for a televised debate, White seemed caught between aggrieved dignity and existential despair. I started to suspect that Perry had somehow caused Shami to run simply to mischief White, and I called Shami to ask as much, but it was a fruitless line of inquiry. Shami told me that the governor loved his campaign and was very supportive, but then Shami was living in a world where everyone loved him and where everyone has manes of tumbling, glossy hair, even in the humid Houston summers, so he probably would have said as much regardless. The whole thing was odd. From his humble beginnings on the dirt farm in Paint Creek, Perry had emerged as some kind of political Zen master, Bruce Lee for dummies. I interviewed Perry again at the end of the primary and reminded him of his earlier prediction. "Yes," he said, reflective in triumph. "That one did follow the plan rather closely."

There are two ways to understand Perry's unprecedented and unanticipated success in Texas politics. The first is that the voters were clearly deranged. The other, painfully, requires some criticism of Texas's long-suffering optimists. Perry's ambition should have been obvious long before. So should his skill. Perry quite clearly has many limitations, some of which were starkly on display during his catastrophic run for the Republican presidential nomination. But he's not completely helpless. "He's a slow learner," one longtime observer told me, "but when he learns something, he learns it." And one thing he's learned is how to win an election, at least in Texas.

Behind closed doors, Democrats readily acknowledge this. They were beginning to recognize that Perry knew something their candidates in 2006 and 2010 didn't—how to win. There was nothing wrong with Bell, but he had very little name recognition and hadn't held office since 2005. White had stronger credentials, but even he had balked at the idea of running against Perry. Hutchison had said that she would leave the Senate to focus on the gubernatorial race, and White initially declared for Senate on the presumption that there would be an election to replace her in Washington. As for other contenders—crickets. No one was willing to risk it. "You can't lose twice," one Democratic staffer explained.[4]

You also can't win if you don't try. That maxim shouldn't need saying, but Texas Democrats still struggle to get their heads around it. Even the first step, running for office, occasionally eludes them.

To be fair, when the Democrats do find a good candidate, it's an uphill slog. In 2002, Peter J. Boyer, writing for the *New Yorker*, took a close look at the race to replace Phil Gramm in the US Senate. On the one hand, he observed, the state's rightward trend had been obvious for some time. George W. Bush was beloved in his home state, and his strategist, Karl Rove, was still keeping a close eye on Texas politics, so surely the Republican candidate, John Cornyn, was a pretty safe bet.

"Yet Texas Democrats," explained Boyer, "even with the weight of money, history, and George W. Bush against them, are looking forward to the Senate election with an almost giddy optimism, centering on a bald, bespectacled black man named Ron Kirk."[5] In 1995, Kirk had been elected mayor of Dallas, becoming the first African American to hold that post. He was reelected in 1999, despite being a black moderate (the mayor's office is nominally nonpartisan) in a city where most of the business and political players were, and are, Anglo conservatives.

In the end, John Cornyn beat Kirk by a 12-point margin. Little has changed in the intervening decade, except that Boyer's story mentioned that Kirk had been reading the third volume of Caro's LBJ epic, *Master of the Senate*, which was published that year. In 2012, the long-awaited fourth volume, *The Passage of Power*, was published.

Texas Democrats, in other words, are even slower than Caro. Despite all the changes that transpired in Texas during the decade in question—the surging population, the changing demographics, the ten additional years of budget cuts and backroom bargains—their strategy for retaking a statewide office, any statewide office, remains the same: statistically dubious optimism with a dash of identity politics.

Some observers had argued to Boyer that Kirk's biggest challenge would be overcoming racism, vestigial or otherwise, among Texas voters. It wasn't an unreasonable suggestion, given that Texas has never sent an African American to the US Senate. After Reconstruction, voters hadn't even sent an African American to the Texas Senate until Barbara Jordan, a Democrat from Houston, was elected in 1966. (In 1972, Jordan became the first black woman from the South to be elected to the US House of Representatives.) At the same time, Republicans did well in the 2002 midterms (in Texas and around the country) and Kirk's party was probably a stumbling block too. "This is as close as a black politician can come to being inoffensive to the Anglo community, without becoming a Republican," said Rufus Shaw, a local political consultant and pundit, who had criticized Kirk for being too conservative.[6] "If Texas doesn't vote for him, it's going to say something about Texas, and it will not be very good." But these days, if asked to pick between two similarly conservative candidates, Texas voters tend to vote for the one labeled Republican, just as they used to prefer the conservatives labeled Democrats.

And in 2002, for that matter, Cornyn was a moderate—a "middle of the roader," as Texan journalist Paul Burka put it—although he tacked right once he got to the Senate.[7] In 2008, in a nod to Texas's carnie tradition, Cornyn released a musical campaign ad, "Big John," depicting himself as a cowboy gone to Washington to tell the Senate there was a new sheriff in town.

Interestingly, this is what happened with Bush, too. He seemed like a moderate in Texas, he *was* a moderate in Texas, but he lurched right once he got to Washington. In the Cornyn case, Burka offered a couple of ideas. Cornyn had replaced Gramm, a staunchly ideological conservative, so maybe Gramm's staffers were whispering in his ear, or perhaps it was "a shrewd political calculation that the shortcut to advancement in the Senate is via the right side of the spectrum." Or, of course, Cornyn's realignment might have been a result of Bush's; the junior senator from Texas was an ally of the president. Cornyn himself disputed the idea that he had changed. "A moderate in Texas is a conservative in Washington," he told Burka.[8] Or maybe the national political scuffle itself activates a reactionary enzyme among a certain subset of Texas politicians. They come up in a state where pragmatic probusiness conservatism is the unquestioned consensus, and when challenged—well, Victory or Death! We saw a little bit of that with Rick Perry, too.

But to Burka's point, if it were a political calculation, it wasn't an incorrect one. Cornyn was reelected in 2008, despite the "Big John" video, which *Burnt Orange Report*, an Austin-based political blog, had confidently assumed would strike voters as "ridiculous."[9]

Maybe Texas Democrats were like frogs in a pot of water: by the time they realized the water was boiling, it was too late. Strong-arm tactics have helped keep them there. The most notorious example would be the 2003 fiasco over redistricting. More recently, Republicans have focused on making it harder for people to vote. In 2011, the state passed a voter ID measure that had been suggested and bitterly contested in the preceding sessions. The official rationale was that photo identification is a necessary precaution against voter fraud. It's one of those arguments that are hard to make with a straight face. Texas does have a history of voter fraud—think back to Landslide Lyndon and his 87-vote victory over Coke Stevenson. But no one's ever stolen an election by the type of voter fraud that the photo ID bill purportedly addresses; if you were going to go to all that trouble, you might as well just win the darn thing. And Texas also has a long history of disenfranchising people and suppressing the vote. So given that the law (which went straight to the Supreme Court) would disproportionately affect voters who support Democrats—ethnic minorities, the poor, and so on—the partisan dimensions are unmistakable.

The greatest advantage that Texas Republicans currently enjoy, however, is that Texans haven't really had a problem with their policies. The evidence is that people keep voting for them. Whether those voting patterns can be considered a rousing endorsement of the current leadership or a temperate vote for the status quo seems to me to be missing the point. During Perry's run for president, for example, one of the critiques from national observers was that Perry had originated no policies, merely continued those of his predecessors. That's largely true, but the value of innovation in government largely depends on who's doing the innovating.

Even among Texas Democrats, the opposition to Republican rule is less pointed than you would think. White, for example, struggled to find an effective message. He argued, fairly, that Texas had been underfunding education and services under the Republican regime, but he never really explained how his administration would rustle up more money. His most specific suggestion for finding some wiggle room in the budget was that the state was wasting a lot of money on Perry's rental house. The rental was expensive—about $25,000 a month—but it was hardly the biggest culprit in the state's budget issues, and arguably a valid expense, with the governor's mansion being uninhabitable. Such vagueness is all too often observed in Texas Democrats. Ask them how they plan to pay for their programs, and they go quiet. Take it a step farther and ask explicitly if they think the state should have a personal income tax, and they're at pains to say that there's no need to take it that far.

It's not as if Texas Democrats never show signs of life. In 2008, the Republican majority in the state House of Representatives was whittled to 2 votes, although the trend was reversed in 2010 and the Republicans returned to the legislature in 2011 with a supermajority. Most of Texas's big cities have Democratic mayors. There are some young Democrats, the Castros among them, who seem like they could run for statewide office at some point and win.

Still, many Texas Democrats sound forlorn when they talk about their political fortunes. John Sharp, who was one of the last Democrats elected to statewide office before losing the lieutenant governor's race in 1998, later observed that running against Rick Perry was "like running against God." Democrats were so thoroughly out of power they couldn't do much in the capitol to make their presence known. "I'm not relevant," said Mark Strama, the state representative from Austin. I asked one Democratic legislator what it would take for his party to win again. A celebrity, he said. Someone who could really get people excited, like Lance Armstrong. (That was before Armstrong was stripped of his Tour de France titles, and Armstrong had, in his heyday, expressed some interest in running for office, so it wasn't *that* desperate a suggestion.)

It's enough to make you wonder if the Texas Democrats have a secret strategy to win by attrition, except they so rarely give the impression of any strategic thinking whatsoever. Still, they might have stumbled on to something despite themselves. My old joke is that Texas Republicans have a card up their sleeve: Texas Democrats. But Texas Democrats have a secret weapon of their own: Texas Republicans.

14

THE COMING CRACK-UP

ON A SUMMER NIGHT in Houston in 1993, Jenny Ertman and Elizabeth Pena, aged fourteen and sixteen, respectively, left a pool party. They were worried about getting home late, so they decided to take a shortcut.

Cutting through a park, they came across six men drinking beer. The men had recently finished a gang initiation ceremony and decided to celebrate by having "fun," as one of them would later put it. But after raping and beating the girls for about an hour, the men started to worry that the girls might recognize them. So they strangled the girls to death. They used a belt. Then the belt broke, so they used shoelaces. Then they started stomping on the girls' necks, to make sure.[1]

All of the men were arrested several days later. The three who were older than eighteen at the time would eventually be executed. But one of them, Jose Medellin, challenged the sentence all the way to the Supreme Court. The issue was that he was a Mexican national, having only moved to the United States when he was three, and none of the Houston police had bothered to notify the Mexican Consulate when he was arrested.

201

This was, of course, a blatant violation of the 1963 Vienna Convention on Consular Relations. Or that was what the United Nations thought, anyway, prompting George W. Bush, then the president, to order Texas to review the case. You can guess how well that went over. In March 2008's *Medellin v. Texas*, the US Supreme Court sided with Texas in a rebuke to the federal government, the United Nations, and the pieties of international law. "Amazingly, however, *three* justices did not agree," Rick Perry would later write, "perhaps believing instead that international law should trump the laws of Texas."[2]

Feeling the same way was Randy Ertman. His daughter had initially managed to run away from the group and probably would have been fine if she hadn't gone back to try to help her friend. "This business belongs in the state of Texas," he told the *Houston Chronicle* in 2008. "The people of the state of Texas support the execution. We thank them. The rest of them can go to hell."

The state solicitor general who argued the case before the Supreme Court was named Ted Cruz. He is a second-generation Cuban American whose father came to the United States as a teenager with $100 sewn into his underwear. After graduating from Harvard Law, Cruz quickly made a name for himself as a rising star in legal circles. The *American Lawyer*, the *National Law Journal*, *Texas Lawyer*—they all bigged him. He would eventually argue nine cases before the Supreme Court during the course of that job, and he won six of them.

In 2011 when Cruz announced that he would run for Kay Bailey Hutchison's Senate seat, national conservatives were on him like flies on pie. The *National Review* put him on the cover. The long-suffering liberals at the *Texas Observer* warned that he could be the next Ronald Reagan. He was endorsed by Rand Paul and Ron Paul and Sarah Palin. It's easy to see why all these people have hearts shooting out of their eyes. Cruz looks like a perfect mix of Marco Rubio, Paul Ryan, and Rand Paul: a smart young Hispanic who is beloved by the Tea Party and doesn't pull his punches.

In Texas, however, Cruz was slower to catch on. When he entered the race, he could muster only a few points in the polls. The heavyweight in the race was David Dewhurst, the lieutenant governor since 2003, a former rodeo champion who made a fortune in the oil and gas industry.

After years in office, Dewhurst still has an oddly low profile; he tends to eschew public appearances, preferring to ensconce himself in his inner chambers, where classical music plays quietly and guests are offered cold cuts on a silver tray. He gives the impression, actually, of mild social anxiety; when compelled to give a speech, his delivery is careful, sometimes halting, and he doesn't seek out the public., Still, Dewhurst was unquestionably favored to win. At the outset he had a commanding lead in the polls, the support of the party establishment, and, of course, his personal fortune to fall back on in the event that campaigning would be necessary.

Cruz's argument was that Dewhurst isn't a real conservative. It was a good year for ideological purification in general—after the Tea Party surge in 2010, the Republican base was emboldened. At a 2012 Tea Party rally in Dallas, Ken Emanuelson, an attorney from Dallas, had told me that even if the Tea Party were risking a short-term backlash, it was worth it to help drive the conversation. "Without entitlement reform," he argued, "you can get rid of all the fish hatcheries or teapot museums you want."[3]

On the merits, Cruz's should have been a hard case to make, because Dewhurst is clearly conservative. He was an incumbent officeholder, but in Texas rather than Washington. He had never voted for any bailouts, and because the lieutenant governor presides over the state Senate, Dewhurst had had a big role in setting the state's legislative agenda.

Still, Cruz's conviction carried the day. The campaign was heated. Toward the end, Dewhurst brought out an ad accusing Cruz of supporting amnesty for illegal immigrants. "That is the act of a desperate man clinging to power," said Cruz, and it did elicit a backlash. Among his defenders was George P. Bush: "When I first heard this false attack ad, I was offended not only as a Hispanic but as a Republican." Cruz's rise in the polls was inexorable. By May, he had enough support to force Dewhurst into a runoff. When the runoff rolled around in July, Cruz won by a 12-point margin.

And with that, the election was effectively decided, although Cruz did, for form's sake, win the general election in November. He will be one of the most ideological national politicians Texas has ever had— and in that sense, he represents a new kind of Texas Republican. Despite their intemperate rhetoric, and occasional red-meat gesture, the state's contemporary Republican leaders have been pragmatic enough in practice. Conservative, sure, but hardly lunatic. Recall that when George W. Bush was running for president, he was considered a moderate. He had occasionally worked with Democrats as governor of Texas. We forget this now because Bush became quite far right as president, but several million Americans, mostly from the more progressive end of the spectrum, were so underwhelmed by the putative difference between Bush and his opponent, Al Gore, that they cast protest votes for Ralph Nader.

Even Perry has been more of an opportunist than an ideologue. On the social issues, for example, he had always struck me as someone who at a fundamental level could not care less. You can practically see him glazing over, in real time, during the televised interview where Evan Smith asked him about abstinence. The words dribble out; the "for rent" sign goes up in his eyes. A small-government conservative could see that as a feature rather than a bug.

Between 2000 and 2012, the Republicans captured more offices, but their agenda didn't really go further to the right than it had been. There are still plenty of traditional Republicans in Texas. Dewhurst wasn't the only high-profile Republican incumbent to face a backlash from the right, and some of the others who were targeted by the Tea Party types won. For that matter, if the moderate Hutchison hadn't decided to retire, it's not certain that Cruz would have beat her. She did lose the 2010 gubernatorial primary to Perry, but she had waged such a halfhearted campaign that it might as well have been run by the Democrats.

On the other hand, some things have changed since 2010.

THE DAY AFTER TEXAS'S 2012 primary election, Joe Straus met with reporters in his office. "Welcome," he said, smiling indulgently and adjusting his cuffs. All the reporters were fiddling with their recorders and muttering among themselves. "You're supposed to say 'thank you,'" he said, still smiling.

Straus, a moderate Republican from a prominent Jewish family in San Antonio, was elected to the Texas House of Representatives in 2004. Prior to that, he had a respectable but low-key career in business and politics. "Respectable" and "low-key," of course, have never been among that legislative body's aspirational ideals. That's one of the reasons people were surprised in 2009 when he announced he had enough votes to become the Speaker of the House.

He did, though—the majority of his supporters, it turned out, were Democrats, who had reasoned that Straus was the most temperate speaker they were going to get. Speaker Straus took the dais, and the legislative session that followed, in 2009, was markedly less dysfunctional than the one that had preceded it. That made some conservatives uneasy, and Straus's tenure as speaker has been dogged by accusations of moderation. At one particularly grotesque moment John Cook, a member of the State Republican Executive Committee, sent a couple of e-mails arguing that Texas needs a Christian conservative as a speaker. Questioned, he explained that he doesn't have a problem with Jews; he just prefers Christians.[4]

On the May afternoon in question, Straus had just shrugged off a primary challenge, which was officially from a Tea Party candidate named Matt Beebe but was effectively from Michael Quinn Sullivan, an Eagle Scout, a self-described fitness nut, and the president and

CEO of a PAC called Empower Texas. The PAC had bankrolled a number of primary challenges to moderate Republicans that year, including Beebe's.[5]

The speaker seemed to be in a slightly punchy mood. He professed that it hadn't bothered him to be challenged in the primary: "Hey, look, it's a free country; it's a free Texas House of Representatives." With that said, he observed that Sullivan's effort to unseat him had been "spectacularly unsuccessful." If Sullivan were so keen to participate in the political process, Straus mused, he should really run for office himself, although such an effort "would be spectacularly unsuccessful too."

I asked him why there had been so many contested primaries this time around, if that was a cyclical phenomenon or a structural one. "I think it's probably down to the success and the growth of the Republican majority," he said. "If you want to be an elected official, the path to it is as a Republican."

Political opportunism has, in the past, been part of the explanation for the Republican Party's growth in Texas—that was clear in the 1980s, when Democrats such as Perry were simply switching sides. But in 2010 and 2012, the people who challenged incumbent Republicans in the primaries weren't coming from the center. They were coming from the right. And the Republican majority in the legislature isn't just getting bigger. It's getting redder. That had been clear in the 2011 session, when the Republicans finally succeeded in passing their voter ID bill.

More illuminating, perhaps, were two other bills from the 2011 session, both of which probably would have failed in 2009, and both of which were backed by Republicans affiliated with the Tea Party. One of them meant to restrict unauthorized immigration; the other meant to restrict access to abortion. The latter passed; the former didn't. Looking at them side by side suggests there's a fault line within the state Republican Party over how socially conservative the state should be.

The first of the bills in question was a measure that would have outlawed sanctuary policies for unauthorized immigrants. It wasn't a very strong bill—the state would have had no ways to force cities to comply—but it nonetheless met with opposition from Democrats, and—more importantly—from the business-minded Republicans, who are not zealous about unauthorized migration. The sanctuary cities bill died quietly, of neglect.

The other was the sonogram bill, the one that requires women seeking an abortion to receive a sonogram first. It had an economic dimension, insofar as a working woman who is planning an abortion would now need to take two days off rather than one. But there aren't many people lobbying on behalf of working-class women, so there was little opposition from within the Republican Party. The sonogram bill, accordingly, passed without much trouble.

It didn't even elicit that much surprise given the state's casual lack of interest in health care in general, and women's health in particular. Texas is heaven for men and dogs, hell on women and oxen, the old saw goes. In 1977, film critic Mary Mackey offered a feminist critique of the state. The text at hand was *The Texas Chainsaw Massacre*. "Texas itself, the location of the film, is the land of male violence par excellence. In US folk mythology, Texas more than any other state embodies the cowboy ideal of the lone male who carves out a place for himself with his trusty Colt 45," she wrote. "Women have never counted for very much in Texas, and in the lives of the slaughterhouse family they don't count at all."[6]

Texans have historically been happy enough for women to have economic rights. The Republic of Texas allowed women to retain ownership of any property they had before marriage, a right inherited from Spanish law and one that most other states lacked.[7] A number of women went into business for themselves as teachers, innkeepers— "inn" often being a euphemism for "brothel"—and even, occasionally, ranchers.

Texas was, relatedly, an early adopter of public education for the second sex. In New England, the civilization of women had long been considered a private affair; if genteel parents wanted elegant daughters, they could make their own arrangements. Texas, lacking the genteel parents, needed to intervene, for everyone's sake. "The *girls*, we will not say young ladies, will grow up like mere parrots," wrote Dr. Francis Moore Jr. in 1841. "What a contrast will there be between these dull, shiftless, stupid females, and the intelligent, refined, active, and accomplished ladies who adorn the first society of the United States."[8]

On the other hand, Texas politicians never took much interest in women's civil rights. Pa Ferguson, the populist but crooked governor from the 1910s who later put his wife up for governor in his stead, was against women's suffrage. It was Texas's restrictive abortion laws that triggered the lawsuit that led to *Roe v. Wade*. (At the same time, it was a Texas woman, Norma McCorvey, who brought the lawsuit, and a Texas woman, Sarah Weddington, who won the case at the Supreme Court.)

The right to vote, the right to reproductive freedom, the right to be seen as equals—no. The right to work, the right to an education (education always being seen as an economic issue in Texas)—suit yourself, little lady.

So the passage of the sonogram bill wasn't a surprise, per se. Voters also weren't surprised when the state announced that it would stop providing any funds for Planned Parenthood, a nonprofit reproductive health care organization that provides access to abortion—never mind that abortion is a tiny part of Planned Parenthood's activities. But the latter, in particular, will probably come to look like an example of the Texas Republicans taking things too far.

The sonogram bill inspired an angry backlash from liberals, but polling found that a majority of voters approved it, and in any case, the details of the process of getting an abortion probably weren't directly visible to enough voters, male or female, to inspire a widespread movement. The attack on Planned Parenthood, however, was different. The majority of Americans, in Texas and elsewhere, support access to contraception in general and Planned Parenthood in particular. It's been around for more than a century and has, over that time, been the reproductive health care provider of first and last resort for millions of women. It elicits some loyalty around the country.

That had become apparent in 2012 when the Susan G. Komen Foundation, a nonprofit that raises money for the fight against breast cancer, announced that it was going to stop contributing money for Planned Parenthood to provide breast cancer screenings, also because Planned Parenthood's offerings include abortions. The move got way more attention than Komen could have intended and turned into a massive windfall for Planned Parenthood, as people around the country, realizing that America was suddenly having a gilded-era-style war on contraception, opened their checkbooks.

Surveys corroborate the point. In 2012, Public Policy Polling did a national poll for Planned Parenthood and found that 56 percent of likely voters supported the idea that employer-sponsored health plans should cover birth control.[9] A separate survey, also by Public Policy Polling, found that 58 percent of Texans thought Planned Parenthood should continue to receive funding from the state's Women's Health Program.[10] It has a higher approval rating in Texas than Rick Perry.[11] (As an aside, the national head of Planned Parenthood is Cecile Richards, who is the daughter of Ann Richards and the founder of the Texas Freedom Network.)

Defunding Planned Parenthood, in other words, was exactly the kind of move that could backfire on Texas Republicans. On social issues, Texans are generally in line with national norms—which is to say, moderate. In a May 2012 Gallup Poll, 38 percent of Americans described themselves as social conservatives.[12] That sounds like accurate self-reporting. There's some variation depending on the particular issue at hand, but as a rule of thumb social conservatives make up a plurality of voters, but not a majority, in both Texas and the United States.

In 2011, for example, according to a national survey from the First Amendment Center, 67 percent of Americans agreed that the First Amendment requires the separation of church and state.[13] In 2010, a Texas survey found 68 percent of likely voters agreeing that separation of church and state is a key constitutional principle.[14] So in 2012, when Rick Perry blamed Satan for the separation of church and state—"Satan runs across the world with his doubt and with his untruths and what have you"—he was well outside the mainstream of both Texan and American opinion.[15]

Texas's political leadership is socially conservative for the same reason that the United States sometimes gets socially conservative leaders: social conservatives are more likely to organize around social issues than moderates or liberals are. We can refer back to that Gallup survey that put the percentage of social conservatives at 38 percent. They're not the majority; they are on the back foot, and some of them know it. "We are in a crisis and so far most of the church fails to recognize we are in a battle," said the demonization PowerPoint that day at Cornerstone.

Social conservatives are, however, the biggest bloc; 31 percent and 28 percent of Americans described themselves as moderate and liberal, respectively. When moderates and liberals agree, they win. That's why abortion is legal, contraception is widely available, and gay marriage—which as recently as ten years ago was barely considered a serious suggestion—is making progress throughout the states as moderates come around to the idea. The social conservatives win, however, when moderates agree with them, which is why gay marriage isn't legal in all the states yet. They also win when they make an effort and moderates and liberals aren't paying much attention.

That's what's happened in Texas. For so many years, the state's Republican majority has been a party driven by business issues. Its sideline in Bible-thumping has mostly been confined to the rhetorical level and has therefore been easy for moderates to ignore, given that in practice Texas isn't noticeably more repressive than any other state.

"The questions were always there between the social conservatives and the business conservatives," says Aaron Wheat of Texans for Public Justice, a watchdog organization.[16] "The all-or-nothing approach of the Tea Partiers is sort of bringing it to a head."

Social conservatives, emboldened as they are, may be at risk of going too far. In 2012, John Carona, a Republican state senator from Dallas, told the *Dallas Voice* that he supported several gay rights measures, including offering partner benefits to employees at state universities. He was even, he allowed, thinking about gay marriage.[17] It was, as the *Voice* put it, "a rare if not unprecedented move for a Republican state legislator," and the response from the religious right was predictably outraged. But while Carona had clearly gone out on a limb, he wasn't out of step with public opinion.

There are other trouble spots looming for Texas's Republican coalition. Immigration is one; while the state party has been more moderate than its national counterparts. As the sanctuary cities bill suggested, some of the newer legislators might want to revive the issue. The budget is going to be another contentious issue between the moderates and the far right. The severe budget cuts of 2011 didn't elicit that much anger among voters at the time. Everyone had heard about the downturn. But in January 2013, the comptroller projected that the state would have $101.4 billion for general purpose spending in the 2014–2015 biennium—including almost $9 billion left over from the previous cycle, because revenues had been higher than projected. If the Tea Party–type Republicans seek further cuts, moderates might balk.

In 2011, the fact that the sanctuary cities bill failed in the legislature showed that the moderate Republicans still had the upper hand. But the fact that the sonogram bill succeeded suggested that the moderate Republicans were choosing their battles. It's not clear which wing of the Republican Party will have the upper hand in 2013. An interesting detail from the 2012 elections, however, was that, although Ted Cruz won his Senate race by a whopping margin, and despite all the attention paid to his candidacy, he got fewer votes in Texas (about

100,000 fewer) than Mitt Romney. The fact that the Republican coalition has gotten so big might, in other words, be a good thing for Democrats over the medium term. If the Republicans keep fighting among themselves, it could create an opportunity for Democrats to make a pitch for moderates. Obama was right, then, to say that Texas is becoming a battleground. In the short term, however, the battle will be within the Republican Party.

15

TWEAKING THE MODEL

LET'S ASSUME, THEN, that Republicans will maintain their control of Texas politics for the next couple of years (through the 2014 elections, at least) but that at some point thereafter (2018, say) Democrats will start retaking statewide offices. The demographic and cultural trends already discussed will, meanwhile, continue. What kind of changes would we expect to see in Texas?

A total overhaul seems unlikely. The Texas model has clearly and incontrovertibly worked. Parts of it are still working. It could use some updates, for reasons I'll describe momentarily. But before that, to defend why I think the model has worked, think about the state's starting position.

"Suppose your country is dirt poor, almost stagnant economically, and that few people are educated," writes economist Paul Collier in *The Bottom Billion*, his 2007 book about the world's poorest countries. "You don't have to try that hard to imagine this condition—our ancestors lived this way. With hard work, thrift, and intelligence, a society can gradually climb out of poverty, unless it gets trapped."[1]

He describes four common traps. First, there's conflict, which works as "development in reverse"; war is expensive and leads to lingering dislocation and disruption. Second, natural resources, which would seem to be an advantage, can have the perverse effect of thwarting other economic activity. Third, having bad neighbors is a problem, especially in landlocked countries. Fourth, there's bad governance.

This is a simplistic summary, and of course nineteenth-century Texas was never as disadvantaged as, say, Chad is today. But Texas has faced versions of all the challenges Collier describes. The Civil War interrupted access to the Southern markets for cattle and cotton. The state's overreliance on natural resources was apparent in the 1980s, when the collapse in oil prices sent Texas plunging into recession. Its neighbors include the poorest states in America and some of the most fragile states in Mexico. Its governance has historically been scattershot at best. And the Texas model, even if it ultimately looks like a historical accident more than a thoughtful approach to government, helped the state overcome all those.

Consider two Fortune 500 companies based in the Austin metro area—Dell, which was number 44 on the 2012 list, with $62.1 billion in annual revenue, and Whole Foods Market, which was number 265 and has $10.1 billion in annual revenue. Both were founded in Austin in the 1980s, and both have been so successful that it's easy to forget how unlikely that would have seemed at the time. People were cottoning on to computers by the time Michael Dell dropped out of college, at nineteen, to try his hand at selling them, but it wasn't clear that personal computing was going to be so popular that Dell could become a billionaire by starting a business based on the idea of building them faster. John Mackey, the founder of Whole Foods, had the even more harebrained idea that what Texas consumers wanted was healthier food. Still, Texas was an easy place to take a risk. When Mackey opened his first vegetarian grocery store, in 1978, he didn't have to deal with an overheated commercial real estate market. He just ran it out of the garage he shared with his girlfriend.[2]

Today, both founders lean to the political right. Dell keeps a low profile, but his campaign contributions corroborate the impression of a garden-variety probusiness Republican—quick to call for tax cuts, happy to take incentives. Mackey, who used to be a philosophy student, is ideologically libertarian. In 2010, he wrote an op-ed for the *Wall Street Journal* attacking Obamacare and confounding progressives, who wouldn't have guessed that Mackey's views tilted that way given his vegan lifestyle and the affluent, educated Whole Foods ethos.

Both companies have been accused of untoward greed; in 2011, for example, the leftist magazine *Mother Jones* published a long list of Dell's less impressive moments—"exploiting tax loopholes, outsourcing production, and laying off American workers."[3] At the same time, both companies have created a lot of wealth and employment in Texas, which is the main thing Texans expect businesses to do.[4] The net social value of either company, or really any company, is debatable, and subjective; but Texans, on balance, would prefer having them to not.

Texas today may not be as rich as Massachusetts or as well educated as Maryland, in other words, but the fact that it is being compared to those affluent, long-established states is in itself a measure of the progress that has been achieved. No one has such high expectations of, say, Louisiana—except for some reformers, entrepreneurs, and economic development officials in Baton Rouge and New Orleans, and that's partly because they're looking at the gains that Texas has made.

THE TEXAS MODEL WILL CONTINUE to work in many cases, and it still has its classically liberal appeal. But two contemporary phenomena suggest that the model could use with an update. The first is that the state's population is changing, in several ways. The second is that the structural economy has changed, in both the United States and Texas.

Texas's surging Hispanic population gets a lot of attention, but there's something else that should be striking about the state's demographics. Texas is younger than the United States as a whole; 27.1 percent of residents are younger than eighteen. So many people have come to Texas and seen a future here that the state is blessed with a young and growing population. Around the country, only 23.7 percent of people are minors. Similarly, 13.3 percent of Americans are older than sixty-five, and only 10.5 percent of Texans are that old.

As you might guess, age and ethnicity are jarringly correlated. In 2010, according to data from the Hobby Center at Rice University, 67.6 percent of Texans older than sixty-five were Anglo; 20.5 percent of old Texans were Hispanic. Slightly more than half (50.6 percent) of Texans under age five, however, were Hispanic. Just 31.7 percent were Anglo.[5] That's significant because in Texas, as in the United States, ethnicity isn't just correlated with age; it's correlated with things like household income and educational attainment. Consider a statistical oddity: in May 2012, the Texas Education Agency put out a press release bragging that students in Texas's three biggest ethnic groups had posted some of the best scores in their respective groups on the eighth-grade science test from the National Assessment of Educational Progress. The Anglo students had the eighth-highest scale score among all America's white students, the Hispanic students were sixth, and the African Americans were fourth. All together, however, and with Asians added in, the state's eighth-grade students ranked twenty-ninth.[6]

The apparent discrepancy, then, was due to demographics. Across the nation, black and Hispanic students had underperformed on the test relative to white students, and Texas has a greater share of black and Hispanic students than most states. For that matter, if you looked at the other ethnically diverse states, Texas's eighth-graders were doing better than most. On the same test, California's African Americans students ranked thirtieth, Hispanics ranked forty-second, and whites ranked forty-third. Overall, California's eighth-graders were forty-ninth, which kind of makes you wonder if parts of the Texas model would work better in other states than they do in Texas itself.

Still, Texas can't just check that it's beating California again and call it a day. The demographics are what they are, and the reasons for America's racial achievement gap are less relevant for policymakers, perhaps, than the fact that the gap exists. Texas needs to do more to pick up Hispanic and African American kids unless it wants to end up as a two-tiered society. Some Texans worry that it already is.

Steve Klineberg, a sociologist based at Houston's Rice University, observes that the issue is particularly acute because of the way that America's structural economy has changed.[7] Most of the fastest-growing occupations in the country require specialized skills or a college education, if not a graduate one. This shift is happening everywhere; economist Tyler Cowen has summarized the situation by saying that America has eaten all of its low-hanging fruit.[8]

But the shift represents a bigger challenge for Texas than for many states, partly because of the state's youth, and partly because, although the state's economy has diversified, Texas is still more dependent on resources, and lighter on knowledge jobs, than some of its peers. Texas's minimalist model coalesced in an era when a man could make his fortune by rounding up feral cattle. That's really not the case today. Even the energy business is increasingly technological.

After finishing his PhD in acoustics at Penn State, for example, Mark Wochner moved to Austin to work at the University of Texas as a research scientist focused on underwater noise mitigation. The subject isn't as arcane as it sounds. When people are pile-driving, or exploring for oil, or installing offshore infrastructure, they need to figure out some way to turn down the volume. Otherwise, they upset marine life—the fish and marine mammals get confused and distressed and so on. Even if you don't care about the fish, the noise is still a problem, because most countries have environmental laws that won't let people pile-drive all willy-nilly.

Wochner and his colleagues had figured out a new approach to the problem at hand. His technology was cheaper, and more effective, than anything that was currently on the market. The university helped

Wochner and his team get the patent. In March 2012, he officially became the CEO of a new company, AdBm Technologies.

The whole thing was pretty Texas-miraculous. Wochner had the idea, and he built the company, but he got some critical assists along the way. The state had supported his research by funding the university, which funds the research labs. The city had chipped in by supporting the various incubators and nonprofits that patrol the streets of Austin. The business community had helped by providing advice, material resources, funding, and contracts, and of course the original research had been partially funded by oil and gas companies headquartered in Texas. Assuming things keep going well, lots of people are going to see a payoff: Wochner, of course, but also the people he hires, and the state he pays taxes to. Companies will lower their costs, consumers should see some surplus, and the fish families will prosper.

At the same time, it wasn't a very good example of the Texas model at work. Wochner himself isn't the paradigmatic Texan entrepreneur. He wasn't even looking to start a business.[9] And this wasn't a situation that any one actor could have engineered. Low taxes and predictable regulations had played a role, of course, but so too had public-sector investments in education and in infrastructure. This is, increasingly, how innovation happens—it arises from public-private collaborations, rather than being pioneered in a company's own R&D department.[10]

If Texas wants to be a top state for innovation and entrepreneurship, then, it should probably invest in its human capital, particularly its public schools and universities. Even if it just wants to remain a top state for business, it should still do that, because the jobs of the American future are, increasingly, highly skilled jobs.

Some observers are pessimistic about whether Texas is willing to make such investments; in 2011, for the first time in memory, the legislature produced a state budget for the 2012–2013 biennium that didn't provide enough money to cover the enrollment growth public schools are projected to have. The correlation between age and ethnicity adds another layer of complication. Most older Texans, the people with money and power, are Anglo. The cohort that needs more public services—the kids, especially the poor kids—is predominantly Hispanic.

Liberals, accordingly, sometimes ask whether old white people are really going to spend their money on poor Hispanic kids. I am more optimistic on this point, partly because I notice that it's the older Texans who are most concerned about whether Anglos are going to insist on racialized austerity measures. The next generations, the majority of whom are not Anglo themselves, seem to have more confidence on this point, particularly as they're coming into power. When we look at the Hobby Center's figures again, about 40 percent of Texans in their thirties are Hispanic, and about 40 percent are Anglo. One of the people in that age bracket is Castro, the mayor of San Antonio, and in the November 2012 elections, voters in his city authorized one of his top priorities: a minor increase in the local sales tax to fund a citywide preschool program.

Besides, despite all the cross-talk about textbooks, and the sorry high school graduation rate, and the 2011 budget cuts, Texans do care about education. Even Texans who aren't particularly educated themselves say that it's important: "Fund an accountable education system so that you have a skilled work force available," as the Rick Perry recipe puts it. And Republicans have, in the not too distant past, been willing to do just that. In 1987, Bill Clements, the oilman who had become the state's first Republican governor since Reconstruction, famously signed the largest tax increase in Texas's history— more than $5 billion—because not doing so would have required severe budget cuts for public schools.

Education has even, on occasion, spurred a spirit of cooperation between the parties. In 1992, when Ross Perot announced that he would run for president as a third-party candidate, Molly Ivins, pointing to his commitment on this issue, announced that he was "the best right-wing populist billionaire we've got."[11] Today, longtime liberals are making common cause with moderate Republicans over the issue.

Aaron Wheat of TPJ sounded slightly bemused when he told me that Bill Hammond—the president of the Texas Association of Business (one of the most powerful lobbyists in the state, and a longtime bête noire for watchdog groups such as TPJ)—had emerged as "a voice of reason" in recent years. Whereas the Tea Party–type Republicans were strictly slash and burn, Wheat explained, Hammond was among those who realized "that it might not make the most business sense to utterly defund and destroy our university system, that that could be conceived, in some quarters, as shortsighted."

If we assume Texas has the will for education reform, the next question will be what can actually be done. Spending more money on schools is a popular suggestion. Texas already spends less per public school student than almost any other state. For the 2011–2012 school year, the figure was $8,908, according to the National Education Association. The national average was $11,463.[12] That was almost $500 less, per capita, than the previous school year, even before the cuts that were made in the 2011 legislative session.

Some Texas leaders, however, dispute the idea that funding is the critical issue. "The question I always ask, and no one can answer—and I realize it's a tough question—is, how much does it cost to provide quality education?" asked Dan Patrick, a Republican state senator from Houston. Texas has some public schools that are poor but effective, he continued, and some that are well funded but mediocre. Then of course there are a lot of home-schooled students who do pretty well and don't cost the state hardly anything.

"It's not always about money," he continued. "It comes down to the quality of the teacher, the quality of the principal, and a commitment by the parents. If you have a good teacher and a good principal and a parent who cares, I'll show you a successful student, no matter if they're funded at $5,000 a student or $7,000 a student."

Patrick also wants more vocational training and more counseling. "We have let the liberal elite of education convince everyone that every child needs to go to college," he remarked. The result is that hundreds of thousands of Texans have graduated from college with degrees in things like history and English—useless, unless an employer happens to be looking for someone to teach history or write the company's manuals. He looked at me, a putatively employed person: "You're the exception to the rule. You have a four-year in *writing*?"

Even if there were a consensus that Texas's educational pipeline needs more money, the skimpy per-student funding isn't strictly a matter of political will. Texas has always been more willing to spend money on education than other things, and until recently, the state wasn't that far off national norms. In the 1990s, Texas ranked in the middle of the pack in terms of spending per pupil. What's changed is that Texas has more kids now than ever before. Aggregate spending has kept pace; about 40 percent of the state's general revenue spending goes to elementary and secondary education, which is higher than the national average.[13]

Spending per pupil has dropped, then, because the number of kids is growing, and given that education already chews up a disproportionate part of the state budget, Texas politicians would actually be hard-pressed to spend *more* money on schools. It's the constitutional problem again. Even if the state's leaders were willing to invest more in education, they'd have to jump through hoops to raise a meaningful lump of cash. And in the absence of some major push for reform, the only way to raise money is by little tweaks to the current matrix of taxes and fees. Similar problems would arise with regard to other reforms that progressive Texans already suggest—even if there were a cultural consensus in favor of systemic change, the state of government is pretty thoroughly limited by design.

But on most issues, Texans aren't really clamoring for change. The state's commitment to small government is widespread and apparently sincere. To give one example, in 2008, during the height of both the national recession and the Texas Miracle, Texas had 2.7 million people receiving food stamps; California had 2.4 million. That's because Texas has more poor people than California does, even though California has a lot more people overall (about 37 million to 25 million at the time).

With regard to welfare, though, Texas had only about 115,000 people receiving funds through the Temporary Assistance for Needy Families program that year. California had 1.2 million—more than ten times as many. The difference, of course, is that the food stamp program is federally administered. It's not up to the states to decide who's eligible. TANF is largely federally funded and is subject to federal standards, but the states get to fiddle with the eligibility parameters. Texas, as you might guess, is strict about the rules—and if voters were asked to draw up a list of the fifty worst things about Texas, stinginess about welfare wouldn't be on it.

If Texas were inclined to tackle poverty, it would have to pursue a strategy other than expanding the welfare state. It could, for example, raise the minimum wage, which is currently the same as the federal minimum wage, $7.25 an hour. As mentioned at the outset, Texas is tied with Mississippi as the state with the highest share of workers earning that much or less. That is genuinely troubling, because a person who works full-time at the minimum wage (forty hours a week for fifty-two weeks a year at $7.25 an hour) earns $15,080 per year—a measly income that helps explain why about 20 percent of Texans live below the poverty line even when only 7 or 8 percent of Texans are unemployed. Even if that strikes you as fair, it's not particularly desirable. No matter how low your cost of living is, if you're making $15K a year, you're poor.

What's more, raising the minimum wage would help the state. A single mother with one child who works full-time but earns the minimum wage would qualify for Medicaid benefits. Given that the state currently spends about 20 percent of its budget on Medicaid, Texas has a fiscal interest in reducing the poverty rate. And there would be a little lagniappe for the state coffers. Minimum-wage workers typically spend all the money they earn; it's hard to save money if you make so little to begin with. In economic terms, their marginal propensity to consume is 100 percent. And Texas, meanwhile, gets about two-thirds of its general revenue funds from the sales tax. Raising the minimum wage would boost consumer spending, which would yield a little bump in sales tax receipts. Not a huge one, but still—$50 million here, $50 million there, and pretty soon you're talking about real money.

The usual objection to such a suggestion is that raising the minimum wage has an adverse effect on employment, but the demand for minimum-wage workers is closely tied to population, and Texas has never had a shortage of population growth.[14] If any state can afford this kind of experiment, it would be this one, and of all the things the state could do to mitigate poverty, it's the only one that seems possible, albeit remotely, from a political perspective.

Still, if Texas is going to focus on any issue, education will be the priority. Let's hope so, at least. If you're severely lagging behind most of the country in most things, as Texas used to be, any improvement is a win. But if you're a miraculous state that has the second-largest economy in a country that is still the world's largest economy, "Thank God for Mississippi" doesn't seem good enough anymore.

16

TEXAS AND THE UNITED STATES

WHEN I STARTED TELLING PEOPLE I was writing a book about Texas, some of them asked if it was going to be like *What's the Matter with Kansas?*, Thomas Frank's book explaining how conservatives hoodwinked working-class people in his home state of Kansas, and across America, into voting for them. As far as I could tell, this line of questioning was because people have been wondering: What on earth is the matter with Texas?

In Frank's account, as discussed, the problem with Kansas, and the country more generally, is that Republican voters are "deranged." The conservative elite—the cronies—started the culture wars in order to trick working-class Americans. By fomenting a populist backlash against the country's liberal elite, red-state voters could be induced to cast their votes on the basis of issues like abortion and gay marriage. They would barely notice if the socially conservative candidates who sided with them on those pet issues were also supporting an economic agenda that favored the entrenched elite—even if the economic agenda in question would have catastrophic consequences for common folk.

"As a formula for holding together a dominant political coalition," Frank writes, "the backlash seems so improbable and so self-contradictory that liberal observers often have trouble believing it is actually happening."

There are, now that he mentions it, a couple of holes in the plot. For one thing, if Republican voters are stupid, why can't Democrats outwit them? Or if Republican leaders are these political masterminds, why did Democrats win the presidency in 2008, and again in 2012?

Frank's argument is provocative, in other words, but it rests on the premise that people are stupid. Or if not stupid, exactly, then easily and predictably misled. "People getting their fundamental interests wrong is what American political life is all about," he says. If this were true, it's surprising that they're not misled more frequently, and for more exciting purposes than the pursuit of electoral office. But Frank's skepticism is well represented in the annals of American political thought, and when we look at the Republican Party circa 2012, with its xenophobic flare-ups and science skeptics and rape apologists, it feels somewhat naïve to disagree.

There is, however, an alternative view. This is that people are reasonably credible observers and arbiters of their own self-interest—that they can largely be trusted with their own affairs and that they have the right to do what they want, for the most part, unless it's going to hurt someone else. This view is also widespread. Economists believe that people are, if not perfectly rational, responsive to incentives and "predictably irrational." Philosophers and biologists argue about whether it's even possible for people to act *other than* in their own interests, whether the behavior we describe as altruistic (caring for your child, perhaps) is actually self-serving (ensuring the perpetuation of your gene pool).

And political theorists, at least the political theorists whose ideas most of us would prefer to live under, say that self-government is more than plausible: it's a right, and one that liberal societies must protect. The United States, the country that created itself in the nimbus of the

Enlightenment, has built this premise into its practical reasoning. The Declaration of Independence asserts that a just government derives its powers from the consent of the governed, who nonetheless retain the right to bin the old government and set up a new one based on whatever principles "shall seem most likely to effect their Safety and Happiness." Our public schools were built on the belief that everyone has the right and capacity to learn. The law is designed to protect us against being trampled by the ambition or aggression of others. Abraham Lincoln, in his second inaugural address, was presiding over a country that was several years into a civil war over the issue of whether humans should be held as slaves, and he nonetheless urged the North to carry on with the war that would free the slaves and save the Union, "with firmness in the right as God gives us to see the right."

Looking at the United States, then, you get the impression of a country that believes people can, for the most part, look after themselves, and that they have the right to do so, subject to certain parameters. Both parties see it this way, in theory. That's why Republicans are so big on free enterprise and why Democrats are so annoyed by conservatives' interest in other people's sex lives. But all of this professed confidence sits uneasily alongside the fact that every time either party gets a setback, it has a tendency to fall back on scare stories: people are stupid or crazy or corrupt or racist or socialist or simply wrong.

So which is it? Are people stupid, or are they not? Is it just Republicans who are stupid, except for the Republicans who fund all the Super-PACs? How about Independents—do they switch from smart to stupid every couple of years?

The truth is somewhere in between. Some people are stupid. Some are easily misled. Everyone makes mistakes. Some of these errors, whether of judgment or of execution, are common and predictable. Collective decisionmaking is difficult. It's good to have certain safeguards—checks and balances, laws and regulations—to protect us from missteps. With all of those caveats, people have a reasonably good track record. The fact that we're governed by the will of our neighbors is an expression of our values and a testament to our national character.

In other words, there's nothing the matter with Kansas. It's not perfect, but no place is perfect. Kansans are probably doing what they think is best. Some people like it well enough to live there, almost 3 million of them. If you don't want to be among them, no one is going to force you. And that brings us back to Texas. No one's going to force you to live there either. But it's a lot bigger than Kansas, so you may be forced to think about it on occasion.

Fortunately, Texas is not nearly as bad as its reputation suggests. Most of its idiosyncrasies are an understandable result of its history. Even after Texas was annexed, after that decade of sovereign limbo, its acceptance as a part of the United States was provisional, tenuous, and arduous. No sooner had Texas become a state than it was plunged into the Mexican-American War and then the Civil War. It staggered into Reconstruction with the stuffing kicked out of it, its economy little more than scraps. It didn't expect, or receive, much help. It wasn't until the cotton and cattle industries took off that Texas got any kind of footing, and it wasn't until oil was discovered at Spindletop, in 1901, that there was a chance the state might be a success.

The state has gotten big assists from the federal government, since then, but for its first hundred years Texas was basically a poor, rural, backward state. Other states hardly even seemed to notice it. When New Yorkers and Chicagoans were neck-deep in bathtub gin, people in Texas were still bumping along on donkeys. What little the early Texans had, they wrestled from the land, often at serious risk. "What really made a panther hungry was the smell of a baby," wrote J. Frank Dobie in a casual aside from his *Tales of Old-Time Texas*.[1]

Compare that to, say, California. That state was a frontier at one point and has been known for individualism, but it has always had a better rapport with the federal government than Texas has. The United

States fought a war partly on its behalf—the Mexican-American War, which is now usually blamed entirely on Texas. California was annexed just a year after Texas, and there was no fight in Congress over whether that should happen. There was no slavery in the territory, and California had the Pacific coast; annexing it would mean completing the continent. Is it really surprising that California would go on to carve out a bigger role for government than Texas? Places, like people, are products of their experiences.

Maybe the reason Texas's eccentricities excite so much suspicion is that Texans themselves are still so belligerently proud of the state. That's a quirk that has annoyed outsiders since the frontier days. An early visitor from France, for example, once noted that the defenders of the Alamo included "the man who invented that deadly weapon, the 'Bowie knife,' which is the tenant of every Texan's bosom, and which should be deposited (dripping, as it is, with human blood), in the museums of Europe, and placed by the side of the weapons of the benighted Indian of the desert, as an emblem of the savage barbarism of the existing Anglo-American race."[2] I heard a similar view expressed more recently by a friend who had been turned away while trying to buy a six-pack. His driver's license wasn't issued in Texas, so the clerk didn't have to accept it. Most states have similar laws, but Texas is the only one where a clerk would stand on principle.

On the other hand, Texas's outsized pride reflects a genuine concept of identity and is, in many ways, an asset. There are fault lines within Texas. It has more centers of gravity than most states—six of the nation's twenty biggest cities are in this state. Internal rivalries abound—Dallas versus Houston, west Texas versus urban Texas, east Texas versus everyone else. Once I even heard some young professionals in Dallas say, somewhat dismissively, that Fort Worth was still full of cowboys. And yet the overriding concept of Texas is stronger than any of its internal divisions. "Texas, as a state, is maybe more properly viewed as a city with Austin, Dallas, San Antonio,

Fort Worth, Houston as the neighborhoods. It has that intimacy and that cohesiveness to it as a geographical place," said Evan Smith, founder and CEO of the *Texas Tribune*, a nonprofit online news site focused on the titular state.[3]

And as one Texas Democrat put it to me, the state's dogged pride isn't simply a psychological non sequitur.[4] Texas's history is genuinely unique among the states. It's the only state that staged a successful revolution against a governing power. It's the only state, other than Hawaii, that existed as an independent republic long enough to be recognized as such by other countries and ultimately had to agree to its own annexation. Even if we're putting aside the hoodoo about culture, that has practical import. It means that Texas had laws before it joined the Union, some of which were carried over. The state pride can, moreover, be channeled on behalf of a good cause. A clear example of that was the "Don't Mess with Texas" campaign. It was designed to get people to quit littering—and it worked, although the hefty fines probably helped too.

It might be jarring, it might seem backward looking, when Attorney General Greg Abbott compares his latest lawsuit against the federal government to the siege of the Alamo. But you also get Texans talking about the 1832 Battle of Velasco, at which dozens of Texan settlers were imprisoned by the Mexican army (Ron Paul explaining why unlawful detention is wrong), or the fact that Sam Houston once ran a one-room schoolhouse (Dan Branch, a state senator, arguing that education is worthwhile).[5]

There's a difference, too, between rooting for your own team and wanting the other guys to fail. And none of this, by the way, is intended to exclude people. A 2009 report from the Pew Research Center found that more than two-thirds of people living in Texas were born in Texas, which leaves about 7 million people who weren't.[6] And this isn't one of those states like South Carolina, where people sit around talking about who your people were. Whatever the Texan identity has been, or is today, it's never been restricted to the people who were born here. None of the people who fought the Texas revolution were born in the state of Texas (not even the *Tejanos*), and they were real enough. Today's Texans are similarly quite accepting of newcomers. Like lackadaisical evangelicals, all they want is a confession of faith: "I wasn't born in Texas, but I got here as fast as I could." Texans are, in fact, unusually open—and on that axis, among others, they're mirroring an American value and amplifying it.

On balance, I would say that outsiders are a little too prone to jump to conclusions about Texas. The interminable controversy over textbooks is a classic (not to say textbook) case. In 2012, the *New York Review of Books* carried a long essay on the subject, which concluded that, although Texas hasn't actually rewritten history and science the way people might think, the state has made textbooks worse for everyone: faced with the possibility that the stubborn and contentious educators of Texas are going to throw a fit, textbook publishers have revised and revised their books until they're all a big, hem-hawing pile of mush.[7]

As well meaning as Texas's critics may be, they're too often overlooking or blurring the facts in favor of the story, which is, incidentally, often what they're accusing the other side of doing. The resulting dismissals and distortions have consequences, and not just for Texas. The opportunity cost of talking about textbooks all the time, for example, is that it cuts into time we might otherwise use to figure out why African American eighth-graders in Texas are doing so much better on national math and science tests than black students in most states.

Or let's consider a more substantive issue, the one that Frank raises: the working class's occasional willingness to vote for the party of big business, despite what progressives understand workers' economic interests to be. Some Americans are, as Frank says, prioritizing social issues over economic ones. But the United States does have a long tradition of what we might call probusiness populism. Texas is unusually disposed to it, not because Texans are unusually crazy, but because of the experiences described throughout this book.

And it's not just Texans. In May 2010, for example, I went to Louisiana to report on the aftermath of the explosion on the Deepwater Horizon. People were, of course, devastated, upset, and afraid. But part of what they were afraid about was the impact on the oil industry. Many Americans felt the same way—in July of that year, a Bloomberg poll would find 73 percent of Americans opposed to the Obama administration's May 28 moratorium on offshore drilling.[8] But it was striking to see such support for the industry in the immediate wake of the disaster in the area most affected by the disaster. The people I met were almost protective. One roughneck told me he was shocked this had happened on a rig run by BP, because he knew, from his experience, that the company was a real stickler for safety and checklists. It was the mom-and-pop operations, he said, that you had to watch out for. A few towns over a woman working at a fast-food chicken restaurant was worried because her husband worked on the rigs; if the government put a moratorium on drilling, he would be out of luck.

This was within forty-eight hours of an accident that had killed eleven people in exactly the same line of work as her husband's. It wasn't as if she didn't care, though; she obviously cared about her husband. It was that the offshore drilling boom had been good for the people of southern Louisiana—during the recession the Houma area had one of the lowest unemployment rates in the country—and despite the accident, people thought the oil jobs were good jobs, which they were, by the regional and historical standard. The people in south Louisiana wanted BP to fix the mess, of course, and to pay for the cleanup, but as long as it seemed like BP was going to do that, they weren't going to turn against the industry.

The local assessment might have been overly generous, or just wrong, but I would be reluctant to dismiss it as deranged. Sweeping dismissals preclude conversations, and while it's sometimes impossible to reason with the other side, it's not always impossible. Texas, for its part, is sometimes impervious to criticism. Complacency has always been the danger arising from the state's self-esteem. One early visitor from Virginia reported that his hosts were friendly enough, but they had "a Munchausen-like idea of Texas prowess."[9] "Such insular pride discourages any feeling that some changes might be desirable," observed Green, the historian, about 150 years later.[10] "Nothing fails like success," observed Klineberg, the sociologist in Houston.[11] Texas has a history of getting into trouble that way, but it also has a history of dusting itself off and, over time, recalibrating.

In 2011, the initial response to Perry's abortive presidential campaign wasn't especially productive for either side. After the 2012 election, however, with Perry safely out of striking distance from Washington, critics allowed themselves to take a more temperate view of Texas: maybe there was a reason that Texas Republicans often win 40 percent of the Hispanic vote, whereas Mitt Romney mustered a feeble 27 percent. Maybe the Texas Miracle was real, even if it was supported by factors that other states can't replicate. Maybe the Texas model makes sense for some states, even if other states wouldn't go for it. Texas will probably have a delayed reaction this time around, as the state's Republican Party tries to sort itself out, but the latest round of national scoffing gave Texas Democrats plenty to think about.

The image I keep coming back to, with regard to Texas and the United States, is the double helical structure of DNA. The molecule has two strands, each made of the same nucleotides. The strands are bonded together, and their connections are reinforced by outside pressures; but the strands are just repulsive enough to each other that rather than aligning side by side, like a ladder, they warp and start to circle around each other. The bonds are strong but not uncomplicated, and DNA's molecular structure reflects that internal tension.

The analogy does break down because DNA replicates itself by "unzipping" down the middle, leaving each strand temporarily alone, which sounds like a metaphor for secession, and it would probably be better for everyone if Texans stopped talking about secession so much. Other than that, though, it seems apt. Texas is made of the same materials as the United States. The two are bonded together, and outside forces help stabilize the bond. There's a mutual and apparently intrinsic wariness that shapes their interactions; anyone can see it. But that doesn't mean that the unit itself doesn't work.

The United States is a big, complicated, heterogeneous country, and politics is the iterative process through which we mediate our differences and articulate our values. Yet on both sides we see people in high dudgeon, arguing that the country is falling prey to socialism or falling prey to fascism and worrying that the future of America will be grimmer than its past. This Manichean outlook is too often on display when people talk about Texas, and when Texans talk about Washington, meaning the federal government. We can afford to be more broad-minded about both.

ACKNOWLEDGMENTS

FOR YEARS, I've been joking that I wanted to write a book that would help people come to terms with the existence of Texas. In August 2011, when Governor Rick Perry's entrance into the presidential race nudged us that much closer to a national nervous breakdown, I realized that I actually wanted to write that book.

I was, at the time, working as the southwest correspondent for *The Economist*, a job I had taken over in 2007. The first people I'd like to thank here are my colleagues and editors there, especially Jon Fasman, Greg Ip, Matthew Bishop, Rachel Horwood, Adrian Wooldridge, Robert Guest, Roger McShane, and my former boss, Christopher Lockwood, who was either very gracious about giving me the space to write this book or secretly sick of me recklessly opining on *The Economist*'s American politics blog.

I say "former" because in November 2012 I became a senior editor at *Texas Monthly*, which has been publishing first-class journalism about Texas for forty years. My new colleagues, especially Jake Silverstein, Brian Sweany, and Paul Burka, have already chipped in with great comments about the ideas and arguments in this book, and I look forward to working with the whole *Texas Monthly* team for years to come. Thanks, guys.

Not having written a book before, I didn't know what to expect when I started this one. There were definitely moments along the way when I found myself wishing for the sunny overconfidence of the governor himself. There would have been more had I not had the good fortune to stumble across an excellent agent, Rafe Sagalyn, who was immediately taken by the idea and whose first order of business was to put me in touch with an excellent editor, Brandon Proia. Brandon's fine touch with prose is matched only by his tough but fair attitude regarding unwarranted leaps of logic. In addition to thanking those two for their hard work on behalf of this project, I want to salute my friend Reihan Salam, who introduced me to Rafe and thereby set the entire chain of events in motion, as he tends to do.

My understanding of Texas is, in part, drawn from countless interviews since 2007; and my thanks and appreciation go to the public and private figures who have given generously of their time.

In addition, I find that people who work in areas related to politics, economics, history, journalism, or any combination thereof are good to talk to, because they're smart and have been made reflective by exposure to absurdity. I was lucky while researching and writing to have lots of people to talk things over with, and I especially want to thank Allison Schrager, Kate Galbraith, Emily Lodish, Evan Smith, Gardner Selby, Jim Henson, Steve Scheibal, Ben Healy, Laurel Wamsley, Jason Stanford, Dave Shaw, Meghan Ashford-Grooms, Julián Aguilar, Drew Dupuy, Julian Sanchez, Josh Treviño, Alexander Betts, and Jeremy Kessler for their thoughts and insights. I'm also indebted to the friends who kept me going by fueling me with snacks and jokes, including Elisa Barquin, Ginny Yang, Puja Ahluwalia, Nara Meli, Ingrid Powell, Gunnar Hellekson, Tom Meaney, Jess Sauer, Craig McCullough, Ava Sanchez, Oscar Sotuyo, Laurent Tran, Mark Wochner, Eva Schmidt, Karan Mahajan, Francesca Mari, Jason Callahan, and Jared LeBoff. Finally, of course, I thank my parents, in this case because they're the people who taught me how to read. It was hard, but worth it.

NOTES

INTRODUCTION

1. T. R. Fehrenbach, *Lone Star: A History of Texas and the Texans* (New York: Da Capo Press, 2000), 347.

2. Marquis James, *The Raven: A Biography of Sam Houston* (rpt., Austin: University of Texas Press, 1994), 255.

3. Binyamin Appelbaum, "Texas Is the Future," *Economix* (blog), *New York Times*, June 5, 2012, http://economix.blogs.nytimes.com/2012/06/05/texas-is-the-future/?hp.

CHAPTER 1:
MAN-MADE MIRACLE

1. Bureau of Labor Statistics, http://data.bls.gov/timeseries/LNS14000000.

2. Bureau of Labor Statistics, http://data.bls.gov/timeseries/LASST48000005?data_tool=XGtable.

3. J. P. Donlon, "Another Triumph for Texas: Best/Worst States for Business," *Chief Executive*, May 2, 2012, http://chiefexecutive.net/best-worst-states-for-business-2012.

4. Mark Arend, "A Better Mousetrap," *Site Selection*, November 2011, http://siteselection.com/issues/2011/nov/cover.cfm.

5. "Business Facilities 2012 State Rankings: Texas Takes Best Business Climate Crown," http://businessfacilities.com/news/business-facilities-2012-state-rankings-texas-takes-best-business-climate-crown/.

6. Jennifer Dauble, "Texas Is America's Top State for Business, According to CNBC Exclusive Study," CNBC, July 10, 2012, http://www.cnbc.com/id/48080934.

7. Milken Institute, http://bestcities.milkeninstitute.org/.

8. They were Dallas (#8), Austin (#9), San Antonio (#13), Fort Worth (#15), and Houston (#20). Kurt Badenhausen, "The 25 Best Places for Business and Careers," *Forbes*, June 27, 2012, http://www.forbes.com/sites/kurtbadenhausen/2012/06/27/the-best-places-for-business/.

9. Binyamin Appelbaum, "Texas Is The Future," *Economix* (blog), *New York Times*, June 5, 2012, http://economix.blogs.nytimes.com/2012/06/05/texas-is-the-future/.

10. http://trailblazersblog.dallasnews.com/2011/08/full-transcript-of-rick-perrys.html/.

11. Bureau of Labor Statistics, http://data.bls.gov/timeseries/LNS14000000.

12. "Alternative Measures of Labor Underutilization for States, 2011," Bureau of Labor Statistics, http://www.bls.gov/lau/stalt11q4.htm.

13. Paul Krugman, "The Texas Unmiracle," *New York Times*, August 14, 2011, http://www.nytimes.com/2011/08/15/opinion/the-texas-unmiracle.html?_r=1.

14. Merrill Goozner, "Rick Perry and the Myth of the Texas Miracle," *Fiscal Times*, August 12, 2011, http://www.thefiscaltimes.com/Articles/2011/08/12/Rick-Perry-and-the-Myth-of-the-Texas-Miracle.aspx#page1.

15. Kevin Drum, "Why Rick Perry Won't Win," *Mother Jones*, August 13, 2011, http://www.motherjones.com/kevin-drum/2011/08/why-rick-perry-wont-win.

16. Harold Meyerson, "The Sad Facts Behind Rick Perry's Texas Miracle," *Washington Post*, August 16, 2011, http://www.washingtonpost.com/opinions/the-sad-facts-behind-rick-perrys-texas-miracle/2011/08/16/gIQAxc3zJJ_story.html.

17. Steven A. Camarota and Ashley Monique Webster, "Who Benefited from Job Growth in Texas?: A Look at Employment Gains for Immigrants and the Native-Born, 2007–2011," Center for Immigration Studies, September 2011, http://cis.org/immigrants-filled-most-new-jobs -in-Texas.

18. A chronological summary of polls for the 2012 Republican presidential nomination may be found at Real Clear Politics, http://www .realclearpolitics.com/epolls/2012/president/us/republican_presidential _nomination-1452.html#polls.

19. Richard Fisher, "Connecting the Dots: Texas Employment Growth; a Dissenting Vote; and the Ugly Truth (with reference to P. G. Wodehouse)," speech in Midland, Texas, August 17, 2011, http://www .dallasfed.org/news/speeches/fisher/2011/fs110817.cfm.

20. The federal minimum wage, as of July 2009, is set at $7.25 an hour, with certain exemptions. Waiters, for example, are usually paid less than the federal minimum wage; the assumption is that they will make up or exceed the shortfall with tips. Very small businesses are also exempt from the federal law and may pay their employees less than the federal minimum wage.

21. "Characteristics of Minimum-Wage Workers, 2011," Bureau of Labor Statistics, http://www.bls.gov/cps/minwage2011tbls.htm#3.

22. Texas Economy at a Glance, Bureau of Labor Statistics, http: //www.bls.gov/eag/eag.tx.htm.

23. Krugman, "The Texas Unmiracle."

24. Anil Kumar, "Why Texas Feels Less Subprime Stress," *Southwest Economy*, November 2008, http://econpapers.repec.org/article/fipfeddse/y _3a2008_3ai_3anov_3ap_3a3-616_3an_3a6.htm.

25. Mike Konczal, "Vermont, Texas, and Subprime Loans," *Baseline Scenario* (blog), August 18, 2009, http://baselinescenario.com/2009/08/18 /vermont-texas-and-subprime-loans/.

26. Tom Fowler, "Texas Energy Employment Returns to Record Highs," *Fuel Fix*, July 25, 2011, http://fuelfix.com/blog/2011/07/25/texas -energy-employment-returns-to-record-highs/.

27. Mine K. Yücel and Jackson Thies, "Oil and Gas Rises Again in a Diversified Texas," *Southwest Economy*, first quarter 2011, http://dallasfed.org/research/swe/2011/swe1101g.cfm.

CHAPTER 2:
THE TEXAS MODEL

1. Scott Drenkard, ed., "Facts and Figures Handbook: How Does Your State Compare?," Tax Foundation, February 15, 2012, http://taxfoundation.org/article/facts-figures-handbook-how-does-your-state-compare-0.

2. Meghan Ashford-Grooms, "Gov. Rick Perry Says He Has a Track Record of Not Raising Taxes," PolitiFact Texas, November 1, 2010, http://www.politifact.com/texas/statements/2010/nov/01/rick-perry/gov-rick-perry-says-he-has-track-record-not-raisin/.

3. "Sorry, Losers," *The Economist*, May 19, 2011, http://www.economist.com/node/18712311.

4. Jonathan Cohn, "Blue States Are from Scandinavia, Red States Are from Guatemala," *New Republic*, October 5, 2012, http://www.tnr.com/article/politics/magazine/108185/blue-states-are-scandinavia-red-states-are-guatemala.

5. "Greek Americans," *The Economist*, July 30, 2011, http://www.economist.com/node/21524887.

6. "Federal Appropriations Earmarks by State," CQ.com, http://innovation.cq.com/media/earmarks2010/.

7. http://www.stateintegrity.org/texas; http://www.texpirg.org/news/txp/texas-first-transparency.

8. Ross Ramsey, "Agencies Ordered to Propose 10 Percent Budget Cuts," *Texas Tribune,* June 5, 2012, http://www.texastribune.org/texas-taxes/budget/agencies-ordered-propose-10-percent-budget-cuts/.

9. http://governor.state.tx.us/ecodev/etf/etf_about/.

10. Perry's Piggybank, http://www.tpj.org/search/label/Enterprise%20Fund.

11. Ibid.

12. "Con Job," Texans for Public Justice, November 2011, http://info.tpj.org/watchyourassets/enterprise4/ConJob.pdf.

13. "What's It Worth to You?," Economist.com, September 16, 2011, http://www.economist.com/blogs/freeexchange/2011/09/job-creation.

14. "An Analysis of Texas Economic Development Incentives 2010," Texas Comptroller of Public Accounts, December 22, 2010, http://www.texasahead.org/reports/incentives/cost.php.

15. Loren Steffy, "Politics Infect A&M Research," *Houston Chronicle*, August 1, 2009, http://www.chron.com/business/steffy/article/Politics-infect-A-M-research-1735057.php.

16. "Building Up the Arsenal," *The Economist*, June 30, 2012, http://www.economist.com/node/21557773.

17. Author interview.

18. http://www.economist.com/blogs/freeexchange/2011/10/great-green-jobs-hope.

19. http://www.census.gov/foreign-trade/statistics/state/data/tx.html.

20. http://www.statehealthfacts.org/comparemaptable.jsp?ind=32&cat=1.

CHAPTER 3:
THE TROUBLESOME TERRITORY

1. William C. Davis, *Lone Star Rising: The Revolutionary Birth of the Texas Republic* (College Station: Texas A&M University Press, 2004), 213.

2. See also T. R. Fehrenbach, *Lone Star: A History of Texas and the Texans* (New York: Da Capo Press, 2000), 214. Texans have also been known to describe Thermopylae as the Alamo of Greece.

3. From Buckingham Smith, trans., *The Narrative of Álvar Núñez Cabeza de Vaca*, excerpted in *Documents of Texas History*, ed. by Ernest Wallace, David M. Vigness, and George B. Ward (Austin: State House Press, 1994), 2.

4. From George Parker Winship, "The Coronado Expedition, 1540–1542," excerpted in *Documents of Texas History*, 7.

5. From Fray José Franco López, "Report and Account That the Father President of the Missions in the Province of Texas or New Philippines Sends to the Most Illustrious Senor Fray Rafael Jose Verger of the Council of His Majesty, The Bishop of the New Kingdom of Leon, in Accordance with the Royal Order that, on January 31, 1781, Was Issued at El Pardo and Was Sent to His Illustrious Lordship, the Bishop, by the Most Excellent Viceroy Count of Galvez, On August 4, 1785, filed [for Permanent Record] in the Archives of this Presidency," in *Documents of Texas History*, 32.

6. "The Declaration of Independence," April 6, 1813, in *Documents of Texas History*, 39.

7. Fehrenbach, *Lone Star*, 750.

CHAPTER 4:
STATE OF HATE

1. Sam Kashner, "A Clash of Camelots," *Vanity Fair*, October 2009, http://www.vanityfair.com/politics/features/2009/10/death-of-a-president 200910?currentPage=1.

2. "Disgraced Dallas Delivers Apologies for Mistreatment of Adlai Stevenson," Associated Press, October 25, 1963.

3. Eric Boehlert, "A President Was Killed the Last Time Right-Wing Hatred Ran Wild Like This," Media Matters for America, September 18, 2009, http://mediamatters.org/blog/2009/09/18/a-president-was-killed -the-last-time-right-wing/154331.

4. Frank Rich, "What Killed JFK," *New York Magazine*, November 20, 2011, http://nymag.com/news/frank-rich/jfk-2011-11/.

5. *Report of the President's Commission on the Assassination of President John F. Kennedy* (Washington, DC: GPO, 1964), 415. The web version is at http://www.archives.gov/research/jfk/warren-commission-report/.

6. Ibid.

7. Lawrence Wright, "Why Do They Hate Us So Much?," *Texas Monthly*, November 1983, http://www.texasmonthly.com/1983–11 –01/feature2–6.php.

8. Robert Bryce, *Cronies: How Texas Business Became American Policy— and Brought Bush to Power* (New York: PublicAffairs, 2004), 49.

9. Seth Kantor, "Lone Star Assault," *Austin American-Statesman*, August 20, 1990, excerpted in *Documents of Texas History*, ed. by Ernest Wallace, David M. Vigness, and George B. Ward (Austin: State House Press, 1994), 316.

10. Brian O'Keefe, "Exxon's Big Bet on Shale Gas," *Fortune*, April 16, 2012.

11. "Legislators Question Border Health," *El Paso Times*, March 6, 2003.

12. Death Penalty Information Center, http://www.deathpenaltyinfo .org/number-executions-state-and-region-1976.

13. Andrew Lubetkin, "Why Joseph Nichols' Execution Must Be Stopped," *Houston Chronicle*, March 4, 2007, http://www.chron.com /opinion/outlook/article/Why-Joseph-Nichols-execution-must-be -stopped-1843009.php.

14. http://www.tdcj.state.tx.us/stat/dr_info/nicholsjosephlast.html.

15. http://www.tdcj.state.tx.us/stat/dr_info/clarkjameslast.html.

16. "Continued Majority Support for Death Penalty," Pew Research Center, January 6, 2012, http://www.people-press.org/2012/01/06 /continued-majority-support-for-death-penalty/.

17. Ross Ramsey, "UT/TT Poll: Texans Stand Behind Death Penalty," *Texas Tribune*, May 24, 2012, http://www.texastribune.org/texas-dept -criminal-justice/death-penalty/uttt-poll-life-and-death/.

18. "State's Prison Population Lowest in Five Years," *Austin American-Statesman*, August 12, 2012, http://www.chron.com/news/houston-texas/article/State-s-prison-population-lowest-in-5-years-3783056.php.

19. Manny Fernandez, "Two Lawsuits Challenge the Lack of Air-Conditioning in Texas Prisons," *New York Times*, June 26, 2012, http://www.nytimes.com/2012/06/27/us/two-lawsuits-challenge-the -lack-of-air-conditioning-in-texas-prisons.html?_r=1&hp.

20. http://www.census.gov/compendia/statab/2012/tables /12s0308.pdf.

21. Calvin Trillin, *Trillin on Texas* (Austin: University of Texas Press, 2011), 99.

22. John Schwartz, "Lee Otis, Free," *Texas Monthly*, August 2002, http://www.texasmonthly.com/2002–08–01/weremember.php.

23. Neil Sapper, "Richards, Dorothy Ann Willis [Ann]," in *Handbook of Texas Online*, http://www.tshaonline.org/handbook/online/articles/fri62.

24. R. G. Ratcliffe, "Guns and Metal Detectors Coexist at Texas Capitol," *Houston Chronicle*, May 21, 2010, http://www.chron.com /news/houston-texas/article/Guns-and-metal-detectors-coexist-at-Texas -Capitol-1697645.php.

25. Molly Ivins, *Molly Ivins Can't Say That, Can She?* (New York: Random House, 1991), 22.

26. W. Gardner Selby, "Gov. Rick Perry Recaps His Comment on Texas Seceding from the United States; Does He Repeat Accurately?," PolitiFact Texas, April 15, 2010, http://www.politifact.com/texas /statements/2010/apr/22/rick-perry/gov-rick-perry-recaps-his-comment -texas-seceding-u/.

27. "In Texas, 31% Say State Has Right to Secede from U.S., but 75% Opt to Stay," Rasmussen Reports, April 17, 2009, http://www.rasmussen reports.com/public_content/politics/general_state_surveys/texas/in_texas _31_say_state_has_right_to_secede_from_u_s_but_75_opt_to_stay.

28. http://www.rasmussenreports.com/public_content/politics /general_politics/may_2012/24_say_states_have_right_to_secede.

29. Steve Benen, "Polling Secession," *Washington Monthly*, May 6, 2009, http://www.washingtonmonthly.com/archives/individual /2009_05/018062.php.

30. Sonia Smith, "The Arguments for (and Against) Texas Secession," *Texas Monthly*, November 14, 2012, http://www.tmdailypost.com/article /politics/arguments-and-against-texas-secession.

31. Erica Grieder, "Everything There Is Big, Including Stereotypes," *New York Times*, July 2, 2012.

32. Rick Perry, *Fed Up! Our Fight to Save America from Washington* (New York: Little, Brown, 2010), 125.

33. http://americanradioworks.publicradio.org/features/prestapes /lbj_haggar.html.

34. Mark Crispin Miller, *The Bush Dyslexicon: Observations on a National Disorder* (New York: Norton, 2001).

CHAPTER 5:
LAND AND CATTLE

1. Oprah Winfrey, "How Oprah Learned to Declutter," *O: The Oprah Magazine*, November 2011, http://www.oprah.com/spirit/How-Oprah -Learned-to-Declutter.

2. Paul Andrew Hutton, "Hell and Texas," in *Forever Texas: Texas the Way Those Who Lived It Wrote It*, ed. by Mike Blakely and Mary Elizabeth Goodman (New York: Forge, 2000), 257.

3. H. W. Brands, *Lone Star Nation: The Epic Story of the Battle for Texas Independence* (New York: Anchor Books, 2005), 4.

4. Margaret Swett Henson, "Anglo-American Colonization," in *Handbook of Texas Online*, http://www.tshaonline.org/handbook/online /articles/uma01, accessed November 21, 2012.

5. J. Frank Dobie, *The Longhorns* (rpt., Austin: University of Texas Press, 1990), 50.

6. Ibid., 37.

7. Ibid., 51.

8. L. B. Anderson in *The Trail Drivers of Texas: Interesting Sketches of Early Cowboys and Their Experiences on the Range and on the Trail During the Days That Tried Men's Souls— True Narratives Related by Real Cowpunchers and Men Who Fathered the Cattle Industry in Texas*, ed. by J. Marvin Hunter, rev. ed. (Austin: University of Texas Press, 1985), 207.

9. Dobie, *The Longhorns*, 71.

10. Ibid., 72.

11. From Richard Irving Dodge, *The Hunting Grounds of the Great West* (London, 1878), excerpted in *Documents of Texas History*, ed. by Ernest Wallace, David M. Vigness, and George B. Ward (Austin: State House Press, 1994), 231.

12. From Charles Goodnight, "Managing a Trail Herd," excerpted in *Documents of Texas History*, 232.

13. Robert E. Zeigler, "Cowboy Strike of 1883," in *Handbook of Texas Online*, http://www.tshaonline.org/handbook/online/articles/oec02, accessed November 21, 2012.

14. John Cornyn, "The Cowboy Strike," *Texas Times*, September 9, 2008.

15. Frank S. Hastings, "Some Glimpses of Ranch Life," excerpted in *Documents of Texas History*, 236.

16. Dobie, *The Longhorns*.

17. J. Frank Norfleet, quoted in Amy Reading, *The Mark Inside: A Perfect Swindle, a Cunning Revenge, and a Small History of the Big Con* (New York: Knopf, 2012), 53–54.

18. Bob Tutt, "Texas Rangers/Lawmen: The Romantic Element of State Mystique," *Houston Chronicle*, March 2, 1986, http://www.chron.com/CDA/archives/archive.mpl/1986_222719/texas-rangers-lawmen-the-romantic-element-of-state.html.

19. S. C. Gwynne, "The Last Ranchers," *Texas Monthly*, November 2012.

20. Wallace Stegner, *Where the Bluebird Sings to the Lemonade Springs: Living and Writing in the American West* (New York: Penguin Books, 1992), 103.

CHAPTER 6:
BLACK GOLD

1. See, for example, Isabel V. Sawhill, "Economic Mobility: Is the American Dream Alive and Well?," Brookings Institution, May 2007; and "Pursuing the American Dream: Economic Mobility Across Generations,"

Pew Charitable Trusts, July 2012, http://www.pewstates.org/uploadedFiles
/PCS_Assets/2012/Pursuing_American_Dream.pdf.

2. Energy Information Administration, "Annual Energy Review 2010."

3. Roger M. Olien and Diana Davids Hinton, *Wildcatters: Texas Independent Oilmen* (College Station: Texas A&M University Press, 2007), 14.

4. Ibid.

5. Ibid.

6. https://play.google.com/books/reader?id=xKkPAAAAIAAJ&print sec=frontcover&output=reader&authuser=0&hl=en&pg=GBS.PA49.

7. Ibid.

8. http://www.eia.gov/dnav/pet/hist/LeafHandler.ashx?n=pet&s =mcrfpus1&f=a.

9. http://www.window.state.tx.us/specialrpt/energy/nonrenewable /crude.php.

10. https://play.google.com/books/reader?id=7aYZAAAAYAAJ& printsec=frontcover&output=reader&authuser=0&hl=en&pg=GBS.PA15.

11. Olien and Hinton, *Wildcatters*, 33.

12. Ibid., 60.

13. From Charlie Jeffries, "Reminiscences of Sour Lake," in *Documents of Texas History*, ed. by Ernest Wallace, David M. Vigness, and George B. Ward (Austin: State House Press, 1994), 255.

14. David F. Prindle, *Petroleum Politics and the Texas Railroad Commission* (Austin: University of Texas Press, 1981), 22–23.

CHAPTER 7:
THE UNGOVERNED

1. http://www.statutes.legis.state.tx.us/Docs/CN/htm/CN.17.htm.

2. http://www2.census.gov/prod2/decennial/documents/1870a-03.pdf.

3. See T. R. Fehrenbach, *Lone Star: A History of Texas and the Texans* (New York: Da Capo Press, 2000), 398.

4. Seth Shepard McKay, "The Making of the Constitution of 1876" (thesis, University of Pennsylvania, 1924).

5. Many years later, Republicans would use the inverse maneuver during the 2003 battle over redistricting. Democrats were trying to leave so that there wouldn't be enough legislators present to hold a vote. Republicans responded by physically blocking the exits to the parking garages around the capitol.

6. McKay, "The Making of the Constitution of 1876," 44.

7. Fehrenbach, *Lone Star*, 1237.

8. Joe B. Frantz, *Texas: A History* (New York: Norton, 1984), 124.

9. http://www.statutes.legis.state.tx.us/Docs/CN/htm/CN.7.htm.

10. http://www.sll.state.tx.us/const/6.pdf.

11. Frantz, *Texas*, 124.

12. "Amendments to the Texas Constitution Since 1876," prepared by the Research Division of the Texas Legislative Council, March 2012.

13. Jaron Lanier, *You Are Not a Gadget: A Manifesto* (New York: Vintage, 2011), 6.

14. http://texashistory.unt.edu/ark:/67531/metapth5862/m1/47/.

15. http://www.census.gov/hhes/www/socdemo/voting/publications/historical/index.html.

CHAPTER 8:
THE SHADOW STATE

1. Griffin Smith Jr., "Why Does Dolph Briscoe Want to Be Governor?," *Texas Monthly*, February 1976, 82.

2. Bill Minutaglio, *City on Fire: The Explosion That Devastated a Texas Town and Ignited a Historic Legal Battle* (New York: HarperCollins, 2003).

3. *Dalehite v. United States*, 346 U.S. 15 (1953).

4. Ibid.

5. William Ransom Hogan, *The Texas Republic: A Social and Economic History* (Austin: University of Texas Press, 1969), 295.

6. Author interview.

7. Ira Ingram, in 1830, quoted in Hogan, *The Texas Republic*, 191.

8. Ibid.

9. Ibid., 193.

10. http://www.statutes.legis.state.tx.us/Docs/CN/htm/CN.1 .htm#1.4.

11. Jonathan Edwards, "Sinners in the Hands of an Angry God. A Sermon Preached at Enfield, July 8th, 1741," in *Electronic Texts in American Studies*, ed. by Reiner Smolinsky, http://digitalcommons.unl.edu /etas/54.

12. Hogan, *The Texas Republic*, 206.

13. James W. Latimer, quoted in ibid., 223.

14. Ibid., 119.

15. Workers of the Writers' Program of the Work Projects Administration in the State of Texas, *The WPA Guide to Texas*, introduction by Don Graham (Austin: Texas Monthly Press, 1986).

16. James L. Haley, *Passionate Nation: The Epic History of Texas* (New York: Free Press, 2006), 279.

17. Jeffrey C. Issac, "Faith-Based Initiatives: A Civil Society Approach," *Essays on Civil Society* 12, no. 1 (2003), http://www.scribd.com /doc/91810937/Faith-Based-Initiatives-and-the-Civil-Society-Approach.

18. Emily Gipple, "How the Chronicle Compiled Its Look at Giving Across America," *Chronicle of Philanthropy*, August 19, 2012, http: //philanthropy.com/article/How-The-Chronicle-Compiled-Its/133667/.

19. "The Politics of Giving," *Chronicle of Philanthropy*, August 19, 2012, http://philanthropy.com/article/The-Politics-of-Giving/133609/.

20. Emily Gipple and Ben Gose, "America's Generosity Divide," *Chronicle of Philanthropy*, August 19, 2012, http://philanthropy.com /article/America-s-Generosity-Divide/133775/.

21. "Faith and Giving," *Chronicle of Philanthropy*, August 19, 2012, http://philanthropy.com/article/FaithGiving/133611/.

22. Eddie Izzard, *Dress to Kill*, DVD, 1999.

23. Wendy Kaufman, "As Gates Foundation Grows, Critics Question Methods," NPR, June 3, 2011, http://www.npr.org/2011/06/03 /136920664/gates-foundation-shows-off-new-headquarters.

24. http://www.economist.com/node/10880952.

25. Prison Entrepreneurship Program, 2011 Annual Report, http: //www.prisonentrepreneurship.org/who/results.aspx.

26. Ibid.

27. Gilbert M. Cuthbertson, "Regulator-Moderator War," in *Handbook of Texas Online,* http://www.tshaonline.org/handbook/online /articles/jcr01.

28. Ibid.

29. C. W. Ackerman, "Exciting Experiences on the Frontier and on the Trail," in *The Trail Drivers of Texas: Interesting Sketches of Early Cowboys and Their Experiences on the Range and on the Trail During the Days That Tried Men's Souls— True Narratives Related by Real Cowpunchers and Men Who Fathered the Cattle Industry in Texas,* ed. by Marvin J. Hunter, rev. ed. (Austin: University of Texas Press, 1985), 153.

30. L. B. Anderson, in *The Trail Drivers of Texas,* 206.

31. Wallace Stegner, *Where the Bluebird Sings to the Lemonade Springs: Living and Writing in the American West* (New York: Penguin Books, 1992), 109–110.

32. Hogan, *The Texas Republic,* 274.

33. Hunter, *The Trail Drivers of Texas.*

34. Willie Newbury Lewis, *Between Sun and Sod: An Informal History of the Texas Panhandle* (College Station: Texas A&M University Press, 1976), 106.

35. Hunter, *The Trail Drivers of Texas,* 573.

CHAPTER 9:
DEMOCRATIC TEXAS

1. http://en.wikipedia.org/wiki/United_States_congressional _delegations_from_Texas#United_States_House_of_Representatives.

2. George Norris Green, *The Establishment in Texas Politics: The Primitive Years, 1938–1957* (Westport, CT: Greenwood Press, 1979), 120.

3. http://www.laits.utexas.edu/txp_media/pr/speaker_series_files /transcripts/200810_patterson.html.

4. http://www.texasalmanac.com/topics/elections/senatorial-elections -and-primaries-1906%E2%80%932008–0.

5. Author interview.

6. Green, *The Establishment*, 3.

7. To take an early example: most antebellum southerners were Jacksonian Democrats who had wanted to annex Texas, but there were also southern Whigs who thought expansion wasn't worth the trouble. Very few Texans, by contrast, would have agreed that the republic's fate wasn't a paramount concern for the United States.

8. George Norris Green with Michael R. Botson Jr., "Looking for Lefty: Liberal/Left Activism and Texas Labor, 1920s–1960s," in *The Texas Left: The Radical Roots of Lone Star Liberalism*, ed. by David O'Donald Cullen and Kyle G. Wilkison (College Station: Texas A&M University Press, 2010), 113.

9. http://millercenter.org/president/lbjohnson/essays/biography/2.

10. Mark K. Updegrove, *Indomitable Will: LBJ in the Presidency* (New York: Crown, 2012).

11. http://www.law.cornell.edu/supct/html/historics/USSC_CR_0321 _0649_ZO.html.

12. http://www.texasalmanac.com/topics/elections/presidential -elections-and-primaries-texas-1848–2012.

13. Leslie W. Gladstone, "Equal Rights Amendments: State Provisions," Congressional Research Service, August 23, 2004.

14. http://www.nytimes.com/2005/12/23/sports/ncaafootball /23texas.html?pagewanted=all.

15. *Harvey v. Morgan*, 272 SW 2d 621 (Texas Court of Appeals, 3rd Dist., 1954), 1, http://www.leagle.com/xmlResult.aspx?page=4&xmldoc =1954893272SW2d621_1771.xml&docbase=CSLWAR1-1950-1985 &SizeDisp=7.

16. http://newdeal.feri.org/survey/39a07.htm.

17. http://books.google.com/books?id=CCSW2UV8ipcC&pg
=PA173&lpg=PA173&dq=%22Maury+Maverick%22+%22Fair+Labor
+Standards+Act%22&source=bl&ots=HC6cTbd3zp&sig=liVYLAtep
L8GEugE8ZvbeOrrLsU&hl=en#v=onepage&q=%22Maury%20
Maverick%22%20%22Fair%20Labor%20Standards%20Act%22&f
=false.

18. http://www.monitor.net/monitor/0012a/copyright/mi-gonzalez
.html.

19. Michael T. Kaufman, "Maury Maverick Jr., Champion of the
Unpopular, Is Dead at 82," *New York Times*, February 3, 2003, http:
//www.nytimes.com/2003/02/03/obituaries/03MAVE.html.

20. Cheryl Dahle, "Social Justice: Ernesto Cortes Jr.," *Fast Company*,
November 30, 1999, http://www.fastcompany.com/39208/social-justice
-ernesto-cortes-jr.

21. Joe Belden, "Daniel's Lead Overwhelming," *Victoria Advocate*, June
5, 1958, http://news.google.com/newspapers?nid=861&dat=19580605
&id=1xtQAAAAIBAJ&sjid=J1YDAAAAIBAJ&pg=4191,3782074.

22. T. R. Fehrenbach, *Lone Star: A History of Texas and the Texans* (New
York: Da Capo Press, 2000), 1861.

23. Martin Tolchin, "How Johnson Won Election He'd Lost," *New
York Times*, February 11, 1990, http://www.nytimes.com/1990/02/11
/us/how-johnson-won-election-he-d-lost.html?pagewanted=all&src=pm.

24. Robert A. Caro, "My Search for Coke Stevenson," *New York Times*,
February 3, 1991, http://www.nytimes.com/1991/02/03/books/my-search
-for-coke-stevenson.html?pagewanted=all&src=pm.

25. Fehrenbach, *Lone Star*.

26. Robert Draper, "Death of a Fixer," *Texas Monthly*, November
1992, 12.

27. Al Reinert, "Should These Men Be Smiling?," *Texas Monthly*, April
1974, 59.

CHAPTER 10:
THE RISE OF THE RIGHT

1. http://www.laits.utexas.edu/txp_media/html/leg/features/0303
_01/slide1.html.

2. Kathryn J. McGarr, *The Whole Damn Deal: Robert Strauss and the Art of Politics* (New York: PublicAffairs, 2011).

3. Steve Bickerstaff, *Lines in the Sand: Congressional Redistricting in Texas and the Downfall of Tom DeLay* (Austin: University of Texas Press, 2007), 221.

4. See author interview with Steve Murdock.

CHAPTER 11:
TWENTY-FIRST-CENTURY TEXAS

1. Steve H. Murdock, Steve White, Md. Nazrul Hoque, Beverly Pecotte, Xuihong You, and Jennifer Balkan, *The New Texas Challenge: Population Change and the Future of Texas* (College Station: Texas A&M University Press, 2003), 14.

2. www.census.gov/newsroom/releases/archives/population
/cb11–215.html.

3. T. R. Fehrenbach, *Lone Star: A History of Texas and the Texans* (New York: Da Capo Press, 2000), 37.

4. Ibid., 77.

5. http://quickfacts.census.gov/qfd/states/48000.html.

6. Murdock et al., *The New Texas Challenge*, 27.

7. E-mail from Steve Murdock.

8. Carlos R. Soltero, *Latinos and American Law: Landmark Supreme Court Cases* (Austin: University of Texas Press, 2006), 41.

9. Ibid., 43.

10. James L. Haley, *Passionate Nation: The Epic History of Texas* (New York: Free Press, 2006), 349.

11. Robert A. Caro, *The Years of Lyndon Johnson: The Passage of Power* (New York: Knopf, 2012), xiv.

12. Ibid.

13. Lyndon Johnson, "Speech to Students at Lyndon B. Johnson School of Public Affairs," December 2, 1972, video, LBJ Library and Museum, quoted in Mark Updegrove, *Indomitable Will: LBJ in the Presidency* (New York: Crown, 2012), 51.

14. Caro, *The Passage of Power*, xix.

15. http://www.forbes.com/sites/danielfisher/2012/04/18/americas -fastest-growing-cities/.

16. http://www.har.com/mls/dispPressRelease.cfm.

17. http://ycharts.com/indicators/sales_price_of_existing_homes.

18. "Changing the Plans," *The Economist*, July 14, 2012, http://www .economist.com/node/21558632.

19. http://stopashbyhighrise.org/.

20. Manny Fernandez, "A Spotlight with Precedent Beckons a Mayor from San Antonio," *New York Times*, September 2, 2012, http://www .nytimes.com/2012/09/03/us/politics/democratic-convention-spotlight -beckons-san-antonio-mayor.html?pagewanted=1&_r=1&seid=auto &smid=tw-nytimes.

21. Claudia Hazlewood, "Archive War," in *Handbook of Texas Online*, http://www.tshaonline.org/handbook/online/articles/mqa02.

22. http://www.utexas.edu/utpress/excerpts/exbragap.html#ex2; http://www.utexas.edu/utpress/books/eckduc.html.

23. Michael Corcoran, "Welcome to Mediocre, Texas," *Michael Corcoran.net* (blog), May 2012, http://www.michaelcorcoran.net/welcome -to-mediocre-texas.

24. Andrea Ball, "Homer the Homeless Goose: Where Is He Now?," *Austin American-Statesman*, December 30, 2010, http://www.statesman .com/news/local/homer-the-homeless-goose-where-is-he-now-1154982 .html.

25. "Lights Down, Curtain Up," *The Economist*, October 29, 2009, http://www.economist.com/node/14753866.

26. Thomas Wilson, "How Marfa, Texas, Got Its Name," *Journal of Big Bend Studies*, 2001. Abridged version at http://www.bigbendquarterly.com /marfa.htm.

27. "Texas Official Warns of Obama Civil War," *Houston Chronicle*, August 22, 2012, http://www.chron.com/news/houston-texas/article /Lubbock-judge-warns-of-Obama-civil-war-3807672.php.

28. "U.N. to Invade Texas? 'Ridiculous,' Says World Body," Reuters, August 24, 2012, http://www.reuters.com/article/2012/08/24/us-un -texas-duel-idUSBRE87N14A20120824.

CHAPTER 12:
VESTIGIAL PARTS

1. Sonia Smith, "Aggies Build Human Wall to Keep Westboro Baptist Church from Protesting Funeral," TexasMonthly.com, July 6, 2012, http://www.tmdailypost.com/article/education/aggies-build-human -wall-keep-westboro-baptist-church-protesting-funeral.

2. Jon Mcacham, "Of God and Gays and Humility," *Time*, July 30, 2012, http://www.time.com/time/magazine/article/0,9171,2119 924,00.html.

3. http://commons.trincoll.edu/aris/publications/aris-2008-summary -report/.

4. David Wiley and Kelly Wilson, "Just Say Don't Know: Sexuality Education in Texas Public Schools," Texas Freedom Network Education Fund, February 2009, www.tfn.org/site/DocServer/SexEdRort09_web .pdf?docID=981.

5. "Sex Education in Texas Public Schools: Progress in the Lone Star State," Texas Freedom Network Education Fund, November 2011, http://www.tfn.org/site/DocServer/Report_final_web.pdf?docID=2941.

6. Like most standard-issue right-wing conspiracy theories, this has a relationship to the truth, but only a glancing one. Seventh-graders are supposed to get a segment on Islamic civilizations, including an account of the life and teachings of Muhammed and an explanation of the

significance of the Qur'an and the Sunnah; sixth-graders are supposed to learn about the life and teachings of Jesus of Nazareth and the central beliefs of Judaism.

7. Timothy Egan, "Rick Perry's Unanswered Prayers," *Opinionator* (blog), *New York Times*, August 11, 2011, http://opinionator.blogs.nytimes.com/2011/08/11/rick-perrys-unanswered-prayers/.

8. Manny Fernandez, "Perry Leads Prayer Rally for 'Nation in Crisis,'" *New York Times*, August 6, 2011, http://www.nytimes.com/2011/08/07/us/politics/07prayer.html?_r=1.

9. http://www.huffingtonpost.com/2011/08/18/rick-perry-says-texas-pub_n_930858.html.

10. Reeve Hamilton, "Campus Carry Debate Likely to Return Next Session," *Texas Tribune*, April 4, 2012, http://www.texastribune.org/texas-issues/campus-carry/campus-carry-debate-likely-return-next-session/.

11. The Innocence Project's list of exonerations in Texas is available online at http://www.innocenceproject.org/news/state.php?state=TX.

12. Steve McVicker and Roma Khanna, "New Tests Urged in HPD Crime Lab Final Report," *Houston Chronicle*, June 13, 2007, http://www.chron.com/news/houston-texas/article/New-tests-urged-in-HPD-crime-lab-final-report-1530898.php.

13. Hilary Hylton, "Texas: The Kinder, Gentler Hang 'Em High State," *Time*, September 19, 2009, http://www.time.com/time/nation/article/0,8599,1924278,00.html.

14. Death Penalty Information Center, http://www.deathpenaltyinfo.org/death-sentences-united-states-1977–2008.

15. Ted Oberg, "Why Rosenthal Had to Turn over Email," KTRK-TV, January 31, 2008, http://abclocal.go.com/ktrk/story?section=news/in_focus&id=5926157.

16. http://www.txdps.state.tx.us/administration/crime_records/pages/crimestatistics.htm.

17. Law Center to Prevent Gun Violence, http://smartgunlaws.org/gun-laws-matter-a-comparison-of-state-firearms-laws-and-statistics/.

18. http://www.laits.utexas.edu/txp_media/html/leg/0205.html.

19. Aman Batheja, "Private Firm Planning Bullet Trains in Texas by 2020," *Texas Tribune*, August 15, 2012, http://www.texastribune.org/texas-transportation/transportation/private-firm-planning-bullet-trains-texas-2020/.

20. "New Trends Emerge in Urban Water Supply Development," *American Water Intelligence*, August 2011, http://www.americanwaterintel.com/archive/2/8/market-insight/new-trends-emerge-urban-water-supply-development.html.

21. Ralph K. M. Haurwitz, "UT System Plan for Incentive Pay Stirs Debate," *Austin American-Statesman*, August 21, 2012, http://www.statesman.com/news/texas/ut-system-plan-for-incentive-pay-stirs-debate-2439602.html.

22. http://www.tpwd.state.tx.us/newsmedia/releases/?req=20120725c.

23. Molly Ivins, "Texas-Style Ethics," in *Molly Ivins Can't Say That, Can She?* (New York: Random House, 1991), 60.

24. Ben Barnes, *Barn Burning, Barn Building* (Albany, TX: Bright Sky Press, 2006), 94.

25. Ibid., 95.

CHAPTER 13:
TURNING TEXAS BLUE

1. Marc Hugo Lopez, "The Hispanic Vote in the 2010 Elections," Pew Hispanic Center, November 3, 2012, www.pewhispanic.org/files/reports/130.pdf.

2. O. Ricardo Pimentel, "Texas Content with Low Latino Voter Turnout," *San Antonio Express-News*, June 16, 2012, http://www.mysanantonio.com/news/news_columnists/o_ricardo_pimentel/article/Texas-content-with-low-Latino-voter-turnout-3639810.php#ixzz24tV3kWSo.

3. Molly Ivins, "Shrub Flubs His Dub," *The Nation*, May 31, 2001, http://www.thenation.com/article/shrub-flubs-his-dub#.

4. Author interview.

5. Peter J. Boyer, "The New Texan," *New Yorker*, August 12, 2002, http://www.newyorker.com/archive/2002/08/12/020812fa_fact#ixzz 23uopkbUz.

6. Ibid.

7. http://www.texasmonthly.com/2007–12–01/feature2.php.

8. Ibid.

9. Karl-Thomas Musselman, "TX-Sen: John Cornyn's Totally Ridiculous Ad," *Burnt Orange Report* (blog), June 16, 2008, http://www.burntorangereport.com/diary/6050/.

CHAPTER 14:
THE COMING CRACK-UP

1. Allan Turner, "Execution of Houston Girls' Killer Still on Track for Aug. 5," *Houston Chronicle*, July 16, 2008, http://www.chron.com/news /houston-texas/article/Execution-of-Houston-girls-killer-still-on-track -1788473.php.

2. Rick Perry, *Fed Up!: Our Fight to Save America from Washington* (New York: Little, Brown, 2010), 101.

3. Author interview.

4. Abby Rapoport, "SREC Member: I Got into Politics to Put Christian Conservatives into Office," *Texas Observer*, December 3, 2010, http://www.texasobserver.org/srec-member-i-got-into-politics-to-put -christian-conservatives-into-office.

5. http://www.michaelquinnsullivan.com/about/.

6. http://www.ejumpcut.org/archive/onlinessays/JC14folder /MassacreWomen.html.

7. William Ransom Hogan, *The Texas Republic: A Social and Economic History* (Austin: University of Texas Press, 1969), 246.

8. Ibid., 143.

9. "Our Polling on the Birth Control Issue," Public Policy Polling, February 10, 2012, http://www.publicpolicypolling.com/main/2012/02 /our-polling-on-the-birth-control-issue.html.

10. Emily Ramshaw: "Poll: Voters Want to Keep Planned Parenthood in WHP," *Texas Tribune*, March 5, 2012, http://www.texastribune.org /texas-health-resources/abortion-texas/poll-voters-want-keep-planned -parenthood-whp/.

11. Thanh Tan, "A Closer Look at UT/TT Poll on Planned Parenthood," *Texas Tribune*, June 6, 2012, http://www.texastribune.org /texas-health-resources/reproductive-health/closer-look-ut-tt-poll-planned -parenthood/.

12. Jeffrey M. Jones, "In U.S., Nearly Half Identify as Economically Conservative," Gallup, May 25, 2012, http://www.gallup.com/poll /154889/nearly-half-identify-economically-conservative.aspx.

13. "Who Knows What About Religion," Pew Research Center, September 28, 2010, http://www.pewforum.org/U-S-Religious- Knowledge-Survey-Who-Knows-What-About-Religion.aspx#Public.

14. "Poll: Texans Back Church-State Separation," Texas Freedom Network, May 20, 2010, http://tfninsider.org/2010/05/20/poll -texans-back-church-state-separation/.

15. Casey Michel, "Rick Perry Blames Satan for Separation of Church and State," *TPMMuckraker* (blog), September 20, 2012, http://tp mmuckraker.talkingpointsmemo.com/2012/09/rick_perry_satan_church _state.php.

16. Author interview.

17. "John Carona Among First Republican Legislators in Texas to Back Gay Rights," *Dallas Voice*, October 23, 2012.

CHAPTER 15:
TWEAKING THE MODEL

1. Paul Collier, *The Bottom Billion* (Oxford: Oxford University Press, 2008), 5.

2. Nick Paumgarten, "Food Fighter," *New Yorker*, January 4, 2010, http://www.newyorker.com/reporting/2010/01/04/100104fa_fact_paumgar ten. A few years ago, I was driving around Austin with demographer

Joel Kotkin, and he offered a theory of why you tend to find a pocket of blue in red states like Texas: cheap land and low taxes mean a low cost of living, which, in turn, means you can get by on tacos while you're starting your band. Entrepreneurs are in some respects different from musicians; they need access to capital, not studio space. Still, Kotkin's logic seems to apply.

3. Josh Harkinson, "Michael Dell: The Making of an American Oligarch," *Mother Jones*, March/April 2011.

4. Mackey's company arguably has some positive externalities beyond that, because Whole Foods has helped promote a variety of sustainability issues by marrying its vaguely conscientious ethos with the kind of supply-chain leverage that you would expect from Wal-Mart or, for that matter, from Dell.

5. Steve Murdock, "Population Change in Texas and the Dallas–Fort Worth Area: Implications for Education, the Labor Force, and Economic Development," presentation to the DFW International Community Alliance, Dallas, Texas, August 24, 2011.

6. http://www.tea.state.tx.us/index4.aspx?id=2147506592.

7. Author interview.

8. Tyler Cowen, *The Great Stagnation: How America Ate All the Low-Hanging Fruit of Modern History, Got Sick, and Will (Eventually) Feel Better* (New York: Dutton, 2005).

9. Author interview.

10. Fred Block and Matthew R. Keller, "Where Do Innovations Come From?: Transformations in the U.S. National Innovation System, 1970–2006," Information Technology and Innovation Foundation, July 2008.

11. Molly Ivins, "The Billionaire Boy Scout: Ross Perot," *Time*, May 1992, http://byliner.com/molly-ivins/stories/the-billionaire-boy-scout-ross-perot.

12. http://trailblazersblog.dallasnews.com/2012/02/spending-on-public-school-stud.html/.

13. Henry J. Kaiser Family Foundation, http://www.statehealth facts.org/comparetable.jsp?typ=2&ind=33&cat=1&sub=10.

14. And if there are people in your state, there are going to be people working the register and stocking the shelves and assembling food according to pictorial instructions. You can't outsource a Whataburger. Texas's population growth is the reason for its increase in minimum-wage jobs, and it's the reason hiking the minimum wage wouldn't hurt business very badly. In any case, Texas's most important industries, such as energy, manufacturing, and the burgeoning tech sector, wouldn't really be affected by a change to the minimum wage. The exceptions would be construction and agriculture, but, again, it's hard to outsource homebuilding, and in any case, those businesses have effectively skirted the current minimum wage by quietly thwarting any move toward E-Verify, which they can of course continue to do.

CHAPTER 16:
TEXAS AND THE UNITED STATES

1. J. Frank Dobie, *Tales of Old-Time Texas* (rpt., Austin: University of Texas Press, 2000), 187.

2. N. Doran Maillard, Esq., *The History of the Republic of Texas, from the Discovery of the Country to the Present Time; and the Cause of Her Separation from the Republic of Mexico* (London: Smith, Elder, 1842), 103.

3. Author interview.

4. Author interview.

5. These examples are taken from the 2012 Republican Party of Texas convention, held in Fort Worth in June 2012.

6. D'Vera Cohn, "Magnet or Sticky?: A State-by-State Typology," Pew Research Center, March 11, 2009.

7. Gail Collins, "How Texas Inflicts Bad Textbooks on Us," *New York Review of Books*, June 21, 2012, www.nybooks.com/articles/archives/2012/jun/21/how-texas-inflicts -bad-textbooks-on-us/?pagination=false.

8. Kim Chipman, "Americans in 73% Majority Oppose Deepwater Drilling Ban," Bloomberg, July 14, 2010, http://www.bloomberg.com /news/2010-07-14/americans-in-73-majority-oppose-ban-on-deepwater -drilling-after-oil-spill.html.

9. William Ransom Hogan, "Rampant Individualism in the Republic of Texas," *Southwestern Historical Quarterly* 44 (July 1940–April 1941): 456.

10. George Norris Green, *The Establishment in Texas Politics: The Primitive Years, 1938–1957* (Westport, CT: Greenwood Press, 1979), 4.

11. Author interview.

BIBLIOGRAPHY

Barnes, Ben. *Barn Burning, Barn Building*. Albany, TX: Bright Sky Press, 2006.

Bickerstaff, Steve. *Lines in the Sand: Congressional Redistricting in Texas and the Downfall of Tom DeLay*. Austin: University of Texas Press, 2007.

Blakely, Mike, and Mary Elizabeth Goodman, eds. *Forever Texas: Texas the Way Those Who Lived It Wrote It*. New York: Forge, 2000.

Brands, H. W. *Lone Star Nation: The Epic Story of the Battle for Texas Independence*. New York: Anchor Books, 2005.

Bryce, Robert. *Cronies: How Texas Business Became American Policy—and Brought Bush to Power*. New York: PublicAffairs, 2004.

Burrough, Bryan. *The Big Rich: The Rise and Fall of the Greatest Texas Oil Fortunes*. New York: Penguin Press, 2009.

Caro, Robert A. *The Years of Lyndon Johnson: Master of the Senate*. New York: Knopf, 2002.

———. *The Years of Lyndon Johnson: Means of Ascent*. New York: Random House, 1990.

———. *The Years of Lyndon Johnson: The Passage of Power*. New York: Knopf, 2012.

———. *The Years of Lyndon Johnson: The Path to Power*. New York: Random House, 1981.

Collier, Paul. *The Bottom Billion*. Oxford: Oxford University Press, 2008.

Cowen, Tyler. *The Great Stagnation: How America Ate All the Low-Hanging Fruit of Modern History, Got Sick, and Will (Eventually) Feel Better*. New York: Dutton, 2005.

Cullen, David O'Donald, and Kyle G. Wilkison, eds. *The Texas Left: The Radical Roots of Lone Star Liberalism*. College Station: Texas A&M University Press, 2010.

Davis, William C. *Lone Star Rising: The Revolutionary Birth of the Texas Republic*. College Station: Texas A&M University Press, 2004.

Dobie, J. Frank. *The Longhorns*. Rpt. Austin: University of Texas Press, 1990.

———. *Tales of Old-Time Texas*. Rpt. Austin: University of Texas Press, 2000.

Draper, Robert. *Dead Certain: The Presidency of George W. Bush*. New York: Free Press, 2007.

Fehrenbach, T. R. *Lone Star: A History of Texas and the Texans*. New York: Da Capo Press, 2000.

Frank, Thomas. *What's the Matter with Kansas? How Conservatives Won the Heart of America*. New York: Henry Holt, 2004.

Frantz, Joe B. *Texas: A History*. New York: Norton, 1984.

Friedman, Milton. *Capitalism and Freedom*. Chicago: University of Chicago Press, 1962.

Goodwin, Doris Kearns. *Lyndon Johnson and the American Dream*. New York: St. Martin's Griffin, 1991.

Goodwyn, Lawrence. *The Populist Moment: A Short History of the Agrarian Revolt in America*. Oxford: Oxford University Press, 1978.

Green, George Norris. *The Establishment in Texas Politics: The Primitive Years, 1938–1957*. Westport, CT: Greenwood Press, 1979.

Haidt, Jonathan. *The Righteous Mind: Why Good People Are Divided by Politics and Religion*. New York: Pantheon Books, 2012.

Haley, James L. *Passionate Nation: The Epic History of Texas*. New York: Free Press, 2006.

Hayek, F. A. *The Road to Serfdom*. Rpt. London: University of Chicago Press, 2007.

Hinton, Diana Davids, and Roger M. Olien. *Oil in Texas: The Gusher Age, 1895–1945*. Austin: University of Texas Press, 2002.

Hogan, William Ransom. *The Texas Republic: A Social and Economic History*. Austin: University of Texas Press, 1969.

Hunter, J. Marvin, ed. *The Trail Drivers of Texas: Interesting Sketches of Early Cowboys and Their Experiences on the Range and on the Trail During the Days That Tried Men's Souls—True Narratives Related by Real Cowpunchers and Men Who Fathered the Cattle Industry in Texas*. Rev. ed. Austin: University of Texas Press, 1985.

Ivins, Molly. *Molly Ivins Can't Say That, Can She?* New York: Random House, 1991.

Ivins, Molly, and Lou Dubose. *Shrub: The Short but Happy Political Life of George W. Bush*. New York: Vintage Books, 2000.

James, Marquis. *The Raven: A Biography of Sam Houston*. Rpt. Austin: University of Texas Press, 1994.

Kay, Jonathan. *Among the Truthers: A Journey Through America's Growing Conspiracist Underground*. New York: HarperCollins, 2011.

Langewiesche, William. *Cutting for Sign*. New York: Pantheon Books, 1994.

Lanier, Jaron. *You Are Not a Gadget: A Manifesto*. New York: Vintage, 2011.

Lewis, Willie Newbury. *Between Sun and Sod: An Informal History of the Texas Panhandle*. College Station: Texas A&M University Press, 1976.

Maillard, N. Doran, Esq. *The History of the Republic of Texas, from the Discovery of the Country to the Present Time; and the Cause of Her Separation from the Republic of Mexico*. London: Smith, Elder, 1842.

McGarr, Kathryn J. *The Whole Damn Deal: Robert Strauss and the Art of Politics*. New York: PublicAffairs, 2011.

McLean, Bethany, and Peter Elkind. *The Smartest Guys in the Room: The Amazing Rise and Scandalous Fall of Enron*. New York: Penguin Group, 2003.

Miller, Mark Crispin. *The Bush Dyslexicon: Observations on a National Disorder*. New York: Norton, 2001.

Minutaglio, Bill. *City on Fire: The Explosion That Devastated a Texas Town and Ignited a Historic Legal Battle*. New York: HarperCollins, 2003.

Minutaglio, Bill, and W. Michael Smith. *Molly Ivins: A Rebel Life*. New York: PublicAffairs, 2009.

Montejano, David. *Anglos and Mexicans in the Making of Texas, 1836–1986*. Austin: University of Texas Press, 1987.

Murdock, Steve H., Md. Nazrul Hoque, Martha Michael, Steve White, and Beverly Pecotte. *The Texas Challenge: Population Change and the Future of Texas*. College Station: Texas A&M University Press, 1997.

Murdock, Steve H., Steve White, Md. Nazrul Hoque, Beverly Pecotte, Xuihong You, and Jennifer Balkan. *The New Texas Challenge: Population Change and the Future of Texas*. College Station: Texas A&M University Press, 2003.

Nackman, Mark E. *A Nation Within a Nation: The Rise of Texas Nationalism*. Port Washington, NY: Kennikat Press, 1975.

Okun, Arthur M. *Equality and Efficiency: The Big Tradeoff*. Washington, DC: Brookings Institution Press, 1975.

Olien, Roger M., and Diana Davids Hinton. *Wildcatters: Texas Independent Oilmen*. College Station: Texas A&M University Press, 2007.

Perkinson, Robert. *Texas Tough: The Rise of America's Prison Empire*. New York: Picador, 2010.

Perlstein, Rick. *Before the Storm: Barry Goldwater and the Unmaking of the American Consensus*. New York: Nation Books, 2009.

Perry, George Sessions. *Texas: A World in Itself*. New York: McGraw-Hill, 1942.

Perry, Rick. *Fed Up!: Our Fight to Save America from Washington*. New York: Little, Brown, 2010.

Prindle, David F. *Petroleum Politics and the Texas Railroad Commission*. Austin: University of Texas Press, 1981.

Ravitch, Diane. *The Death and Life of the Great American School System: How Testing and Choice Are Undermining Education*. New York: Basic Books, 2010.

Reading, Amy. *The Mark Inside: A Perfect Swindle, a Cunning Revenge, and a Small History of the Big Con*. New York: Knopf, 2012.

Rodriguez, Gregory. *Mongrels, Bastards, Orphans, and Vagabonds: Mexican Immigration and the Future of Race in the United States*. New York: Pantheon Books, 2007.

Rostow, W. W. *The Stages of Economic Growth: A Non-Communist Manifesto*. Cambridge: Cambridge University Press, 1971.

Shlaes, Amity. *The Forgotten Man: A New History of the Great Depression*. New York: HarperCollins, 2007.

Sibley, Joel H. *Storm Over Texas: The Annexation Controversy and the Road to Civil War*. Oxford: Osford University Press, 2007.

Soltero, Carlos R. *Latinos and American Law: Landmark Supreme Court Cases*. Austin: University of Texas Press, 2006.

Stegner, Wallace. *Where the Bluebird Sings to the Lemonade Springs: Living and Writing in the American West*. New York: Penguin Books, 1992.

Stephanson, Anders. *Manifest Destiny: American Expansionism and the Empire of Right*. New York: Hill and Wang, 1995.

Trillin, Calvin. *Trillin on Texas*. Austin: University of Texas Press, 2011.

Updegrove, Mark K. *Indomitable Will: LBJ in the Presidency*. New York: Crown, 2012.

Wallace, Ernest, David M. Vigness, and George B. Ward, eds. *Documents of Texas History*. Austin: State House Press, 1994.

Weisberg, Jacob. *The Bush Tragedy*. New York: Random House, 2008.

INDEX

PHOTO BY ROXANNE RATHGE

Erica Grieder is a senior editor at *Texas Monthly*, and formerly the southwest correspondent for *The Economist*. Her writing has also appeared in *The New York Times*, the *Spectator*, the *Atlantic*, *Foreign Policy*, and the *New Republic*. She lives in Austin.

PublicAffairs is a publishing house founded in 1997. It is a tribute to the standards, values, and flair of three persons who have served as mentors to countless reporters, writers, editors, and book people of all kinds, including me.

I. F. STONE, proprietor of *I. F. Stone's Weekly*, combined a commitment to the First Amendment with entrepreneurial zeal and reporting skill and became one of the great independent journalists in American history. At the age of eighty, Izzy published *The Trial of Socrates*, which was a national bestseller. He wrote the book after he taught himself ancient Greek.

BENJAMIN C. BRADLEE was for nearly thirty years the charismatic editorial leader of *The Washington Post*. It was Ben who gave the *Post* the range and courage to pursue such historic issues as Watergate. He supported his reporters with a tenacity that made them fearless and it is no accident that so many became authors of influential, best-selling books.

ROBERT L. BERNSTEIN, the chief executive of Random House for more than a quarter century, guided one of the nation's premier publishing houses. Bob was personally responsible for many books of political dissent and argument that challenged tyranny around the globe. He is also the founder and longtime chair of Human Rights Watch, one of the most respected human rights organizations in the world.

·　　·　　·

For fifty years, the banner of Public Affairs Press was carried by its owner Morris B. Schnapper, who published Gandhi, Nasser, Toynbee, Truman, and about 1,500 other authors. In 1983, Schnapper was described by *The Washington Post* as "a redoubtable gadfly." His legacy will endure in the books to come.

Peter Osnos, *Founder and Editor-at-Large*